Drums

FOR

DUMMIES®

2ND EDITION

by Jeff Strong

WILEY

John Wiley & Sons, Inc.

Drums For Dummies,® 2nd Edition

Published by
Wiley Publishing, Inc.
111 River St.
Hoboken, NJ 07030-5774
www.wiley.com

For general information on our other products and services, please contact our Customer Care Department within the U.S. at 877-762-2974, outside the U.S. at 317-572-3993, or fax 317-572-4002.

For technical support, please visit www.wiley.com/techsupport.

Wiley also publishes its books in a variety of electronic formats. Some content that appears in print may not be available in electronic books.

Library of Congress Control Number: 2006926113

ISBN-13: 978-0-471-79411-0

ISBN-10: 0-471-79411-2

Manufactured in the United States of America

11

2B/RR/QX/QW/IN

WILEY

About the Author

Jeff Strong graduated from the Percussion Institute of Technology at the Musician's Institute in Los Angeles in 1983, where he studied with Joe Porcaro, Ralph Humphrey, Efrain Toro, and Alex Acuna. A drummer for more than 35 years, Jeff began his professional career at the age of 14. His professional experience ranges from live performance to studio drumming to music research. Jeff has performed or recorded with artists as diverse as '60's crooner Gene Pitney, R&B singer Cynthia Johnson (Lipps, Inc.), the country-rock Daisy Dillman Band, and the reggae band Macumba, to name a few. He has released a dozen solo CDs, including *Calming Rhythms 3* — a therapeutic tool currently used by thousands of institutions and schools worldwide.

Jeff is currently President of the REI Institute, a Music Medicine research organization and therapy provider. His pioneering work using drumming for children with autism has been featured in many publications, including many scientific journals and several books. Jeff has spoken at dozens of professional conferences and has been called upon as an expert on music and sound healing, appearing on numerous radio programs and in two documentaries. The REI Institute's therapy program for people with neurological disorders, of which Jeff is the creator, is available through hundreds of Authorized REI Providers located around the world.

Jeff is a sought-after drum clinician focusing on world rhythm techniques and is the author of eight books. You can find out more about Jeff at www.jeffstrong.com and www.reiinstitute.com.

Dedication

For Tovah and the next generation of drummers.

Author's Acknowledgments

My thanks go to all the people at Wiley, especially Mike Baker and Sarah Faulkner, whose hard work and technical skill are obvious in the pages of this book. I'm also grateful for my agent Carol Susan Roth and acquisitions editor Tracy Boggier for making the second edition of this book a reality.

Publisher's Acknowledgments

We're proud of this book; please send us your comments through our Dummies online registration form located at www.dummies.com/register/.

Some of the people who helped bring this book to market include the following:

Acquisitions, Editorial, and Media Development

Project Editor: Mike Baker

(Previous Edition: Allyson Grove)

Acquisitions Editor: Tracy Boggier

Copy Editor: Sarah Faulkner

(Previous Edition: Billie Williams)

Editorial Program Coordinator: Hanna K. Scott

Technical Reviewer: Wade Parish

Media Development Specialist: Laura Moss

Editorial Manager: Christine Meloy Beck

Editorial Assistants: Erin Calligan, David Lutton

Cover Photos: © Digital Vision/Getty

Cartoons: Rich Tennant
  (www.the5thwave.com)

Composition Services

Project Coordinator: Tera Knapp

Layout and Graphics: Claudia Bell, Carl Byers, Andrea Dahl, Joyce Haughey, Barry Offringa

Proofreaders: John Greenough, Leeann Harney, Christine Pingleton, Aptara

Indexer: Aptara

Contents at a Glance

Table of Contents

Introduction

· ·

*A*ll the drummers I've ever met (and I've met quite a few) started out by tapping or pounding on just about anything they could get their hands on. Chances are that if you picked up this book, you fit into this category as well. So, even if you've never played an actual drum or studied drumming in any formal sense, you're a drummer.

With drumming, you've chosen the world's oldest and most popular musical instrument. There isn't a place on this planet that doesn't have some sort of drumming tradition. In fact, as you'll discover in the following pages, playing drums is a universal pastime that anyone can enjoy, regardless of his or her taste in music.

My purpose with this book is to introduce you to as many types of drums and drumming styles as I can in 384 pages. If you're like me, you can find joy in each of them. And by knowing a variety of playing techniques, you can end up being a much better and more versatile drummer.

About This Book

This book allows the drumset player to develop all the skills needed to play a variety of drumming styles from rock to Latin and jazz to R&B. I also expose you to traditional techniques that you can easily incorporate into your drumset playing.

Unlike most drum books, *Drums For Dummies,* 2nd Edition goes beyond the modern drumset and also includes a variety of traditional drums and percussion instruments. For the traditionalist or drum circle enthusiast, *Drums For Dummies,* 2nd Edition includes descriptions of how to play a variety of traditional hand and stick-played drums as well as some common percussion instruments. So, whether you're interested in playing a drumset in popular music or being involved in drumming ensembles using traditional drums and percussion instruments, this book is for you.

Drums For Dummies, 2nd Edition is able to contain all this information because you won't find any exercises that you can't use in real-world situations. The result: You can learn how to actually play the drums much sooner and without learning unnecessary stuff.

This book is also a handy reference for drumming. You can find a variety of drums from around the world that you may not have ever seen or heard of before now. I explain each of these drums, and I describe their technique so that you can play them in the traditional way using traditional rhythms. I also discuss how you can use each of these drums in a musical situation today.

By no means does this book cover all the different drums and percussion instruments played today, but it does cover more than a dozen of the drums that I see most often. And, with the techniques that I describe, you can easily play any drum that I don't present in this book. Just find a drum that looks similar to yours and start there.

Conventions Used in This Book

I use a few conventions in this book to make it easier for you to understand and navigate. Here's a list of those conventions:

- You'll see many of the rhythms in this book marked with a *track bar* that tells you where to find that rhythm on the book's companion CD when you play it as a standard, music CD. The CD and book together allow you to hear as well as see how to play each rhythm, making the learning process that much quicker. As with the 1st edition of this book, many of the tracks have been included as regular CD files. But with the 2nd edition, we're now able to make *all* the rhythms available as MP3 files.

- All the drumset grooves are written for the right-handed player. Well, not exactly right-handed people, but rather people who set up and play their drums in a right-handed way. I do this because it's the most common way to play a drum. Lefties take heart — playing right-handed can actually be better for you. You end up having an advantage because your left hand is as strong as your right (trust me on this one — I'm a lefty who plays right-handed, and so are a lot of other great drummers).

- The musical notation in this book is written so that you can read drumming music. I don't cover those areas (key signatures, melodies, and so on) that are present in music notation unless they specifically apply to the drum rhythm presented.

What You're Not to Read

If you're pressed for time (for example, you have an audition tomorrow), you don't have to read this entire book word-for-word. I can't promise that you'll nail that audition, but I do make it easy for you to know which parts of this book you can skip. Don't read the following unless you have ample time and a real thirst for drumming knowledge:

✔ **Sidebars:** These gray-shaded boxes are filled with fun, interesting information, but it's all nonessential.

✔ **Technical stuff:** You can skip any paragraph marked with a Technical Stuff icon (see "Icons Used in This Book" later in this introduction). This information may be too technical the first time you read through this book, but come back to it as you get more comfortable with your drumming — it will only enhance your knowledge of the subject.

✔ **Drum history:** Don't worry; I don't give you any quizzes on the history of drumming. If you're one of those rare souls who finds history fascinating, dive right in. If you're like the rest of us, this icon lets you know that you don't have to read these sections.

Foolish Assumptions

I really don't make any assumptions about you, the reader. I don't assume that you're interested in a certain type of drum. I don't assume that you want to play a specific style of music. I don't even assume that you already have a drum or that you know what kind of drumming you want to do. In fact, if you don't know these things, this book can help you decide.

The only assumption I make is that you're reading this book because you want to learn how to turn your aimless tapping into music.

How This Book Is Organized

This book is organized so that you can get the information you want quickly and not be burdened with stuff you don't need or want to know. Each section contains chapters that cover a specific area of drumming.

Part I: Setting a Solid Foundation

Part I contains four chapters that cover the basics of drumming. Chapter 1 introduces you to the world of drums and shows you some of the most common drums used today. Chapter 2 provides you with a vocabulary that allows you to read drumming music quickly (you don't need to read music in order to play the rhythms in this book if you don't want to — you can pop the CD into your stereo and listen to some of the rhythms, or download the MP3 files and listen to all the rhythms). Chapter 3 introduces you to the proper way to hit the drums with a stick, and Chapter 4 explores many ways that you can play a drum with your hands.

Part II: Digging into the Drumset

Part II explores the modern drumset. In Chapter 5, you discover how to set up your drumset as well as some basic drumset skills that will help you move your limbs independently of one another. Chapter 6 shows you how to play the drumset in the rock style, and Chapter 7 introduces you to blues drumming. Chapter 8 presents the way to drum in the R&B and funk drumming techniques, and Chapter 9 explores jazz and fusion styles. In Chapter 10, you uncover the secrets to playing Latin and Caribbean rhythms. And, in Chapter 11, you can expand on your rock skills by looking at the rhythms of some great drummers.

Part III: Dressing up Your Drumset Skills

Part III helps you express your own personality on the drumset. Chapter 12 examines what makes a rhythm groove and how to put together a beat that fits your musical situation. In Chapter 13, you can explore how to use licks and fills to complement the music and make a personal statement. Chapter 14 gives you some ideas and guidelines to help you solo effectively.

Part IV: Pounding Out the Beat: Traditional Drums and Percussion

Part IV presents a variety of drums and percussion instruments from around the world. In Chapter 15, you get a chance to discover a bunch of drums that you play with your hands. Chapter 16 explores some drums that you play with either a stick or a combination of a stick and your hand. Chapter 17 presents other percussion instruments, such as the cowbell and the triangle. Chapter 18 builds on Chapters 15, 16, and 17 and shows you how you can combine these instruments to create polyrhythms.

Part V: Choosing, Tuning, and Caring for Your Drums

Part V provides information to help you choose, tune, and care for your drums. Chapter 19 shows you what to look for when buying a drum or drumset. Chapter 20 explains how to tune and take care of your drums so that they sound their best and last a long time.

Part VI: The Part of Tens

Part VI is a staple of *For Dummies* books. Chapter 21 shows you ten ways that you can continue on in the world of drumming, and Chapter 22 offers some tips on choosing a private drum instructor.

Appendix

The appendix explains the organization of the CD that comes with this book.

Icons Used in This Book

As with all *For Dummies* books, I use a few icons to help you along your way.

This icon highlights expert advice that can help you become a better drummer.

This icon lets you know ahead of time about those instances when the way you hit a drum can cause damage to the instrument or your ears. You also see this icon when I present you with a technique or rhythm that is challenging to play.

Certain techniques are very important and stand repeating. This icon gives you those gentle nudges to keep your playing on track.

Throughout the text, I include some technical background on a specific technique. This icon shows up in those instances so that you know to brace yourself for some less inspiring information.

This icon directs you to fun facts about drumming that you can use to impress your friends.

Where to Go from Here

Drums For Dummies, 2nd Edition is set up so that you can either read it from cover to cover and progressively build your drumming knowledge, or you can jump around and read only the parts that interest you. I recommend that either way, you check out Chapters 2 and 3 first. These chapters lay the foundation from which all drumming is built. Knowing this stuff allows you to understand the information in all the other chapters faster and easier.

After you look over Chapters 2 and 3, you can either go to Part II if you're interested in the drumset or you can jump to Part IV to learn about traditional drums.

If you don't have a drum but know what you want, you can find out how to buy one in Part V. If you don't know what kind of drum you want to buy (well, besides a drumset), start with Part IV for some ideas.

Part I
Setting a Solid Foundation

The 5th Wave   By Rich Tennant

"I told you to be careful around the snare drums."

In this part . . .

At last, you've discovered that you're a drummer at heart. Now you want to move beyond those kitchen utensils to an actual drum. Well, this part introduces you to the world of drums and drumming. In Chapter 1, you find out what makes a drum a drum and you get a glimpse of the most common styles available. Chapter 2 gives you a foundation from which to develop your drumming skills by showing you how easy it is to read music. Chapter 3 introduces you to the myriad of ways to hit a drum with a stick and shows you the fundamentals of all drumming: the rudiments (well, a few anyway — the complete list is on the Cheat Sheet). Chapter 4 helps you get a handle on hitting the drums with your hands in case you want to move beyond the drumset to more traditional drums.

Chapter 1

Drum Basics

. . . .

. . . .

Drums are members of the *membraphone family* of musical instruments and are considered one of the world's oldest, dating back thousands of years . . . *yawn*. Bottom line, a drum is a musical instrument that creates a sound when you hit it. What distinguishes a drum from, say, a soup pot, is a membrane (I call it a *head* from now on) strung across a hollow chamber (called the *shell*).

Don't get me wrong. I have nothing against soup pots. Or garbage cans or matchboxes or any other improvised drum for that matter. They can be just as fun to play and listen to as a regular drum — just look at the rhythm group Stomp; now *they* have fun. Face it though, a soup pot may be satisfying to hit for a little while, but sooner or later you're gonna want a more refined sound. Enter the drum. A well-made and well-tuned drum can produce all the subtle dynamic textures of a finely crafted violin and create a variety of pleasing sounds, whereas a soup pot only clanks when you hit it.

In this chapter I introduce you to some drums, both the modern drumset and traditional styles. I also show you the difference between a drum and those kitchen appliances that you've probably been banging on for a while now. (It's okay to admit it. Most drummers spend their careers exploring the rhythmic possibilities of household objects — I'm tapping on my computer mouse right now.) I also explain why a drum sounds better than a cardboard box, and I let you know when you should use your hands, or when arming yourself with sticks works better.

Picking a Drum Apart from Head to Shell

Like pots, pans, and garbage cans, drums come in all shapes and sizes. Most are round, but some are octagonal. Some are shallow and others are deep. Some are shaped like bowls or cylinders, others like goblets or an hourglass. Some you beat with sticks, while others you strike with hands or fingers. (See Figure 1-1 for a few drum shapes and sizes.) But, regardless of their shape or size, all drums consist of three basic components:

- The head (the membrane strung across the shell)
- The shell (the body of the drum)
- The hardware (the stuff that holds the other two parts together)

The look of drum hardware can vary in a lot of ways. The hardware can be as simple as tacks nailed through the head into the shell, or it can be as elaborate as gold-plated cast metal rims with bolts that are tightened to precise torque tolerances (try saying that ten times fast). Either way, they all do the same thing: They create tension on the head so that it can vibrate freely against the edge of the shell. Check out Figure 1-2 for a few hardware styles.

Figure 1-1:
Drums come in all shapes and sizes.

Exploring How Drums Create Sound

When you hit a drum, the head vibrates much the same way as a guitar string vibrates when you pluck it. And like the electric guitar when it's not plugged into an amp, not a lot of sound comes out of the head itself, which is where the shell comes in handy. The shell acts like the amplifier that your friend uses with his or her guitar — only you don't need to plug it in. So, you hit the

DRUM HISTORY

The power of one

Here's a story of a Vietnamese village that was about to be attacked by an enemy: The village had no soldiers available, so one man, a drummer, gathered the entire village's drums and began pounding them all as loud and fast as he could, making a huge ruckus. The attackers retreated and fled figuring that the village's army had to be very large and powerful to have command of such a group of drummers.

drum, the head vibrates, and the sound bounces around inside the shell. This motion makes the shell vibrate too. All the sound is then projected out of the opening in the drum and, *voilà!* The result is the sound of sweet music. Amazingly enough, this action all happens in a fraction of a second.

How the drum sounds depends on the circumference of the head, how tightly it's tuned, and the size, shape, and hardness of the shell. All these factors determine why drums can sound so many different ways and still be just a head, a shell, and some hardware. Without getting too technical, the size and tension of the head dictates the drum's *pitch* (how high or low the drum's tone is) while the size, shape, and hardness of the shell control the volume and timbre of the drum. *Timbre* is a fancy word for the quality of sound produced by an instrument. This timbre is why not all acoustic guitars or violins cost the same amount. For these instruments, the better the timbre, the higher the price. Luckily, this idea isn't necessarily true for drums. (To find out more about the relationship between a drum's timbre and its cost, go to Chapter 19.)

Figure 1-2:
A variety of hardware styles.

I can go on and on about how the relationship between the head and the size and shape of the shell creates particular sounds, but doing so won't help you play the darn thing. So, the important thing to remember here is that the larger the diameter of drum, the deeper the sound, and the longer the shell, the louder the sound. As always, some exceptions exist, but for the most part you can count on this idea being true.

Deconstructing the Drumset

Once upon a time, you played drums one at a time. Each drummer played only one drum, and in order to make bigger and better noise — er, music — more drummers were needed. Then somewhere along the way, innovative drummers started putting groups of drums together and beating them all at once. Today's drumsets consist of the following (see Figure 1-3):

A. Bass drum. The bass drum usually sits on its side on the floor and is played by stepping on a pedal with the right foot. This drum is generally between 18 and 24 inches in diameter and between 14 and 18 inches deep. Its sound is the foundation of the rhythm of a band, often pounding out the basic pulse of the music or playing along with the bass player's rhythm.

B. Snare drum. The snare drum is a shallow drum (typically between 5 and 7 inches deep) that's 14 inches in diameter and has a series of metal wires (called *snares,* hence the name *snare drum*) stretched against the bottom head. When you strike the drum, the bottom head vibrates against the snares. What you hear is a hissing sound. The snare drum creates the *backbeat* (the driving rhythm that you hear in most popular music; you can find out more about backbeats in Chapter 6) of the music and is what makes you want to dance.

C. Tom-tom. The tom-toms are pitched drums that are usually between 9 and 18 inches in diameter. A drumset commonly has at least two, if not three, of them (some drummers, such as Neil Peart from the 1970s rock band Rush, have dozens of tom-toms, so go wild if you want to). Generally, the largest tom-tom (called a *floor tom*) is set up on the floor with legs that are attached to the shell of the drum. The smaller tom-toms (often called *ride toms*) are attached to a stand, which extends up from the bass drum or from the floor next to the bass drum. These drums are used for *fills* (a fill is a break in the main drumbeat, as I cover in Chapter 13) or as a substitute for the snare drum in some parts of songs.

D. Hi-hat cymbals. The hi-hats are cymbals that are mounted on a stand, one facing up and one facing down, and are 13, 14, or 15 inches in diameter. The stand has a pedal that pushes the cymbals together (closed) or pulls them apart (opened). Your left foot controls the opening and closing of the hi-hats with the pedal while you hit the cymbals with a stick. The hi-hats can make either a "chick" sound when closed or a "swish" sound when open. You use them with the bass drum and snare drum to create the basic drum beat.

Figure 1-3:
The modern
drumset.

E. Ride cymbal. The ride cymbal is an alternative to the hi-hats. Ride cymbals range in size from about 16 inches all the way up to 24 inches across (20- and 22-inch ride cymbals are the most common). The ride cymbal is traditionally used to create a louder, fuller sound than the hi-hats and is often played during the chorus of a song or during a solo.

F. Crash cymbals. The typical drumset usually has one or more crash cymbals used for accentuating certain parts of the music, usually the beginning of a phrase or section of a song. These cymbals create a sound that resembles — you guessed it — a crash, not unlike the sound of a frying pan lid hitting a hard floor, only more musical. Crash cymbals generally range in size from 14 inches to around 20 inches in diameter.

The following aren't included in Figure 1-3, but many sets include them.

✓ **Splash cymbals.** Crash cymbals aren't the only accent cymbals that drummers use with today's drumsets. Other cymbals include the splash cymbal, a small cymbal usually between 8 and 14 inches in diameter, which makes a little splash-type sound. The splash cymbal is kind of a softer, watery-sounding version of the popular crash cymbal.

✓ **Chinese cymbals.** These accent cymbals have become common over the last couple of decades or so. Chinese cymbals have a slightly rougher, clangier sound than a crash cymbal (more like a garbage can lid). They range in size from around 12 inches to 20 inches and usually have an up-turned outer edge. They're often mounted on a stand upside down.

✔ **Gongs.** These cymbals were really popular additions to drumsets during the stadium rock era in the 1970s when drumsets were huge and drum solos were a staple. Gongs actually come in many shapes and sizes, but the most popular are large (up to three feet across) and very loud.

You can find many other additions to drumsets, which are limited only by the drummer's imagination and budget. In fact, many of the traditional drums and rhythm-makers that I describe throughout this book are showing up in many drummer's kits (*kit* is another word for a drumset).

Although it's the new kid on the block, the drumset has found a home within all the popular music genres that have emerged over the 20th and 21st centuries. You can put a drumset to work playing rock (see Chapters 6 and 11), the blues (see Chapter 7), R&B (see Chapter 8), jazz (see Chapter 9), and Latin and Caribbean music (see Chapter 10).

Appreciating the Old-timers: Traditional Drums

People have been playing drums since they discovered that banging a stick against a log made a pleasing sound (or at least a loud one). Unlike most musical instruments, you can find drums in all parts of the world. Different cultures created different drums based upon the materials they had on hand, their rhythmic sensibilities, and whether they were nomadic or agrarian people (people who moved around a lot developed smaller, lighter drums). As a result, you see an awful lot of different types of drums in the world.

The dawn of the drumset

Early forms of drumsets consisted of two or three hand drums lashed together and played by one person. Today's drumset, on the other hand, is a highly evolved grouping of specialized instruments, designed to allow one drummer to make as much noise as humanly possible. (I'm just kidding about that last part, but the current design of the modern drumset does have a specific purpose.)

The modern drumset was first developed with the emergence of jazz music early in the 20th century. Early jazz drummers put together the drums and cymbals used in military bands and folk music in order to be able to play all of these instruments by themselves. This setup allowed one drummer to use a variety of drums and cymbals that best complemented the music of the other musicians in the band. The drumset is indispensable in popular music today, and is the image formed in many people's minds when they think of drums.

The most common traditional drums include the *conga,* which is a barrel-shaped drum from Cuba; the West African, goblet-shaped *djembe;* the *Surdo* bass drum from Brazil; and the *frame drum,* which has a very narrow shell and comes from a variety of places all around the world (see Figure 1-4). (In Chapters 15–17, I introduce you to a wide variety of drums and other traditional percussion instruments.)

Figure 1-4:
Traditional drums that you're likely to see today.

Just as you have a wide variety of drum styles in the world, you also have a bunch of ways to play them. Some drums require hands or fingers while others require the use of sticks to produce their characteristic sounds. Still others utilize both hands and sticks.

Swingin' Sticks and Slapping the Skins

The most common and recognizable drumstick is used on the drumset and for playing *rudiments* (used for classical music and in drum corps; see Chapter 3). This stick is generally about 16 or 17 inches long with a diameter ranging from about ⅜ inch to almost one inch. The stick tapers down at about the last 2 or 3 inches (called the *shoulder*) to a beaded tip, which is what strikes the drum. The tip is made of either wood or nylon. The nylon-tipped stick produces a crisper and brighter sound than the wood-tipped stick. Figure 1-5 shows you a typical drumstick.

Some of the more traditional drums have other types of sticks. Some are wrapped in felt or fleece, some are just straight sticks with no tip, some are curved, and others have *beaters* (the part that actually "beats" the drum head) on both ends. See Figure 1-6 for a variety of stick shapes and sizes.

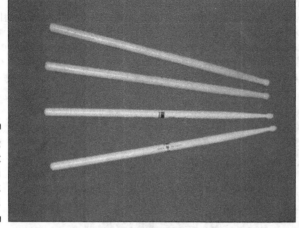

Figure 1-5:
The most
common
drumstick
used today.

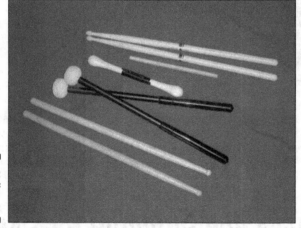

Figure 1-6:
A variety of
drumsticks.

Regardless of its shape or size, a stick can create a louder, sharper sound
than a hand, but a hand can create more subtle textures than a stick. With
your hand, you can *slap, pound, brush, fan,* or *tap* (for more about these and
other hand strokes, check out Chapter 4). You can use your whole hand or
just your fingertips. In many ways, this versatility allows hand drummers to
create an almost limitless variety of sounds on a drum.

Chapter 2

I've Got Rhythm . . .

● ●

In This Chapter

▶ Noting drum notation

▶ Reading music for drums

▶ Picking up on pulse and meter

● ●

A long-standing debate exists on whether drummers need to learn how to read music. To be honest, they don't. You can be a great drummer and never set your eyes on a piece of music. However, being able to decipher what's on the written page can open a lot of doors for you as a drummer. You can sit down with other musicians whom you've never met, play a song you've never heard before, and make it sound like it was meant to sound. Or you can walk into a store and get a transcription of that great drum solo that you've always wanted to learn but couldn't figure out by listening to the CD. Or you can trade rhythms with other drummers over the Internet. Or you can . . . well, you get my point. Read this chapter, and I think you'll find that reading music isn't that difficult. And I guarantee that any time that you spend learning the basics of music notation is well worth it.

As you'll find out, people use many different ways to describe how to play drumming rhythms. In this book, I use regular musical notation and terms. Doing so has two advantages: First, if you ever decide you want to read music for other instruments, you'll already know the basics; second, this way is much easier and clearer than some of the other ways out there.

You don't have to figure out how to read music to get through the rest of the book. All the rhythms written in this book are on the CD. All you need to do is listen to the CD track marked next to the rhythm and you can hear how it sounds. Then you can play along.

You can even use the CD to speed up your reading abilities. Just look at the rhythm in the chapter as you listen to it on the CD. In no time, you'll be reading music like a pro.

Developing a Sound Vocabulary

Think of reading music the same way you think of reading this book. You have letters that form words, which then form sentences, which form paragraphs, and so on. In music, you have notes and *rests* (later in this chapter, you can see all the notes and rests used in music), which form *measures* (a measure is a unit of time on musical notation). The measures then form phrases, and these phrases link together to create a song.

The first step to reading is forming a vocabulary from which to draw. Figure 2-1 shows your basic music vocabulary, which includes the following terms:

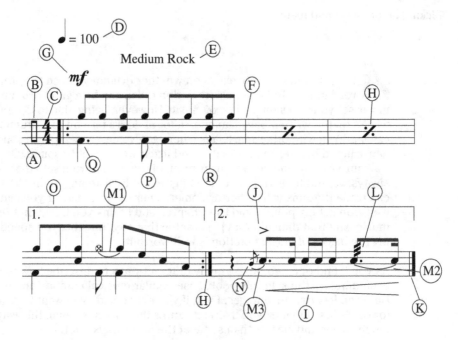

Figure 2-1:
Your basic drum music vocabulary.

A. Staff	G. Dynamic marking	M. Tie
B. Clef	H. Repeat	N. Grace note
C. Time signature	I. Crescendo	O. Ending brackets
D. Tempo marking	J. Accent	P. Notes
E. Style marking	K. End bar	Q. Dotted note
F. Bar line	L. Roll	R. Rest

✔ **A. Staff:** These five lines (and four spaces) contain all the notes, rests, and other pertinent information that you need to play music. Where a note falls within these lines (or spaces) tells you which drum or pitch to play.

Drum music doesn't always have five lines on the staff. It can have as few as one or two lines, depending on how the music is notated and the type of drum being notated. Single drums and percussion instruments — such as the ones I describe in Chapters 15, 16, and 17 — are notated this way.

✔ **B. Clef:** The *clef* refers to the range of notes that the composer wants you to play. For drummers, the *drum clef* merely means that the notes don't reference specific pitches. Instead you can find a legend somewhere on the page (usually at the top but sometimes at the bottom) that describes what drums you need to play and where they're notated on the staff.

✔ **C. Time signature:** This is by far the most important symbol on a piece of music. The time signature tells you how to treat all the notes. Figure 2-1 indicates that the music is written in 4/4 time. Four/four time, by the way, is the most common time signature used and is sometimes indicated by a large "C" instead of a 4 over 4 symbol. (See the "Embracing Odd Meter" section later in the chapter for more on other time signatures.)

The top number of the time signature tells you how many beats are in each measure. The bottom number tells you which note receives one beat (count). An easy way to remember how to get the length of the bottom note is to imagine a one above it. For example, putting a one above the four makes it a ¼ (quarter) note. So, for 4/4 time, a quarter note gets one beat and you have four of them in each measure. Simple, huh?

✔ **D. Tempo marking:** This symbol tells you how fast to play each note in reference to a *metronome* (a device many musicians use to help keep time. To find out more about metronomes, go to Chapter 19) or the clock. In Figure 2-1, the number refers to how many beats per minute you play the quarter note.

✔ **E. Style marking:** The style marking describes the *feel* or musical style in which the music should be played. Depending on the composer, a music score may or may not include the style marking.

✔ **F. Bar line:** The bar line separates the measures. Each *measure* is one grouping of notes that the time signature designates. In Figure 2-1, the bar lines come after four beats. Having measures allows the composer to divide the music up into small sections, making it easier to read and reference.

✔ **G. Dynamic marking:** The dynamic marking tells you how loud or soft to play. In Figure 2-1, the *mf* refers to *mezzo forte,* which means moderately loud. Other dynamic markings designate other volumes. Figure 2-2 shows some common dynamic markings.

Figure 2-2:
Dynamic
markings
found in
music.

pp = pianissimo (very quiet)

p = piano (quiet)

mp = metzo piano (moderately quiet)

mf = metzo forte (moderately loud)

f = forte (loud)

ff = fortissimo (very loud)

✔ **H. Repeat:** This symbol tells you to repeat the previous measure or section contained within the double bar lines.

✔ **I. Crescendo:** The crescendo is a dynamic marking that tells you to increase your volume gradually over the notes above it. Another dynamic marking related to volume is called the *decrescendo*. You play the decrescendo exactly the opposite way. Instead of gradually increasing your volume, you decrease it.

✔ **J. Accent:** The accent is another dynamic marking that refers only to the note below it. You play the accent louder than the surrounding notes.

✔ **K. End bar:** The end bar tells you that the song is over.

✔ **L. Roll:** This symbol refers to the drumroll. As in, "Drumroll, please." Rolls last as long as the note(s) to which they're attached.

✔ **M. Tie:** This symbol connects two notes together. For drummers, ties can be used several ways. They are as follows:

   • **M1:** This is the way ties work with most instruments. Here you sustain the note and hit only the drum on the first note of a tied series. If you're playing with brushes, the tie symbol means you slide the brush along the drumhead in a circular motion (this is one way drummers create sustained notes).

   • **M2:** When ties are connected to rolls, you play your roll (see previous bullet) through the tie and stop at the last note in the series (this technique is another way drummers sustain a note).

   • **M3:** When the first note in a tied series is smaller (a grace note; see the following bullet), you play both notes at nearly the same time.

✔ **N. Grace note:** You occasionally see a little note with the tie attached to a larger note, particularly when you have to play a *flam*. (A flam is a drumming rudiment.) I explain more about rudiments in Chapter 3.

✔ **O. Ending brackets:** The ending brackets tell you how to end a certain section of music. Notice that Figure 2-1 has two ending brackets. Ending 1 has a repeat that goes back to the beginning. The second time through the first three bars, you go to the measure in the second ending bracket instead of the first.

✔ **P. Notes:** These symbols describe what to play. Each note represents a different length of time. Figure 2-3 shows how many of these notes equals one measure in 4/4 time. Notice that one 4/4 measure consists of one whole note, two half notes, four quarter notes, eight eighth notes, or sixteen sixteenth notes. Do you notice something? When you have four quarter notes, each one of them fills up one *quarter* of a measure. The name of the note tells you how many of each note fits into one measure in 4/4 time.

The exception to this rule is an unusual note called the *triplet*. As you can see in Figure 2-3, the eighth notes are marked with a little "3" above them. These notes are triplets. Triplets are an artificial group of eighth notes — instead of two equaling one beat, three make up a beat. That's what the number three above them means. The triplet is a pretty common note grouping.

Other triplets include groups of quarter notes and groups of sixteenth notes. Three quarter-note triplets equal two beats. Three sixteenth-note triplets equal half a beat.

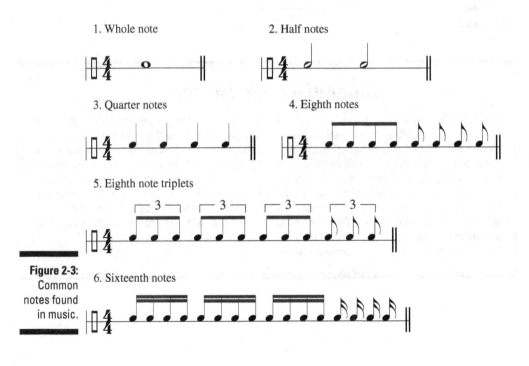

Figure 2-3: Common notes found in music.

✓ **Q. Dotted note:** The dotted note has a value that is one-half longer than its non-dotted counterpart. The dotted eighth note equals three-quarters of a beat rather than half a beat.

✓ **R. Rests:** These symbols tell you when not to play (you *rest* your instrument). Figure 2-4 shows the different types of rests.

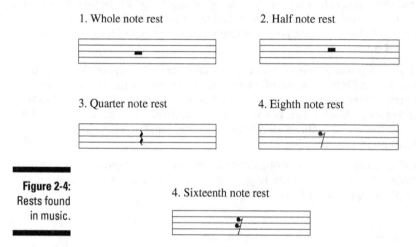

1. Whole note rest

2. Half note rest

3. Quarter note rest

4. Eighth note rest

4. Sixteenth note rest

Figure 2-4:
Rests found
in music.

Singing a different song

Until just a few hundred years ago, music was an oral tradition. Drumming rhythms were passed down through elaborate vocal phrases. Even today, if you study from some African or Indian teachers, you learn strictly through singing. In West African music, for example, an open tone (this tone is one of the many drum strokes that you can make; I describe drum strokes in Chapter 4) on the right hand is called "Go." The left hand is "Do." The vocalizations of the strokes in these cultures closely mimic the sound that the drum makes when it's played with that stroke. This method allows drummers to practice without actually having to play. In fact, I studied with a teacher for almost a year who never let me play the drum during the lessons. Instead, we sang the rhythms. This technique allowed me to really learn the rhythms well.

Adding Some Drumming Definitions

Even though drum notation follows regular music notation, I use some other symbols in this book to help you play rhythms. Figure 2-5 shows you many of them, and the following is an explanation of the terms:

Figure 2-5:
Music
notation just
for drums.

A. Count	E. Snare drum	I. Meduim tom-tom
B. Stroke	F. Bass drum	J. Floor tom-tom
C. Sticking	G. Hi-hat with foot	K. Higher pitched drum
D. Cymbal	H. Small tom-tom	L. Lower pitched drum

✔ **A. The count:** This isn't some aristocrat living in a castle somewhere, but rather a way to say or *count* the rhythm. For a drummer, the count is one of the most useful things to know, not just for reading music, but also for playing any rhythm. My teachers used to say, "If you can't count it, you can't play it."

Counting is really easy. In Figure 2-5 you essentially say out loud the counting pattern notated above the rhythm. For example, just say, "1 and 2 and . . . " for the top rhythm and "1 ee and ah . . . " for the bottom rhythm in the figure as you play the rhythm that's marked below. The purpose of the count is to help you place each note in the rhythm in its correct place within the measure.

✔ **B. Stroke:** This symbol shows the hand position or stroke to play. You use the stroke mainly for hand drums.

The strokes that you find in this book are as follows (I explain each of these strokes in detail in Chapter 4):

- **O:** Open tone
- **B:** Bass tone
- **M:** Muted tone
- **S:** Slap tone
- **H:** Heel movement
- **T:** Tip movement
- **P:** Palm stroke
- **Br:** Brushing stroke
- **Dr:** Drone tone
- **Sn:** Snap
- **Tr:** Trill

✔ **C. Sticking and hand pattern:** This information tells you which hand to use. "R" refers to the right hand and "L" refers to the left hand.

✔ **D. Cymbal:** Cymbals and hi-hats are generally placed on the top line of the staff. The particular cymbal that you should play is designated with the following (these notations vary depending on the composer, but in this book they look like this):

- D1: Hi-hat
- D2: Ride cymbal
- D3: Crash cymbal

✔ **E. Snare drum:** The snare drum part is often in the third space from the bottom of the five-line staff.

✔ **F. Bass drum:** The bass drum usually occupies the bottom space of the staff.

✔ **G. Hi-hat with foot:** When the hi-hat is played with the foot, it's marked with an "x" under the staff.

✔ **H. Small tom-tom:** This space is usually used for the smaller of the two ride toms on a drumset.

✔ **I. Medium-sized tom-tom:** This line refers to the larger of the two ride toms on a drumset.

✔ **J. Floor tom-tom:** This space signifies the drumset's floor tom-tom.

✔ **K. Higher-pitched drum:** When you're asked to play hand or stick-played drums, such as the congas or timbales (go to Chapter 15 for more about congas and Chapter 16 for more about the timbales), they're often notated on a staff with only one or two lines. In this case, the higher pitched drum lies above the line.

✔ **L. Lower-pitched drum:** The lower pitched drum goes below the line on single-line drum notation.

Becoming One with the Pulse (and I'm Not Talking Heartbeat)

All music, whether Mozart or Metallica, has a basic beat that carries it. This beat is called the *pulse.* In most popular music, the pulse follows the quarter notes in the 4/4 measure. You can tap to it and dance to it. The pulse basically drives the music. In other types of music, however, the pulse can be more obscure (such is the case in African music; see Chapter 15).

As a drummer, one of the most important things you need to do — aside from actually *playing* the drum — is tap into the pulse of the music, whether it's prominent or not. Developing a strong inner pulse isn't that difficult. Here are a few steps that you can take to start growing this pulse within you:

✔ Practice to a *metronome.* A metronome is a device that creates a steady beat to which you can play. (Go to Chapter 19 for tips on buying a metronome.)

✔ Tap your foot to the beat while you play.

✔ Count out loud. Use the count that I describe in the previous section and show in Figure 2-5.

✔ Listen to the type of music that you intend to play.

After you develop a strong inner pulse, playing any drum in any situation becomes a lot easier. In fact, if you can comfortably and confidently follow the pulse of the music and support it in your drumming, you'll find that other musicians love playing with you.

Feeling the Meter

Meter is another word for time signature (as in "This song has a 4/4 meter") or it can refer to the overall feel of the music. For example, you may hear the terms *duple* and *triple* meter. These terms refer to the feel of the rhythm and how the pulse of the music is divided. All music has either a duple or triple feel (and sometimes both — see the next section on odd meter). In other words, you can divide the meter into groups of two or three beats. Most 4/4 music has a duple feel (counted like 1–and–2–and–3–and–4–and), but in the case of triplets, you get a triple feel (counted 1–tuh–tuh–2–tuh–tuh–3–tuh–tuh–4–tuh–tuh). Figure 2-6 illustrates duple and triple meter.

Double meter

Triple meter

Figure 2-6:
Duple and
triple meter
(feel).

You may also run across music that you must play with a *shuffle* feel. This term means that you play the eighth notes as a broken triplet — that is, play the first and last notes of the triplet and rest on the second note of the triplet. Check out Figure 2-7 to see how to play the shuffle feel.

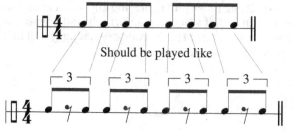

Should be played like

Figure 2-7:
How to
interpret
eighth notes
in a shuffle.

Embracing Odd Meter

When someone says that a song is in *odd meter,* he or she means that the song isn't in 4/4 time. It may be in 3/4 or 6/8 time (these time signatures are the most common odd meters, making them not so odd, actually). Or it can be in 7/8, 11/8, or even something like 21/16 time. Hopefully the person describing the time signature will also tell you the song's meter in addition to just saying, "this is in odd meter"; otherwise, you won't know what to play.

If you plan to play in odd meters, get comfortable with the combinations. Although most people agree that playing in odd meter is more difficult than playing in 4/4 time, you can get used to it. Check the denominator (the bottom number of the time signature — the number that tells you which note receives one beat). If it's 4, the time signature isn't much different than play-ing in 4/4 time — you still have eighth notes and sixteenth notes. The pulse has the same quality as 4/4, but instead of counting to 4 before returning to one, you count to whatever the top number is.

Denominators of 8 or 16 throw most people off. The pulse becomes irregular because the speed of the rhythm makes it difficult to tap on all the beats of the measure. Break up the measure into a pulse that you can tap. You can divide all these odd meters into groups of two and three, and most composers follow these groupings throughout the song. Look at Figure 2-8 to see the grouping combinations that you find in some of the more common odd meters.

As you play these rhythms, accent the first note of the grouping. That gives you the pulse of the rhythm. Being able to feel groupings of two and three notes allows you to really *play* with the rhythms in a song, and that's when drumming gets fun.

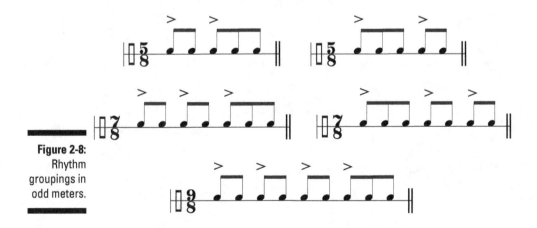

Figure 2-8:
Rhythm
groupings in
odd meters.

Chapter 3

Tapping into Drumming Techniques

● ●

In This Chapter

▶ Preventing injuries while playing

▶ Understanding basic stick playing techniques

▶ Discovering the rudiments

▶ Maximizing your practice sessions

● ●

*Y*ou'll find two aspects to playing the drums, or any other instrument for that matter. The first is knowing how to produce a quality sound on the instrument, and the second is having the muscular dexterity and coordination to make music. This chapter explores both of these areas.

This chapter also helps you prevent injuries by explaining the proper techniques for stretching and warming up before you play. I also tell you how to practice effectively and gain the most improvement for your efforts.

Talkin' Technique: What You Need to Know

With the huge number of different drums available in the world, you may expect a variety of ways to play them. That's true, but with some basic skills, you can pick up nearly any drum and create a decent sound on it. So, without further delay, here are the basics about drumming technique.

The first thing to keep in mind is to relax. Your shoulders and arms should have no tension except during the instant that your hand, foot, or stick contacts the drum's surface. This looseness allows you to play longer and faster and helps keep you from injuring yourself. Contrary to what you may have heard or seen (you know, the familiar images of the drummer who sits behind his drumset sweating and grimacing), playing the drums should be a relaxed and fluid process. Remember that drummers' grimaces are often an act — good drummers know how to stay loose behind their drums; otherwise, they wouldn't be able to play night after night.

Perfecting your posture

You've probably heard this directive a thousand times, but at the risk of sounding like your mother, I'm going to say it again — sit (or stand) up straight. You'll thank me later. And your back will thank you by being pain-free. Besides, with good posture you can play louder, faster, and longer. Isn't that what all drummers want? You bet.

When you're playing, occasionally check in and be aware of how you're holding your shoulders. Are they scrunched up around your ears or are they hanging loose? Chances are your shoulders will creep up as you play, especially when you concentrate or push the limits of your speed or endurance. So, occasionally check in and consciously relax your shoulders. Over time you'll notice that you're less tense overall, even though you'll probably still need to remind yourself to relax your shoulders once in a while.

Before you start playing your drum, sit or stand with your hands or stick resting on the drum and close your eyes. Take a deep breath and as you let it out, feel how you're sitting or standing. Adjust your posture, and then take in another deep breath. This time, as you let your breath out, drop your shoulders and relax your arms. Repeat this exercise two or three times, and then start playing. You can even do this workout once in a while during your practice session. This exercise helps you stay loose and become more aware of how you sit or stand behind your drums.

Preventing injuries

Drumming is a very physical activity, not unlike most sports. And like athletes playing sports, you need to prepare yourself for the demands that drumming can put on your body. This is true for practicing as well as playing a gig. In fact, stretching and warming up may be even more important for practicing. After all, you spend a heckuva lot more time practicing than you do performing.

Injury among musicians is a real problem. Some doctors specialize in the types of injuries common to musicians, and some researchers study nothing but how to prevent and repair these injuries. The most common injuries to befall drummers are *repetitive stress injuries* (*RSI*). As the name suggests, these injuries result from performing the same movement over and over again. Unfortunately, this repetition is what drumming is all about, whether you're perfecting a new rhythm or jamming on a groove with the guys (or gals).

The key to avoiding RSIs is to avoid playing when you're hurt (being sore is okay though) and to stretch, just like athletes do. A few rounds of yoga every day can do wonders. In fact, you may even want to take up yoga if you get really serious about drumming. (And, if you do, check out *Yoga For Dummies,* written by Georg Feuerstein, Larry Payne, and Lilias Folan, and published by Wiley.) If you're not interested in becoming a yogi, the following sections have a few simple stretches to help save you from a lot of pain.

When you're stretching, remember not to get overzealous. You don't want to hurt yourself; the goal is to prevent injuries, not create them. Ease into the stretch, and if it hurts, back off a little. If you practice or play for a long time, taking a break every once in a while to do these stretches is a good idea.

Hand stretch

Any drummer will tell you that hand cramps are a necessary evil in drumming. This reality is especially prevalent when playing with sticks. But by periodically stretching your thumbs and fingers, you can make yourself a lot more comfortable. Try, for example, the following:

- ✔ **Working your thumbs:** To stretch your thumbs, hold your hand with your thumb pointing up like you're hitchhiking. Relax your fingers, and then gently apply pressure to your thumb with your other hand (push it backwards) until you feel a slight burn in the muscle at the base of your thumb. Hold this stretch for 30 seconds and then switch hands. Repeat several times. Figure 3-1 shows you this thumb stretch.

- ✔ **Flexing your fingers:** To stretch your fingers, put your hands together at chest level (index finger presses against index finder, middle finger against middle finger, and so on). Next, put your elbows out, straighten your wrists and bend your fingers at their base. (Take a look at Figure 3-2 to see this position.) Push down on your wrists to stretch. You should feel the stretch in your palm. Hold for 30 seconds, and then rest for 30 seconds. Repeat this stretch a few times.

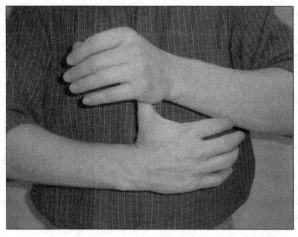

Figure 3-1:
Stretching
the thumbs.

Figure 3-2:
Finger
stretch.

Forearm stretch

As you play you notice that your forearms and wrists take a lot of abuse. If you're going to get injured, your forearms and wrists are likely to be the first casualty. The most important thing you can do to prevent injuries in your wrists is to avoid overflexing them as you play.

This stretch starts the same way as the finger stretch (see the previous section), except that this time, when you put your elbows out, your palms stay together. Figure 3-3 shows this position. Again, hold the stretch for 30 seconds, relax, and repeat.

Shoulder stretch

Because most drummers tend to hunch up their shoulders as they play, this stretch is a really great way to loosen up those shoulders. It can help you become more aware of your shoulders and prevent you from getting a sharp pain in your upper back that makes you want to stop playing.

To do the shoulder stretch, raise one arm straight up over your head and bend it at the elbow. Next, grab that elbow with the other hand and gently push down on the arm. Make sure that you align the hand of the arm that you're stretching with your spine. Figure 3-4 shows you the shoulder stretch position. Like the other stretches, do both arms and repeat (remember to hold the stretch for 30 seconds).

Figure 3-3: Forearm stretch.

Figure 3-4: Stretching your shoulders.

Back stretch

If your back often hurts when you play, you probably have poor posture. However, if you do the stretches that I mention in this section consistently, your posture will improve (if for no other reason than you're more aware of how you hold yourself up).

To stretch your back, bend over and touch your toes. To start, raise your arms up over your head and reach as high as you can. Then slowly bend over from the waist and reach for the floor. (It's okay if your legs bend a little — not too much though). Check out Figure 3-5 to see the back stretch.

Figure 3-5:
Back
stretch.

Hitting the drum: It's (not) all in the wrist

Remember when you're playing a drum to think in terms of *drawing the sound out of rather than driving it into the drum.* Again, this idea relates to relaxation. If your hands and arms are relaxed, your hand or stick will rebound off the head and allow the sound to resonate. If you're tense and your hand or stick presses into the head after you strike it, the sound dampens (sometimes you want this sound, but you need to be able to control it).

You've heard the saying, "It's all in the wrist", right? Well, this saying doesn't hold true for drumming. Instead, you want to control the movement of your wrist and let your whole arm move naturally when you play. Limit your wrist movement to about 2 to 3 inches. When you want to play louder, you can then lift your hand from the elbow. Doing so gives you more power, control, and endurance.

Speaking Softly and Carrying Big Sticks

When playing drums with sticks, you have fewer basic strokes from which to draw when compared to hand drumming. But this deficit doesn't mean that you're limited in what you can do. Drumsets overcome this deficit by providing more drums to get a larger variety of sounds. (Check out Chapter 4 for more on all the stroke options that hand drums provide.) But before you can hit the drum with a stick, you need to know how to hold the sticks.

Holding the sticks

Two basic ways to hold the drumsticks exist: *matched grip* and *traditional grip.* The right-hand position is the same for both these grips, but the left hand's position varies greatly.

Many people want to know which grip is better, the traditional grip or the matched grip. The answer really depends on who you ask. Personally (and I'm not alone here), I suggest the matched grip for most beginners. This grip takes less time to get comfortable with and allows you to play any kind of drum or music that you want. The matched grip also takes fewer muscles to perform a stroke. And you're better able to get a consistent sound between the two sticks using this grip.

On the other hand, if you already know how to play with the traditional grip, you really have no reason to stop using it. The fact is that both grips allow you to play the drums equally well (I sometimes switch between grips when I play).

Traditional grip

The *traditional grip* comes from military drumming. In military bands, a strap held the snare drum over the shoulder, and it rested on the left leg. The drum was tilted with the left side higher than the right. Because the left side was raised up and closer to the left arm, the drummer needed to use a different technique with the left hand. You hold your right hand the same way you do with the matched grip technique, which I describe in the next section.

To hold the sticks in the traditional grip with your left hand, take a look at Figure 3-6. You can see that the left hand basically grips the stick between the thumb and index finger (cozy it up to the inside corner) about a quarter of the way up from the butt end of the stick. This is the *fulcrum* of the grip, and the stick pivots from here. The stick cradles between the middle and ring fingers. The middle and index fingers wrap gently over the stick. These fingers control the lateral movement of the stick. To make the stroke, twist your wrist and rotate your arm from the elbow.

The important thing to remember about the traditional grip is that the stick rests *loosely* in your hand. You apply only enough pressure on the stick at its fulcrum (the thumb–index finger point) to keep it from flying out as you play. To keep the stick from flying out of your hand, squeeze the stick slightly when it hits the drum and release the pressure after it bounces off the head.

Figure 3-6:
Holding the drumsticks with the traditional grip.

Matched grip

The *matched grip* is the most common stick-holding technique used today. The matched grip developed as alternate ways of drumming appeared. Early rock 'n' roll drummers started using the same grip for both hands because they didn't have the constraints of the drum's position to contend with. Also, drum corps drummers started holding the snare drum in front of them with support at the waist. The drum no longer hung to the side, making the matched grip possible.

You hold both sticks the same way in the matched grip, as you can see in Figure 3-7a. Hold the stick between your thumb and index finger at the last knuckle joint of your finger (see Figure 3-7b), about a quarter of the way from the back end of the stick. The rest of the fingers curl around the stick and lightly hold it in place (see Figure 3-7c). The stick pivots from your index finger–thumb point while the fingers control the movement from beneath. Move the stick straight up and down to make the stick stroke.

One trick to holding the sticks with the matched grip is to think of your fingertips. If you use your fingertips, you can feel the drum better. You can also do some advanced techniques that allow you to play faster and with less effort. In Figure 3-7a you can see the gap between the thumb and finger (it looks like an oval space). This gap lets you know that you're holding the stick correctly. Take a look at Figure 3-8 — you don't see a gap. This person isn't using his fingertips. This position limits what he can do on the drum.

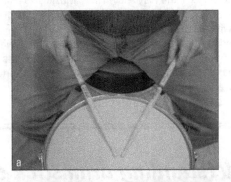

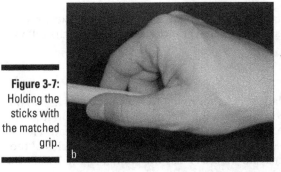
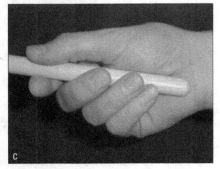

Figure 3-7: Holding the sticks with the matched grip.

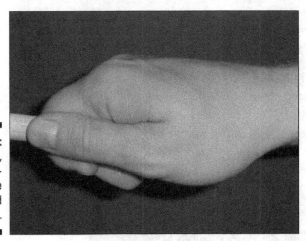

Figure 3-8: A common, but less-effective way to hold the sticks.

Getting a good grip

I learned to hold the sticks in the way shown in Figure 3-8 (the less-effective matched grip). For nearly ten years, while studying classical and jazz music, I worked my chops using this technique. I felt pretty comfortable and became quite accomplished at rudimental drumming (I even won a few awards). But the day I showed up for my first class with Joe Porcaro at the Musician's Institute, he suggested that I switch my grip from the one shown in Figure 3-8 to the grip shown in Figure 3-7. It took me weeks to get comfortable with this new grip, but after about a month, I was a believer. I played faster and with less effort, and I was able to play just as loud. Thanks Joe!

Understanding drumstick strokes

The drumming world has basically four drumstick strokes: the basic stroke, rim-shot, rim-tap, and dead-sticking. Discover more about each in the following sections.

Basic stroke

The *basic stroke* is the standard way to approach the drum, as well as the way you hit it most of the time, regardless of the volume. The best sound that's made from a drum hit with a stick is from the very center of the head. The closer you hit the drum toward the rim, the more *overtones* (multiples of the fundamental tone) it produces and the less clear the sound. Figure 3-9 shows you the basic stroke.

Figure 3-9:
The basic stick stroke.

Within the basic stroke, you see two special notations (check out Chapter 2 to see what the musical notation looks like for each):

✔ The first is the *grace note* (the miniature note on the staff). You play the grace note very softly. Like the muted tone, it's often nearly inaudible. The best way to get this sound is to lift your stick off the head only about an inch. Doing so forces low volume.

✔ The second special notation for the basic stroke is the *accent.* You make this note when you really hit the drum (go ahead and smack it!). Instead of lifting the stick just an inch off the head, you want to lift it a foot or more, depending on the overall volume that you're playing.

Rim-shot

The rim-shot is often associated with a loud sound, but you can play rim-shots at any volume. The trick is to hit the drum away from the center of the head and strike the *rim* (the metal hoop that holds the head on the drum) at the same time that you hit the head. Doing so creates overtones and gives the drum a higher pitched sound. By moving the tip of the stick closer to the rim, you get a thinner and quieter sound. (For rock drummers, you often want to hit the center of the drum when you do a rim-shot. This position gives you that extra punch to cut through even the most obnoxious guitar solo.) Figure 3-10 shows the stick placement for the rim-shot.

Positioning for volume control

Rudimental drummers (drumstick players who focus on playing the rudiments) have a concept called *positioning.* Positioning simply relates to how far you lift your sticks off the drum's head when you play to create a specific volume. Positioning allows a drummer to consistently repeat a volume day after day. The following are the basics for positioning:

✔ For low volumes like those marked *piano* (p), and for grace notes, lift your stick about an inch off the drum.

✔ For moderate volumes, such as those marked with a *mezzo forte* (mf), lift your stick about six inches off the head.

✔ For louder volumes like *forte* (f), start your sticks about 12 inches from the drumhead.

✔ For really loud playing, such as those marked *fortissimo* (ff), lift your sticks 18–24 inches.

Of course, these distances vary depending on the speed at which you're asked to play. (To see what those dynamic markings look like in music, check out Chapter 2.)

To play accented notes, go to the next higher position. For example, if a piece of music is marked as *mezzo forte,* you play the unaccented notes at about six inches from the head and accented notes about 12 inches.

Figure 3-10:
Getting the
rim-shot
right.

Cross-stick

Another rim stroke is the rim-tap or cross-stick (sometimes mistakenly called a rim-shot). Like its name implies, this is a quiet stroke used in jazz, Latin music, and ballads. With this stroke, you turn your stick around, place the tip against the drum head close to the rim, and pivot the stick up to strike the drum. With the tip pressed into the drum, you drive the bottom end of the stick into the opposite rim. Many people rest their left hand on the head while they hold the stick. Doing so helps dampen the overtone when the stick hits the rim. See Figure 3-11 for the rim-tap.

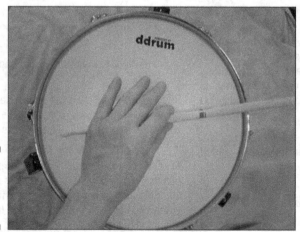

Figure 3-11:
The rim-tap
or cross-
stick.

Dead-sticking

Another commonly used technique is called *dead-sticking*. Dead-sticking is just pressing the stick into the surface after you hit the drum. With this technique, your index finger presses on the top of the stick. Figure 3-12 shows you how to hold the stick for dead-sticking. You use this technique mainly on traditional stick-struck drums and rarely on a drumset. The idea is to mute the head (or shell) after you hit it.

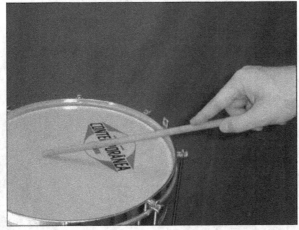

Figure 3-12:
Dead-
sticking
technique.

Painting a Variety of Textures with Brushes

Most drummers who play contemporary music think of playing only with sticks, but there are many more textures that you can create on a stick-played drum by using brushes. Brushes soften the sound of the drum and are often used in jazz drumming and some quieter styles, such as ballads in small clubs.

Brushes work only on *coated heads*. *Clear heads* don't have any texture for the brushes to rub against, so if you intend to use brushes on your drums, make sure that you use one of the coated varieties. Chapter 20 has more on coated versus uncoated heads.

Getting to know brush styles

There are a variety of types of brushes available. Each produces its own unique sound. Figure 3-13 shows a couple of the more common styles of brushes. The ones on the left are wire brushes, and the ones on the right are plastic brushes. You can also find wooden brushes that have larger diameter "brushes" than the plastic ones you see in Figure 3-13. As a general rule, the thinner the brush material, the softer the sound you get. So, the wire brush provides the softest sound while the wooden brush has a much louder, almost stick-like sound to it. The plastic brush material creates a sound in between these other two.

Aside from different brush materials, you can find brushes with different tools on the end of the handle. These tools include a rubber mallet (seen in the wire brush in Figure 3-13) and a wire ring (not shown) and are used to add accents or alternate textures on drums or cymbals.

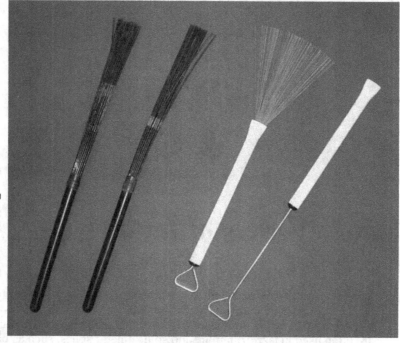

Figure 3-13: Brushes create a more mellow sound on a drum than a stick does.

Getting a grip on brushing techniques

There are tons of ways to play brushes, limited only by your imagination. However, you can find a handful of techniques that are pretty common, two of which I talk about in this section. You can use brushes two ways:

- ✔ **Hit it:** You can strike the drum with the brush in the same manner as you do a stick. This provides a softer sound than a stick but still contains the attack of the brush hitting the head.

- ✔ **Slide it:** By sliding the brush along the surface of the drumhead, you create a sustained (*legato*) sound that is quiet and has no attack like the one you get by hitting the head. You do this by sliding the brushes along the drumhead, often in a circular motion.

Dozens of different brush techniques use one or both of these approaches, and a few really good books and videos dig deeply into a bunch of them. Here are two videos that I particularly like:

- ✔ Ed Thigpen's *The Essence of Brushes*
- ✔ Clayton Cameron's *The Living Art of Brushes*

Sampling a slow-tempo technique

Ballads, some jazz standards, and other quiet, slow-tempo songs sound great when played with a pair of brushes. For these types of songs, you rarely hit the drum with the brush; instead, both hands use a circular sliding motion. Figure 3-14 shows the basic movement. This technique essentially consists of overlapping circles at a tempo where each beat of the measure equals one time around the circle. Your left hand moves in a counterclockwise direction while your right hand moves in a clockwise direction. This circular pattern keeps your brushes from getting tangled up with one another.

The key to masking this pattern groove (creating a musical sound) is to give a little extra push when you hit the top of the circle where the beat of the music happens. You do this by pressing down slightly harder on the head as you round the top of the circle and speeding up over the first third of the circle. You can hear a sample of this sound by checking out the slow-tempo brush pattern in Chapter 9.

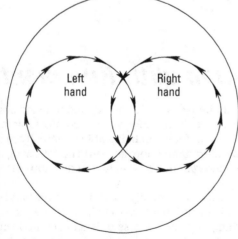

Figure 3-14:
A basic slow-tempo brush pattern uses overlapping circles to create the groove.

Making sense of medium- and fast-tempo techniques

Medium- and fast-tempo brushwork often consists of both the sliding movement and hitting the head with the brush. The pattern illustrated in Figure 3-15 has the left hand sliding around the head in a circle over the course of two beats. On beats 1 and 3 your left hand is positioned in the 10 o'clock point of the head and beats 2 and 4 are played while positioned in the 4 o'clock point. You want an even swishing-type sound as you move around this circle with the brushes.

The right hand plays the song's hi-hat pattern rhythm while moving from left to right in the upper portion of the head. The 1 and 3 beats are played at the 2 o'clock position and the 2 and 4 are played in the 10 o'clock position. Moving your strokes this way keeps your right and left brushes from hitting each other. Chapter 9 has a few grooves that use this technique.

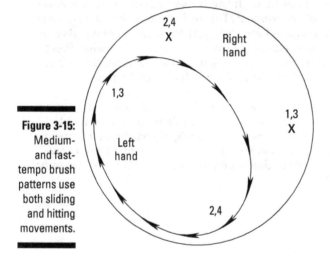

Figure 3-15:
Medium- and fast-tempo brush patterns use both sliding and hitting movements.

Forging a Foundation with Rudiments

As a drummer, your main challenge is to develop a fluid, relaxed sound. The only way to do this is to play the drum. After you get comfortable making the basic sounds on a drum, you can focus on being able to actually *play* it. What you need at this point is hand-to-hand coordination. The following are some tried-and-true exercises, called *rudiments,* to help you develop this skill.

Rudiments are sticking patterns traditionally used by military bands and classical percussionists. The role of rudiments is to help drummers become fluent in a variety of sticking patterns. Percussionists developed rudiments as a way to teach the basics of hand-to-hand coordination. Rudiments represent the foundations for all drumming, whether you play an African *djembe* or a classical *snare drum.*

Figure 3-16 illustrates the most basic and commonly used rudiments — the rudimentary rudiments, if you will. (You can find all 26 American Standard Rudiments on the Cheat Sheet in the front of the book.) No matter how you feel about these classical exercises, you will end up playing a few of them whether you like them or not. So, you may as well know what they are.

1. Single Stroke Roll

2. Double Stroke Roll

3. Paradiddle

4. Flam

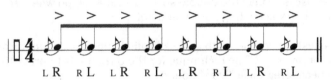

5. Ruff

Figure 3-16: Rudimentary rudiments.

The traditional way to practice these rudiments is to start out really slowly and gradually build up speed until you hit the maximum speed that you can play them and still be in control. Hold that tempo for a few minutes and then slowly reduce your speed until you're back where you started. You'll find that over time, your maximum speed increases. Another way to practice rudiments is to set your metronome (or play along to some music) at a comfortable tempo and play steadily for a few minutes or longer.

The single-stroke roll

This set of strokes is pretty simple: just RLRL ("R" is for your right hand and "L" is for your left hand). The key here is to make sure that both hands sound the same when they hit the drum and that you keep the time between each note even. As silly as it may seem to practice this simple stroke, the single-stroke roll is the foundation upon which you build all your drumming skills. With a solid single-stroke roll, the rest of the rudiments (and everything else you play) will be easier.

The double-stroke roll

RRLL is all you need to know for the double-stroke roll, but as you play this rudiment, your technique varies depending on your tempo. At slower speeds, you can make two deliberate strokes, but when you get to a certain point (this speed is different for everyone), you need to start bouncing the stick once to get the second stroke. In order to get the second bounced stroke to sound the same as the first stroke, boost the bounce with the tips of your fingers by bringing your fingers into the stick as it strikes the drum the second time. One good exercise is to play the double-stroke roll at a tempo where the bounces just start and try accenting the second note.

At the fastest speed, the double-stroke roll changes again and turns into the *buzz roll* or *press roll*. The technique for the buzz roll is to press the sticks into the head, creating a "bzzz" sound.

One thing to keep in mind is that as the roll gets faster, your sticks get closer to the drumhead.

The paradiddle

The *paradiddle* is a combination of the single and double stroke rolls. When you play this roll, make sure to evenly space all the strokes (single and double).

The flam

The *flam* is both hands hitting the drum at nearly the same time. The grace note indicates that you should place the stick close to the drumhead and make the sound of the first note softer than the second. Figure 3-17a shows you how the right flam looks, and Figure 3-17b shows you how the left flam looks. In order to do more than one flam in a row, you need to lift up the hand that plays the grace note to prepare for next stroke. You also need to leave the accented note down to prepare for its next stroke.

Figure 3-17:
The flam.

The ruff

The *ruff* is a lot like the flam (see the previous section) except that you have two grace notes instead of one before the accented notes. You play these two grace notes with one hand. So to play the ruff, do a flam with a double stroke.

Getting the Most Out of Your Practice Sessions

Like it or not, you'll spend more time practicing your drums than performing. This is the sad reality of playing a musical instrument. The good news is that you can increase the efficiency and effectiveness of your practice sessions and save yourself tons of time and energy. And, as I explain in this section, all it takes is a few basic skills. Practicing can be fun!

Starting slowly

The idea of starting slowly may seem obvious, but a reminder never hurts. When you're learning something new, always start really slowly. I mean really, *really* slowly. Painstakingly slow. Doing so forces your brain to organize the movement properly. Starting slowly makes playing fast much easier, and you can progress much more quickly than if you start out too fast. Playing slowly takes discipline, but I guarantee that it helps you learn to play new rhythms much quicker and much better in the long run.

Counting out the rhythm

While you're going slowly, count the rhythm out loud. Doing so helps you place each note more precisely than if you don't count out loud. After you get the rhythm down, you don't need to keep counting, but doing so every once in a while to check yourself is a good idea.

Thinking it through first

What do the world's greatest athletes, musicians, scientists, and business people have in common? The ability to effectively visualize their goals. The greatest athletes know that when it comes to practice, your mind doesn't distinguish between actual physical movement and imagined movement. You send the same signals to your muscles, no matter what. This characteristic of the human nervous system is probably your greatest ally. If you can learn to mentally practice effectively, you dramatically reduce the number of hours you sit behind your drum and keep improving even when you can't get to a drum.

The key to developing this skill is being able to clearly visualize your goal. In the case of drumming, imagine yourself at your drum playing the rhythm. Slowly think through all the steps. See your hands and feet moving in your mind. Imagine how the rhythm feels in your body. Play it perfectly in your mind and you'll be able to play it perfectly for real.

Toughing out practice

Becoming good at a musical instrument takes practice and consistency. Try to practice every day. I know that on some days you just don't feel like practicing. My recommendation: Sit down for just 15 minutes. No matter how much you want to stop, stick with it for those 15 minutes. Sometimes, just getting started is the hard part. If you find that after your 15 minutes are up you still don't want to play the drums, you can walk away knowing that you at least gave it a try. Most of the time though, you'll find that you want to keep practicing.

Knowing when to stop

I know. In the previous section I told you to stick it out when practicing. Now I'm suggesting that you stop playing sometimes. Stopping is the hardest thing to do when practicing (aside from starting on those tough days). Often, you get so wrapped up in the desire to get something perfect that you keep trying something over and over and without getting it right. In these instances, the best thing to do is to stop and take a break. Move on to something else. Such a break can last five minutes or a whole day. Besides, if you keep doing something over and over again incorrectly, guess what? You'll learn it wrong and have to relearn it later. (Relearning something that you did incorrectly is *much* harder than learning it right in the first place.)

When you get frustrated, letting go for a while is best so that you don't start resenting your instrument. Also, most times just taking a break allows your mind and body to process what you've been trying to learn. You may be surprised the next time you try the thing that was so hard and you find out that you can play it.

Some days when you sit down to play, you just can't get it right. As frustrating as this fact is, I do have some good news. On the days when you play poorly, you're actually learning and processing the most. So sit back and take joy in the fact that when your playing stinks, you're actually becoming a better drummer. (Of course, this is no fun when the day happens to be the most important gig of your career.)

Chapter 4

Getting a Handle on Hand Drumming Techniques

Most people in the West instantly think of the drumset when they think of drumming. From a worldwide perspective, however, most drummers play by using their hands. Hand drumming techniques are the world's oldest styles, and a stunning variety of different approaches have developed over the centuries. In this chapter, I introduce you to some of the most common ways to strike a drum with your hands to help you develop the skills to play a bunch of different hand drums.

Taking Matters (and Tones) into Your Own Hands

You can create a wide variety of different tones and sounds on any given drum. A conga drum, for example, can create about a dozen different sounds. Where and how you strike each drum has a direct influence on how it sounds. As a general rule, when you hit a drum toward its edge (or *rim*), you get a high tone, and when you hit it toward the center, you produce a lower tone.

For all the different sounds a drum can create, basically two types of tones exist:

▶ **Open tones:** Open tones allow the head to vibrate after you strike it.

▶ **Muted tones:** Muted tones, or *closed tones,* keep the head from vibrating after you hit it.

Work on each of the hand positions I cover in this chapter until the stroke feels natural and you get a consistently good sound out of the drum. You can then go on to combine these strokes, going from one to the other.

After you can create a clear clean sound, work on each of the rudiments with each stroke technique (see the Cheat Sheet and Chapter 3 for the rudiments). And after you get comfortable with the rudiments, try alternating stroke techniques. For example, go from an open stroke to a muted tone and back again. After you master going from one stroke to another you can combine multiple strokes.

Opting for Open Tones

Several open tone strokes exist. Some are traditionally used with particular types of drums, but you can play them all on any drum (with greater or lesser results).

The key to creating a good open tone is to let your hand bounce off the head as you strike it. Doing so allows the head to vibrate freely.

Basic open tone stroke

For most hand drums, hitting the edge of the drum with the knuckly part of your palm (where your fingers meet your palm) and letting your fingers bounce off the head gives you the best basic open tone (this stroke puts your fingers about 4 inches in from the edge of the drum). Experiment by moving your fingers closer to the center or the edge and see how the sound changes. You want a sound that's rich, clear, and without any *overtones* (those annoying ringing sounds that get in the way of a clear tone).

Every drum sounds a little different depending on the diameter, tension, and thickness of the head. Thinner heads tend to create more overtones than thicker heads. (Check out Chapter 1 for more information on various parts of a drum, including the head.) With thinner heads, you may need to move your fingers closer to the center of the head to get the best quality sound. When you find the best spot, practice hitting it awhile and get used to how it feels. Figure 4-1 illustrates the basic open tone hand position.

Figure 4-1:
Basic open
tone hand
position.

Thumb stroke

You mainly use the thumb stroke on drums with thin heads, although you can use it to play any drum. To make this stroke, strike the knuckle midway up your thumb against the drum about 2 to 3 inches in from the rim (exactly how far depends on your drum). You want a full, open, deep sound that's similar to the basic open stroke. Figure 4-2 shows you the proper way to make the thumb stroke.

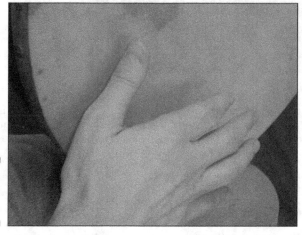

Figure 4-2:
The thumb
stroke.

The open slap tone

The open slap is an accent (louder) note that adds color to your drumming. This tone is also the most difficult sound to make on some drums. To make this sound, cup your fingers slightly as you strike the head. (Figure 4-3 shows the hand position for the slap stroke.) After your hand contacts the drum, relax your fingers and let them bounce off the head. The slap stroke makes a "pop" sound of a higher pitch than the basic open tone stroke. When you hit the drum just right, the sound is bright and projects clearly.

The proper slap sound is like the perfect golf swing or the perfect baseball pitch; some days you have it, and other days you don't. This inconsistency is one of the beauties of drumming. No matter how long you play or how much you practice, you always have something new to discover or some basic skill to perfect.

Figure 4-3:
The open slap.

Having trouble making the slap sound? One of the most important factors in getting that elusive slap sound out of your drum is making sure that the head is tuned properly. If the head is too loose or too tight, the sound is choked. (Go to Chapter 20 for more information on tuning your drum.)

Bass tone

To create the bass tone, strike the center of your drum with the palm of your hand. Like the open tone, you want your hand to bounce off the head as soon as you make contact with it so that the head can vibrate freely. One trick here is to hit the drum on a slight angle, brushing past the head as your palm hits it. This trick also helps get your hand out of the way of the head's vibration. For most drums, this position is also the most natural way to hit the bass tone because you have to move your hand at an angle toward the drum to get to the center of the head. Figure 4-4 shows the hand position for the bass tone.

Some drums are more conducive to creating bass tones than others. Generally, goblet shaped drums, such as the African *djembe* or Middle Eastern *doumbek,* make a more pronounced bass sound than a barrel-shaped drum, such as the conga.

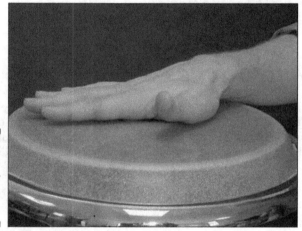

Figure 4-4:
Proper hand position for creating the bass tone.

The rim stroke

The rim stroke is a higher-pitched sound than the basic open stroke. Strike the drum's head close to the rim (in most cases, you actually hit the head where it meets the shell) to play the rim stroke. You want a clear, bright sound, so you need to experiment with each drum that you play to get the best sound. The pitch gets higher as you get closer to the very edge of the drum. After you get comfortable with this stroke, you discover a huge palate of variations in tone that you can use in your playing. Figure 4-5 shows the rim stroke.

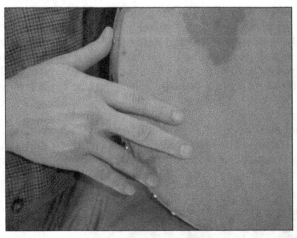

Figure 4-5:
The rim
stroke.

Mastering Muted Tones

Muted tone strokes add dynamic variation to your drumming. They're all much quieter than the open strokes (see "Opting for Open Tones," earlier in the chapter), and you can think of them as unaccented notes. Certain drums require specific techniques, and each different stroke creates a slightly different sound.

Basic muted tone

The muted tone differs from open tone in that you let your hand or fingers rest on the head after you strike it. Think of the muted tone as carrying you to the next accented note. Keep your hands relaxed and barely move them. Figure 4-6 shows this position. You generally play muted tones softer than open tones. All you really hear with a muted tone stroke is a light touch of your fingers against the head.

The purpose of the muted tone stroke is to subtly provide the pulse of the rhythm. Muted tones are the unaccented notes of hand drums that you feel rather than actually hear. They're the background patter that gives a rhythm its sense of movement.

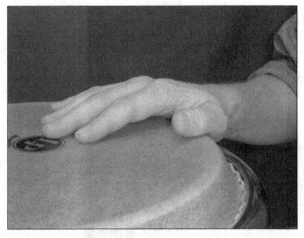

Figure 4-6:
The basic
muted tone.

The closed slap stroke

The closed slap is similar to the open slap except that you press your fingers into the drumhead when you make contact with it, keeping the head from vibrating. To play the closed slap on some drums, such as frame drums, you slap your hand into the center of the head. Figure 4-7 shows this variation on the closed slap.

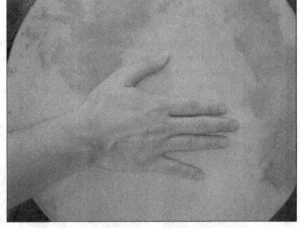

Figure 4-7:
The closed
slap
variation.

The palm stroke

The palm stroke is like a variation of the muted slap that's played in the center of the head except that you lay the palm of your hand into the center of the head instead of cupping your fingers. Drummers most often use this stroke with conga drums. Check out Figure 4-8 to see the palm stroke in action.

Figure 4-8:
The palm stroke.

The heel-tip stroke

The heel-tip stroke is a staple for conga drummers. To play this muted tone, rest your hand on the head and rock from the heel of your palm to the tip of your fingers. Remember to always keep your hand in contact with the head when you play the heel-tip stroke. Figure 4-9 shows the heel-tip stroke.

Figure 4-9:
The heel-tip stroke uses the heel (a) and the tip (b).

Venturing into Some Alternative Strokes

Occasionally, you want to add to some of the basic strokes that I mention previously in this chapter with some unusual variations. You can add the following alternative strokes when you feel comfortable with the basics.

Brushing stroke

To play the brushing stroke, strum your fingers against the head by moving your arm up and down at the elbow. This quiet, light stroke adds texture to your playing. You can use either the pads of your fingers or your fingernails for a brighter, louder sound. Figure 4-10 shows the brushing stroke.

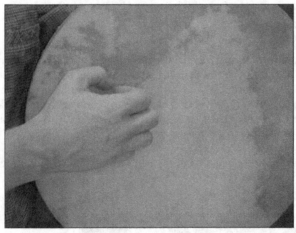

Figure 4-10:
The brushing stroke.

Drone tone

Dampen your finger against your tongue and slide it (your finger) lightly against the head of your drum to make the drone tone. Like the open slap stroke, this tone is often elusive. You need just the right amount of moisture (how much varies depending on the head and the relative humidity in your environment) and a textured head (natural hide works better than plastic). A smooth plastic head doesn't make this sound. See Figure 4-11 for the drone tone.

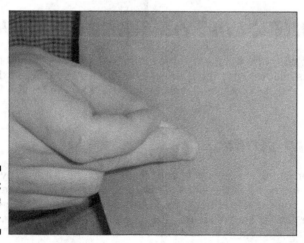

Figure 4-11:
The drone
tone.

The snap

The snap is an alternative stroke that drummers don't use very often. You play the snap at the rim of the drum (usually a frame drum). Performing this stroke is as easy as snapping your fingers. In fact, you do snap your finger (didn't I say it was easy?). What makes this move into a drum stroke is that you snap your finger into the rim of the drum. Go easy, though. You don't need to snap very hard to get a loud sound.

The snap stroke sounds like a brighter rim stroke. Figure 4-12 shows the hand position for this stroke.

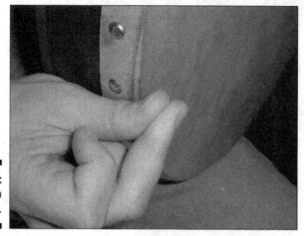

Figure 4-12:
The snap
stroke.

Trills

Tap the fingertips of your ring, middle, and index fingers against the drumhead in succession to make a trill. You can do just one round (ring, middle, index) for a three-beat stroke, or you can repeat it to make a *drumroll* out of it (a *drumroll* is just a succession of notes played fast). Figure 4-13 shows the hand placement for this stroke.

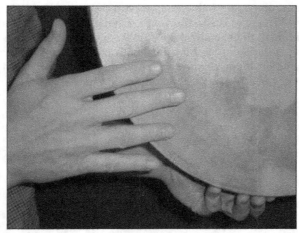

Figure 4-13:
The trill.

One-handed rolls

To make a one-handed roll, rock your hand back and forth by twisting your wrist between the knuckle of your thumb and your ring finger. Check out Figure 4-14 to see how to play this stroke.

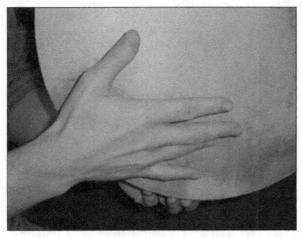

Figure 4-14:
The one-handed roll.

Keeping Your Options Open

You can find many more hand drumming techniques used around the world than I list in this chapter and in Chapter 15. I've been playing drums for more than 35 years and every year I discover a new way to play a drum. This discovery is one of the most exciting parts of playing drums for me — I always have something new to learn.

I encourage you to be open to the many ways a drum can be hit and to explore the variety that exists in the world. Even if you don't consider yourself a hand drummer, the skills you develop from working on these new techniques increases your ability to play musically and to perform on your instrument of choice. If you're interested in discovering more hand drumming techniques, I offer some great resources in Chapter 21.

Part II
Digging into the Drumset

"Kid down here is practicing his drums...wants to know if we could coordinate our hammering to coincide with his backbeat."

In this part . . .

*E*ver since you decided to be a drummer, you've probably been itchin' to get your hands (and feet) on a
drumset. Well, this section is for you. In Chapter 5, I introduce you to the quintessential drumming tool: the drumset. You find out how to set up your kit and take your first
steps toward rhythm independence. In Chapters 6 through
10, you start developing the skills to play many styles of
music, including rock, jazz, blues, R&B and funk, and Latin.
To end this section on a high note, Chapter 11 shows you
the rhythms and techniques of some of today's best rock
drummers.

Chapter 5

Settling In Behind the Drumset

Are you one of those people who wants the guitar player or singer at a club to get out of the way so that you can see what the drummer's doing? At a concert, do you find yourself giving up your tenth-row seats and moving to the nosebleed section behind the band so that you can watch the drummer? Do you love the grace that comes with a nicely played groove or a beautifully executed *fill* (see Chapter 13 for more on fills)? Well, if so, the drumset is the instrument for you (but you probably already knew that or you wouldn't have picked up this book).

This chapter helps you set up your drumset so that you look great sitting behind it. You also get your feet wet, so to speak, and discover how to attack the bass drum and hi-hat pedals. Likewise, you can begin developing the skills necessary to move all four of your limbs (your hands and feet) independently.

Setting Up Your Drumset

You have many ways to set up a drumset. In fact, there are almost as many ways to set up a drumset as there are drumset players. In this section, I help you set up your drums so that they're as comfortable and easy for you to play as possible.

The vast majority of drummers set up their drums right-handed — even many left-handed people (such as myself). So, in this section, I walk you through the right-handed setup (if you intend to drum left-handed, just reverse the positioning of each of the instruments). This is often called playing with a right-hand lead. Playing this way basically means that you play the bass drum with your right foot, the hi-hat pedal with your left foot, the snare drum with your left hand, and the hi-hat or ride cymbal(s) with your right hand. (Your right hand crosses over your left hand in order to play the hi-hats.)

The first thing you want to do is set up your drums as I outline in Chapter 1. You can then go through the rest of this section and make the minor adjustments that fit you.

Sitting on the throne

As you set up your drums, the first and probably most important position is how high you sit on your *throne* (the throne is the stool). The height that you choose depends on your comfort level. For instance, drumming great Vinnie Caliautta (he's played with Frank Zappa and Sting, among many others) sits really low, with his knees way above his hips. I also know some drummers who have their thrones set so high that they're almost standing behind the drums. Although you can play the drums at almost any height, a certain height range does seem to make playing easier and more efficient.

A good rule to follow when adjusting your throne is to have your hips even with or just slightly higher than your knees, so that the top of your thighs is parallel or slightly above parallel to the ground (see Figure 5-1).

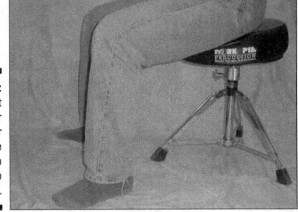

Figure 5-1:
A throne fit for a king or queen: Your thighs are close to parallel to the ground.

Having your hips too low causes your muscles to work harder because you have to lift your knees farther in order to make a stroke. You're also more easily thrown off balance when you use both feet. If you sit too high, you have more difficulty generating a lot of power with your feet, especially if you want to play with your heels down.

Positioning the pedals

Getting the pedals adjusted essentially means setting your throne the proper distance away from the bass drum and hi-hat stands. This task is pretty simple. You get the most power, speed, and endurance if your ankle joint lies directly beneath your knee. Figure 5-2 shows you this position.

If your knee sits too far beyond your ankle, you create an uncomfortable stress on your ankle joint when you play. If your knee is farther away from the drum or hi-hat stand than your ankle, your playing will lack power.

Figure 5-2:
Proper
pedal
position:
Place your
knee
directly
above your
ankle.

Securing the snare drum

The snare drum sits on a stand positioned between your legs and is, without a doubt, the drum you hit most often, so its position is very important. With the snare drum stand, you can adjust both the height and angle of the drum. In most cases, you want to have the drum at as flat of an angle as possible and the height such that you can play both rim-shots and open strokes easily (see Chapters 3 and 4 for descriptions of these techniques). Check out Figure 5-3 to see the best position for the snare drum on its stand. Notice how the drum tilts slightly toward you.

Figure 5-3:
The snare
drum stand
position.

Placing the tom-toms

How high and at what angle you place your mounted tom-toms determine how long your drumheads last and how easily you can reach them. Like the snare drum, you want to keep your tom-toms as close to level as possible. Place them at an angle, but make sure that the angle matches your sticks' angle. You want your stick to hit them at a relatively flat angle so that it doesn't drive tip-first into the head. Figure 5-4 shows a good tom-tom position. Notice how they're not set up so high above the snare drum that you can't reach them, but they're high enough that the rims of the snare and small tom-tom aren't touching.

Figure 5-4:
A good
position for
the tom-
toms.

Adjusting the ride cymbal

Adjusting your cymbals properly allows you to get a variety of sounds from each of them and also lengthens the useful life of your sticks. You want to hit the ride cymbal with either the tip or shoulder (the part that narrows) of your stick. You also want to reach the *bell* (the little "crown" at the center of the cymbal) easily. Figure 5-5 shows you the most popular position for the ride cymbal. In addition to having one on the right side of the drumset, some people put a ride cymbal on the left side near the hi-hats.

Figure 5-5:
A common
ride cymbal
position.

Angling the crash cymbals

Unlike the ride cymbal, the crash cymbals sound best when you strike them on their edge with the shoulder of your stick. This kind of hit chews up your sticks pretty badly, but that's the price you have to pay for a full crash cymbal sound. Check out Figure 5-6 to see one of the many angles at which you can set your crash cymbals.

When you set up your crash cymbals, make sure that you can reach them easily and that they look good from the audience's viewpoint. Some drummers like to position them so that they can be seen by the audience while others like to hide behind their cymbals. Choose the way that you like best.

Figure 5-6:
A good angle for your crash cymbals.

Be careful not to hit the bow of the crash cymbal (located halfway between the center and edge of the cymbal) with the shoulder of your stick (see Figure 5-7). Doing so increases the likelihood that your expensive cymbal will crack.

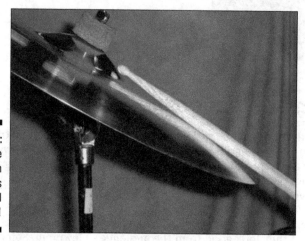

Figure 5-7:
Don't hit the crash cymbals this way. They'll crack!

Raising the hi-hats

Playing the hi-hats is easiest when you position them high enough so that you can hit the snare drum with some force and not have your right hand in the way. Check out Figure 5-8 for an idea about where to position your hi-hats. Notice how, at this height, the shoulder of your right-hand stick can hit the hi-hats toward their edge and leave plenty of room for your left hand to play the snare.

Figure 5-8:
Hi-hat cymbal position.

Putting Your Foot Down

Some drummers play with their heels down while others play with their heels up. Each way has advantages, and only you can decide what's best for you. Personally, I almost always play the bass drum with my heel up and play both ways on the hi-hat, depending on the situation. I assume that you'll do the same things with your feet because that's what every drummer I know does. Playing this way is also the most efficient way to play today's music (all styles — yes, even jazz).

Beating the bass drum

Although some people play the bass drum with their heel down, the vast majority of drummers keep their heel up. The heel-up position allows you to play faster, louder, and longer (don't worry — you can still play softly with the heel up, too). Figure 5-9 shows the typical heel-up position. Notice that you apply pressure on the ball of the foot.

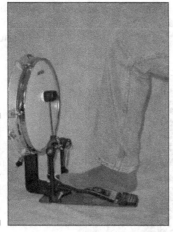

Figure 5-9:
The typical
heel-up
position for
the bass
drum.

To make the bass drum stroke, lift your knee and drop your foot into the pedal. If you apply a little forward pressure as you push down on the pedal, you get a solid sound. Most of the time, you want the pedal's beater to bounce off the head of the drum so that it can ring freely.

As you get comfortable playing the bass drum and get a few grooves under your belt, you'll probably want to play some *double strokes* (for more on double strokes, go to Chapter 3). Here's where the heel-up position comes in handy. With it you can play double strokes with very little effort.

Check out Figure 5-10. It shows you how to play a double stroke. Notice the position of the foot in Figure 5-10a. The heel is way up and the pressure is applied on the very front of the ball of the foot and the toes. This is the first stroke. Figure 5-10b shows the second stroke. You can see that the heel is lower and the pressure is more toward the back of the foot's ball. To play the second stroke, move your foot slightly forward as you bring your heel down after the first stroke.

To play the double stroke, play the first stroke on your toes with your heel way up. Then drop your heel and move your foot forward slightly. Kick lightly into the drum. To do triple or quadruple strokes, repeat the first stroke position (heel stays up and foot stays back) for all but the last stroke (heel comes down and foot moves forward).

Playing the hi-hats

You can play the hi-hats either with your heel up or down, depending on what you're doing. Whenever you play the hi-hats with your sticks, you want your heel down. To open the hi-hat, raise your toes slightly and release some of the pressure on the cymbals. Figure 5-11a shows this position.

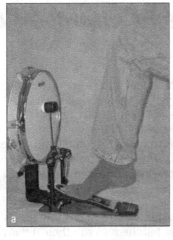

Figure 5-10:
The double bass drum stroke.

How much you lift your toes determines just how much your hi-hats will open and how long they will ring when you hit them. Most of the time you want a full swish sound. To create this sound, don't open the cymbals too much. You have to experiment to find the swish sound that you like best.

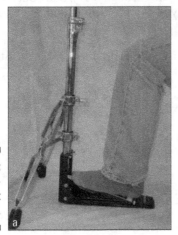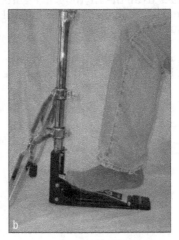

Figure 5-11:
The heel-down hi-hat position.

At times, you may want to use your left foot to play the hi-hat while you're playing the ride cymbal or another drum with your right hand. In this case, playing with your heel up is the way to go. This technique is pretty much the same as the heel-up bass drum stroke (see the previous section). You can even do double strokes on the hi-hat pedal the same way. Check out Figure 5-11b to see the heel-up hi-hat position

Working Out: Exercises to Improve Your Hand- and Footwork

Being able to move your hands and both feet independently is the foundation of all drumset playing. At this point, you become as much an athlete as a musician. The drumset drummer has the distinction of being the most coordinated and physically trained of the musicians in a contemporary musical setting. Sure, the guitar player strums or picks with one hand while fretting with the other and maybe singing too, but the drummer is back there essentially running laps with his or her legs while at the same time using both hands, often doing two different things.

Don't let the other musicians in the band tell you that drumming is easier than playing the guitar. If they do, just tell them to rub their tummy and pat their head while salsa dancing.

The following series of exercises can help you mentally separate each of your limbs. The first group, shown in Figure 5-12, alternates single-stroke patterns (right, left, right, left) among your four limbs. Take a look at the legend at the top of the figure to see which hand or foot plays which note (this legend applies to all the rhythms in Figures 5-12 through 5-17). Start out slowly and gradually build up your speed until you can play them fluidly at a tempo of about 120 beats per minute.

The next set of rhythms (see Figure 5-13) uses double strokes (right, right, left, left) on each of your extremities.

Figure 5-12: Single stroke four-way independence exercise.

Figure 5-13: Double stroke four-way independence exercise.

The rhythms in Figure 5-14 contain some exercises that double up your limbs, which helps you figure out how to use two limbs at the same time. Playing the notes that use a right foot and a right hand together or a left foot/left hand combination is easier than mixing a left hand and right foot or right hand and left foot.

Figure 5-14: Combination exercises.

The series of rhythms shown in Figure 5-15 uses double strokes and double limbs. Like the rhythms in Figure 5-14, you may find mixing a left foot with a right hand or a left hand with a right foot tricky at first. Just take your time and go slowly. You'll get the hang of it.

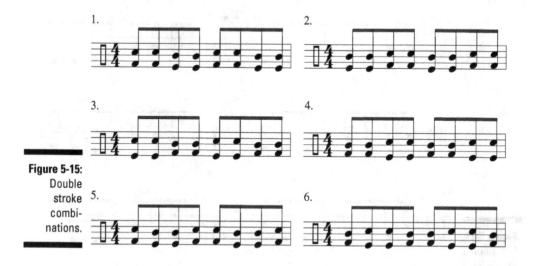

Figure 5-15: Double stroke combinations.

The exercises in Figure 5-16 are definitely the most difficult (that's why I put them toward the end of the chapter), utilizing double strokes on each limb but in combinations where you play the first stroke with one limb and the second with another.

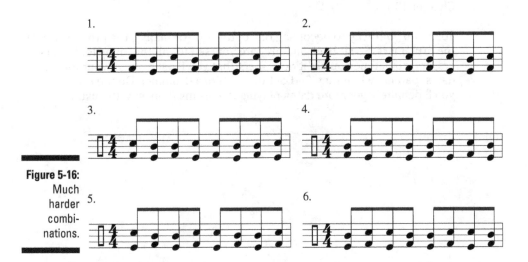

Figure 5-16:
Much harder combinations.

Figure 5-17 shows you a few more difficult combinations in case you haven't had enough yet.

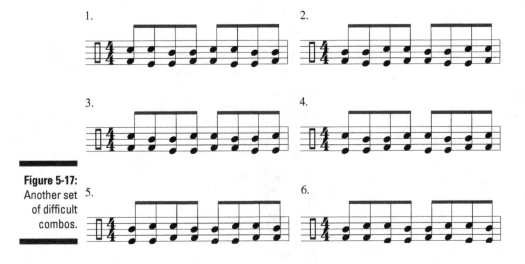

Figure 5-17:
Another set of difficult combos.

I love these exercises and often use them as a warm-up. Some of these rhythms also make cool fills. As you learn the rhythms in the following chapters, you can incorporate them into your drumming by playing three bars of time (your main drum rhythm) and then one of the patterns in this chapter. Doing so helps you get into and out of a fill. (For the full scoop on fills, see Chapter 13.)

You're on your way to becoming one of the few (or many), the proud (or not), the drummers. So sit back and prepare yourself for all the funny looks, snickers, and sometimes outright disrespect that you'll get from all your future dates' parents when they find out that you're a drummer. On the other hand, you'll definitely get more dates playing the drums than, say, the ukulele.

Chapter 6

Rolling into Rock Drumming

• •

• •

*I*mages of Ringo Starr (you know, from the Beatles) sitting behind his drums in front of tens of thousands of screaming fans or Rush's Neil Peart wowing the audience with his 15-minute drum solo and huge drumset have stirred many people to want to pick up a pair of sticks and join a rock band. Who can blame them? Rock drumming can be both creatively stimulating and physically gratifying. And, as Ringo demonstrated to the world, rock drumming can be a whole lotta fun.

This chapter explores what is probably the most popular drumming style today. Rock music is comprised of many different styles, including rhythms from jazz, blues, Latin, and Caribbean styles. Variations among these diverse styles abound, and rock drumming encompasses everything from straight-ahead styles to progressive, rhythmically diverse approaches.

When the band The Police showed up in the 1970s, drummer Stewart Copeland broke a lot of rock drumming rules by integrating the little-known reggae style of playing complex hi-hat patterns and playing the kick drum where the snare drum would usually play. This rule-breaking not only gave The Police a unique sound but also opened many doors for young drummers like myself who were thinking (and playing) outside the box. In another example, the Dave Matthews Band drummer Carter Beauford draws heavily from the influences of the 1970s progressive rock and jazz-fusion styles in his playing. So, even if you intend to play drums only in a rock band, I highly recommend that you check out the chapters on other styles of drumming — these chapters may help you define a sound that's uniquely your own.

In this chapter, you discover the basics of rock drumming and develop the skills that you need to play most rock music. I introduce you to some basic rhythms in all the different feels that encompass the rock genre. You can even get fancy with a few grooves that make you sound like a pro. Finally, you also find out that rock drumming isn't all about bashing and banging; it's as dynamically rich and texturally varied as any other style of drumming.

Harnessing the Backbeat

Without a doubt, the backbeat is the foundation of all rock drumming. The *backbeat* is the driving rhythm that the snare drum plays. You almost always play this rhythm on the second and fourth beats of the measure. The backbeat gives rock music its characteristically driving feel. As a rock drummer, you need to play the backbeat with conviction. No limp-wristed, drop-the-stick-on-the-head stuff here. You need to really hit the drum.

Practice hitting the snare drum solidly in the center of the head. The sound should be deep and full. One of the best ways to create a driving backbeat is to play a rim-shot. As I cover in Chapter 3, you play a rim-shot by hitting the rim of the drum at the same time that your stick strikes the head. Because it makes the shell vibrate more, the rim-shot adds depth to your drum's sound.

You don't have to play loudly in order to get a great backbeat sound. With a rim-shot, you can play an almost infinite variety of dynamics and still have a good sound. You can experiment with where you hit your sticks on the drumhead to see the different sounds that you can get. As a general rule, the deepest, fullest pitch results from hitting the center of the head. As you hit closer to the edge, the sound of the drum gets thinner and higher in pitch.

Hitting the drum toward the edge creates *overtones*. Overtones are higher-pitched, "ringy" sounds that the drum makes all the time, but are usually covered up by the main tone of the drum (that is, if it's tuned properly; go to Chapter 20 for more on tuning). Hitting the drum off-center allows these overtones to ring more loudly compared to the main tone of the drum.

Mastering the Basic Beats

With the command of just a few basic rhythms, you can make your way in a rock band. The rhythms in this section cover nearly all the styles that you may encounter (and a few that you won't see very often). The key to these rhythms is creating a tight, hard-driving feel. Your backbeat should be strong, the bass drum solid, and the hi-hat smooth. And, you should play all these instruments (snare drum backbeat, bass drum, and hi-hat) in sync with one another.

Rock music (and its close relatives blues, R&B, and funk) consists of a variety of styles or *feels*. The feel basically refers to the way that the rhythm is composed and interpreted. Different feels include eighth-note feels, sixteenth-note feels, shuffle feels, and regular and half-time feels. I refer to these feels many times in the next few chapters, so I'm listing them here for easy reference. The basic drumset feels are as follows:

- ✓ **Eighth-note feel:** The eighth-note feel consists of eighth notes played on the hi-hat or ride cymbal. This feel is also called the straight eighth-note feel because you play the eighth notes straight (as written). You play the snare drum on the second and fourth beats of the measure.

- ✓ **Sixteenth-note feel:** The sixteenth-note feel is similar to the eighth-note feel except that you play sixteenth notes or variations on the sixteenth note on the hi-hats or ride cymbal instead of eighth notes. You also play the snare drum on beats two and four.

- ✓ **Shuffle feel:** The shuffle feel uses triplets as the base instead of eighth or sixteenth notes. The shuffle also uses what are called *broken triplets*. With a broken triplet, you don't play the second note (you play only the first and third notes) of the triplet. You also play the snare drum on beats two and four for the shuffle feel.

In each of the previous feels (eighth-note, sixteenth-note, and shuffle) you play a variety of rhythms on the bass drum, depending on the song.

When you play the snare drum on beats two and four, you're playing what's called a *regular-time feel*. But, the eighth-note, sixteenth-note, and shuffle feels can each be played in a *half-time feel*. The half-time feel essentially means that you play the snare drum *half* as often as in the regular-time feel. Instead of twice in a measure (beats 2 and 4), the snare drum is played only once, usually on the 3 but sometimes on the 4 (depending on the song).

Unless I state otherwise, you play all the rhythms in this chapter with a *right-hand lead*. That is, you play the hi-hat (top line of the musical staff) with your right hand and the snare drum (third space from the bottom) with your left hand. Chapter 5 has more information on playing with a right-hand lead.

With all the rhythms in this section, experiment with how much you close the hi-hat. Applying a lot of pressure to the hi-hat pedal creates a tight, "chick" sound when you hit the cymbals, while releasing that pressure slightly gives the hi-hats a fuller, louder "chshh" sound.

Practice all the rhythms and their variations one at a time until you can play them steadily and fluidly at a variety of tempos.

Eighth-note feel

The vast majority of all rock music is played with an *eighth-note feel*. This feel essentially means that the music is in 4/4 time and that you play eighth notes on the closed hi-hats. The snare generally occupies beats two and four, and the bass drum plays variable eighth-note patterns (usually playing along with the bass player's rhythm).

The rhythms in Figure 6-1 contain some of the most common bass drum patterns. Rhythms 1 and 3 are arguably the most used rock beats. In fact, if you turn on your radio or put on a rock CD, I bet you don't have to listen to more than a couple songs before you hear one of these beats (you can find a few more basic rock beats in Chapters 7 and 8).

Figure 6-1:
Basic eighth-note feel rock beats.

After you get comfortable with all these variations, try playing them with the hi-hat accent patterns in Figure 6-2. You play accented notes louder than the surrounding note.

Figure 6-2: Alternate hi-hat accent patterns for eighth-note feel rhythms.

Sixteenth-note feel

The *sixteenth-note feel* uses sixteenth notes as the basis for the rhythm. Instead of playing eighth notes on the hi-hat, you play sixteenth notes or variations based upon the sixteenth note. You still play the snare drum on the second and fourth beats. Generally, songs using this feel are slower than those that use an eighth-note feel.

At slower tempos, you play the hi-hat with your right hand (or your left hand if you play left-handed), but at faster tempos, you have to ditch the right-hand lead technique (the right hand plays the hi-hat) because these rhythms work best with alternating strokes (right, left, right, left . . .). When you play these rhythms using an alternating stroke pattern, you play the snare drum with your right hand. Because you play the hi-hat with both hands, you won't be able to hit the snare drum and the hi-hats at the same time. So to play the backbeat, your right hand has to come off the hi-hat in order to strike the snare drum.

Figure 6-3 contains some common basic sixteenth-note feel rhythms. These rhythms are written for a slow tempo. (That's why the music notates that you play the hi-hat when you play the snare drum.)

Figure 6-3:
Sixteenth-note feel rock beats with a slow tempo sticking pattern.

Take a look at Figure 6-4. Here you can see the sticking pattern for the faster tempos. Which pattern you use is determined by how fast you can comfortably play and which pattern sounds better in the song that you're playing. You should get comfortable playing each of the bass drum patterns in Figure 6-3 at both slow and fast tempos.

Figure 6-4:
Sticking
pattern for
fast tempo
sixteenth-
note feel
rhythms.

After you get fluid with the rhythms in Figures 6-3 and 6-4, try using the hi-hat accent patterns in Figure 6-5. Accent pattern 3 is very challenging, so take your time and go slowly until you get the hang of it.

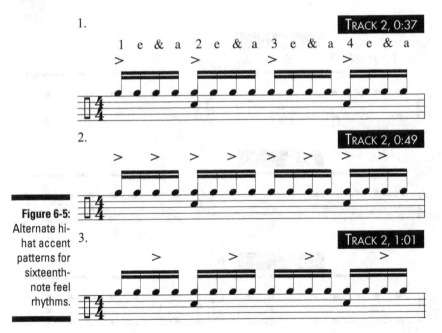

Figure 6-5:
Alternate hi-
hat accent
patterns for
sixteenth-
note feel
rhythms.

Half-time feel

The half-time feel gives a song the feeling of being slower than it is. Drummers often use this type of rhythm during verses or quieter, mellower parts of songs (see Chapter 12 for more on the parts of a song). The half-time feel can use either eighth or sixteenth notes. What distinguishes the half-time feel from the regular-time feel (grooves with backbeats on two and four) is that you play the snare drum on the third beat of the measure instead of the second and fourth. This technique makes the rhythm seem half as fast as its regular counterpart.

Figure 6-6 shows some common half-time feel grooves using an eighth note hi-hat pattern. As you can see in Figure 6-6, rhythms 5 and 6 have their backbeat on the four instead of the three. This is another interpretation of a half-time feel and is very common for the verses in rock ballads.

Figure 6-7 contains some common half-time feel rhythms using a sixteenth-note hi-hat pattern. Take a look at rhythms 4 and 5. They both have the backbeat on the four instead of three. Notice how different they sound from others. Practice each of these rhythms using both the slow and fast sticking patterns from Figures 6-3 and 6-4.

Figure 6-6:
Half-time feel rhythms using an eighth-note hi-hat pattern.

Figure 6-7:
Half-time
feel rhythms
using a
sixteenth-
note hi-hat
pattern.

After you get really comfortable playing all the rhythms in Figures 6-6 and 6-7, try switching back and forth between the half-time feel and a regular-time feel rhythm (those rhythms in Figures 6-1 through 6-5).

The rock shuffle

The rock shuffle is a fairly uncommon feel, although it was much more common during the blues/rock era of the late 1960s and early 1970s. The *rock shuffle* is simply a regular eighth-note feel with the eighth notes interpreted as a *broken triplet* (you play only the first and last notes of the triplet beat; go to Chapter 2 for more on triplets). The trick in playing this feel is to make it swing. (You can find out more about how to swing a groove in Chapter 10.) Basically, the feel should have a feeling of forward movement.

You may find the right-hand shuffle pattern somewhat challenging when you begin to play it. One good trick to getting the shuffle feel right is to play a quiet left hand stroke on the rest (the second note of the triplet) while your right hand plays the broken triplet (just tap your left hand against your leg so it doesn't make any noise). Figure 6-8 shows how you play this rhythm. When doing this exercise, concentrate on how your right hand's rhythm feels and sounds. After the rhythm becomes fluid, eliminate your left hand and see whether it sounds the same. If it does, move on to the rhythms in Figure 6-9.

Figure 6-8:
Right-hand shuffle pattern exercise (your left hand plays silently).

Figure 6-9 contains a few rock shuffles to familiarize you with this playing style. You see rhythms 1, 5, and 6 most often in rock music. Some rock shuffles require that you play them very fast (as in the case of early punk or speed metal styles), and you won't be able to play the broken triplet pattern with your right hand. In this case, use one of the hi-hat patterns in Figure 6-10 instead. You may also find situations in which the song calls for one of the alternate patterns even when the tempo is slow enough to play the broken triplet. Make sure that you can play all the bass drum patterns from Figure 6-9 with these two alternate hi-hat patterns (Figure 6-10).

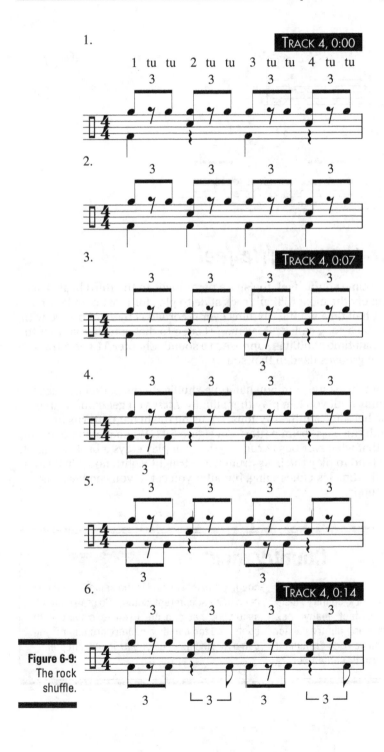

Figure 6-9:
The rock
shuffle.

Figure 6-10:
Alternate hi-
hat patterns
for the rock
shuffle.

The half-time shuffle feel

During the half-time shuffle feel, the snare part moves to the third beat. This shuffle is arguably the most difficult rock style to play for most people. One of the greatest half-time shuffle rhythms ever recorded is by Jeff Porcaro with the band Toto on a song called "Rosanna." (Listen to that song if you want to hear how the half-time shuffle is supposed to sound. Chapter 11 has a transcription of the grooves used in that song.)

Figure 6-11 contains some common half-time shuffle rhythms. Practice each of these rhythms until you can play them fluidly. After you get comfortable with the basic half-time shuffle rhythms, try using the hi-hat patterns in Figure 6-12 with the bass drum patterns in Figure 6-11. When playing pattern 1, make sure that whatever bass drum rhythm you play stays a broken triplet. (Most people tend to play the bass drum with straight eighth notes instead of shuffling it.) Rhythm 3 is challenging, but after you get it, you can hear just how cool it sounds.

Country rock

As its down-to-earth lyrics and showmanship blended with the rhythms of rock, country music became hugely popular. In fact, many rock drummers found their niche in country music. You can use most of the basic rock drumming grooves exactly as they are in contemporary country music. The feel is the same — you just need to wear different clothes. So grab yourself a cowboy hat and get used to playing with boots. You too can be a country drummer if you can play the basic rock beats in this chapter.

1.

2.

3.

4.

5.

Figure 6-11:
The half-
time shuffle.

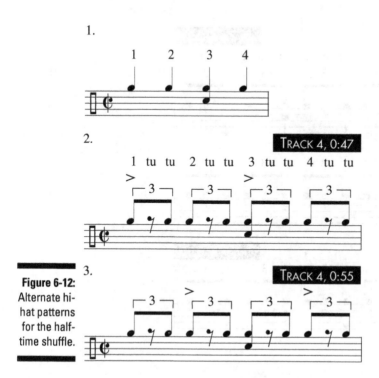

Figure 6-12:
Alternate hi-hat patterns for the half-time shuffle.

Dressing Up the Basic Beats

If you think that you have the hang of playing some basic rock patterns, you can now start thinking about adding some personality and texture to your drumming. The following exercises give you a palate from which to draw. You can use some of these rhythms as your basic groove, while others are better suited for only occasional use as fills and embellishments (see Chapter 13). The rhythms and techniques in this section are where you really get to shine as a rock drummer. Use these variations to the basic beats effectively (this often means using them sparingly) and you'll sound like a pro.

Mixing up the hi-hat

You can choose from an almost infinite variety of open and closed variations. Figure 6-13 shows a few (the "o" notates that you open the hi-hat slightly before you hit it to create a swish-type sound and the "+" indicates when you close the hi-hat with your foot to choke the swish sound off).

Figure 6-13:
Rock beats
with open
and closed
hi-hat
patterns.

Because you haven't used your left foot with the basic rock beats, except to keep the hi-hats closed, it may take you some time to get used to incorporating it into your playing. Just go slow and you'll get it in no time at all.

When you open the hi-hat, keep your heel on the pedal and lift your toes slightly. You're trying to make a "swish" sound. Both cymbals should still touch when they're open. The "swish" often sounds better if you hit the edge of your cymbals with the shoulder of your stick. Doing so gives you a fuller sound.

With these rhythms, you use all four limbs, and your posture is really important. Falling off balance just a bit throws off your playing. So sit up straight and lean forward slightly. For more tips on the right kind of posture to use while playing, check out Chapter 3.

Moving the backbeat

At times, moving the backbeat from its typical position on the two and four (or the three for half-time feel rhythms) can make your groove more interesting. This move is usually most effective when you do it sparingly; however, a few recent, popular rock songs use rhythms like numbers 3 and 5 in Figure 6-14 throughout the song very effectively. Moving the backbeat has a tendency to completely change the feel of the music. Figures 6-14 and 6-15 contain some grooves that allow you to get comfortable altering your backbeat placement.

Figure 6-14 contains eighth-note grooves. Notice how the snare drum beats in rhythms 7 though 12 fit in between the eighth notes of a hi-hat stroke.

The rhythms in Figure 6-15 have a sixteenth-note feel. They're written for a slow tempo with your right hand playing the hi-hat pattern.

Figure 6-16 shows you how to approach the rhythms in Figure 6-15 using an alternating stroke pattern on the hi-hats.

Figure 6-14:
Eighth-note feel rock beats with an offset backbeat.

Figure 6-15: Sixteenth-note feel rock beats with an offset backbeat.

Figure 6-16: Another approach to the rhythms in Figure 6-14.

Notice how you play the first snare drum beat (written on the "a" of 1) with your left hand. Getting your left hand past your right hand in order to hit the snare drum may be tricky at first but with practice it gets easier.

Adding syncopations

More and more, rock drumming draws from other styles of music. Syncopated (notes played on the "e" or "a" of the beat) bass drum and snare drum patterns are becoming more commonplace and give the music a funky feel.

Figure 6-17 shows a few rock beats with the bass drum playing syncopation. Some of these rhythms are a bit tricky to play because you play the bass drum both between the beats of the hi-hat as well as on the adjacent beat.

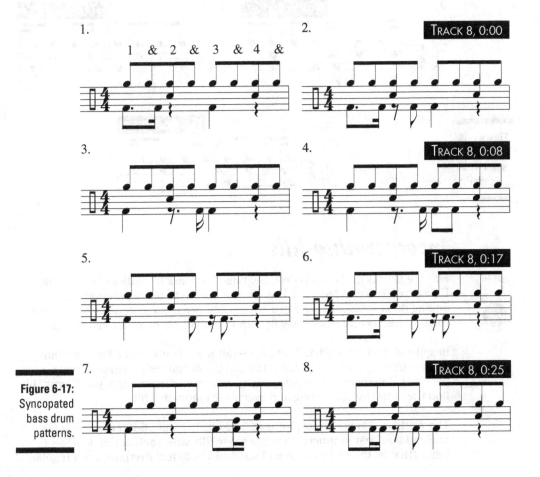

Figure 6-17: Syncopated bass drum patterns.

Figure 6-18 contains some syncopated snare drum accents. This type of playing is very common in the alternative, modern style of rock music. In each case, you play the syncopated snare beat between two hi-hat beats. You should play these additional snare drum beats slightly softer than the backbeat.

Figure 6-18: Syncopated snare drum patterns.

Incorporating fills

Fills are breaks in the main drumbeat used to mark transitions in the song. Unless you're Keith Moon of The Who, you want to use discretion when adding these breaks to your drumming. Fills are most effective when you use them sparingly and when they fit with the music of the other instruments.

In spite of their somewhat limited use (after all, you spend a lot more time playing basic grooves than fills), fills are the drummer's chance to make a personal statement. If you get really serious about drumming, you'll probably find the most joy in creating and executing innovative fills.

The world of fills is almost limitless. The fills in Figure 6-19 are some basic one and two beat numbers. Practice these fills with each of the *duple-feel* beats (that is, the eighth-note and sixteenth-note feel rhythms, both regular time and half time). After you get comfortable with them, try *changing the orchestration* (using a different drum). For instance, play rhythm 1 on a tom-tom rather than the snare.

Figure 6-19:
Some basic fills in duple feel.

The set of rhythms in Figure 6-20 has one and two beat fills for triplet-feel rhythms (the shuffles).

Figure 6-20: Some basic fills in triplet feel (shuffles).

You should play all the fills in Figures 6-19 and 6-20 as written until you get comfortable with them. After you're comfortable, add three bars of a groove before them to create a *four-bar phrase*. Figure 6-21 shows how to play this phrase. Try all the fills with each of the drum beats in this chapter. For more fills, check out Chapter 13.

Figure 6-21:
Creating a
four-bar
phrase with
the fills.

Chapter 7

Beating the Blues

A aahhhh, the blues. The blues is probably one of the most loved styles of music and also one of the most fun to play. And the great thing about the blues is that you can play it successfully in no time! Of course, you have to develop a few skills, but this chapter can help you so you don't have to experience the heartache that often typifies the blues in order to really *feel* this style of music.

In this chapter, I explore blues drumming and introduce you to some of its most common rhythms and styles. I also tell you what it takes to play the blues effectively and what makes a great blues drummer great. To top it off, I also explain how to fit your playing into the most common blues song structure so that you can play the rhythms in this chapter.

Finding the Pocket and Staying in It

Blues music is all about the feel of the rhythms. Technical skill is less important than how you interpret what you're playing. When you play the blues, you want to make sure that you're *in the pocket*. Being *in the pocket* means playing the rhythm solidly and keeping it simple.

You don't want to clutter up your playing with a bunch of fills (see Chapter 13 for more on fills). Blues music also tends to have very extreme dynamic variations, so closely following the dynamics of the tune is important. When the volume is loud, you need to whack the backbeat on the snare drum; when the volume is low, you need to barely hit it.

Here are some other key ideas to remember when playing blues:

✔ As you play, you should lock in with the bass player. Try to match your bass drum rhythm to the bass player's. Closely watching (and listening to) what the bass player does often helps, and in most cases, a good bass player watches (and listens) to you too.

✔ The singer or lead guitar player often cues the dynamic changes by motioning with his or her hand or body, so keep an eye on him or her as well (you'll be able to tell when he or she wants to play louder or softer). You want to offer support to the singer as he or she pours his or her heart out.

If you really want to learn how to connect with the other musicians in the band and to play with heart and soul, playing the blues will teach you a lot. These skills easily translate to any other style of music that you may want to play. As always, watching a band play live can teach you a lot about how musicians interact and communicate on stage, so go see as much live music as you can. Doing so only improves your ability to play well with others.

Playing Blues

Most traditional blues music has a triplet feel and is written in either 4/4 or 12/8 time. Regardless of how it's written, the sound is the same. Check out Figure 7-1 and notice how both 12/8 and 4/4 time with triplets are actually the same. In fact, if the music is written in 12/8 time, it's usually still counted like it's in 4/4 time. To count this way you divide the 12/8 measure into four groupings of three. The four beat pulse lands on the one, four, seven, and ten. Take a look at the accents in the top rhythm of Figure 7-1. They correspond to the four beat pulse. All the rhythms in this chapter have this pulse.

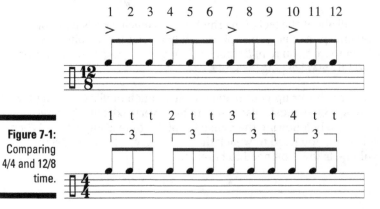

Figure 7-1:
Comparing
4/4 and 12/8
time.

Slow tempo

The basic groove for slow blues is pretty easy to play. Figure 7-2 shows this rhythm. Notice that the hi-hat plays eighth notes while you play the bass drum on the first (counted as one) and seventh beats (counted as three) and the snare drum on the fourth (counted as two) and tenth beats (counted as four). If you can play this rhythm solidly, you can play the blues.

Figure 7-2:
Basic slow blues rhythm.

TRACK 10, 0:00

The most common slow blues rhythm adds a few additional bass drum notes to the rhythm in Figure 7-2, creating a shuffle-type feel between the bass drum and the snare. Figure 7-3 shows this rhythm.

Figure 7-3:
The most common slow blues rhythm.

TRACK 10, 0:11

Of course, you can play many variations to the bass drum rhythm on the main groove that will (if used correctly) add to the song. If you listen to the rhythms that the bass player plays, they'll guide your bass drum beat. Try to match your bass drum with the bass player's groove. Figure 7-4 contains some slow tempo bass drum variations to the main groove. If you have a mastery of each of these rhythms, you can *lock in* (play along) with what most bass players play.

1.

TRACK 10, 0:23

2.

TRACK 10, 0:34

3.

4.

TRACK 10, 0:46

Figure 7-4:
Variations
on the slow
blues
rhythm.

Medium tempo

The shuffle (see Chapter 6) rules in medium-tempo blues. Your snare drum
and bass drum patterns remain the same as with the slower blues beats I
describe earlier in this chapter while the hi-hat pattern changes to reflect the
faster tempo. Figure 7-5 shows a bare-bones medium-tempo blues groove
using a shuffle hi-hat pattern. To get used to playing this hi-hat rhythm (and
to help get your right hand to play a solid shuffle rhythm), check out Figure
6-8 in Chapter 6. Playing the shuffle pattern correctly is really important in
order for the shuffle to sound right.

Like the slow blues rhythms, the basic medium-tempo pattern can have a
variety of bass drum patterns. Figure 7-6 shows a few.

Figure 7-5:
Basic
medium-
tempo blues
rhythm.

TRACK 11, 0:00

1.

TRACK 11, 0:07

2.

3.

4.

TRACK 11, 0:14

Figure 7-6:
Variations
on the
medium-
tempo blues
rhythm.

5.

More and more, blues players use a straight eighth-note feel (see Chapter 6 for more on this and other feels) with their music. This music is often classified as *blues-rock*, and as the name implies, most straight-ahead rock beats fit nicely. Figure 7-7 has a few blues-rock rhythms to get you started, but you can go to Chapter 6 to see more basic rock beats that you can use in blues music.

Figure 7-7:
Straight eighth-note feel blues rhythms.

Fast tempo

Sometimes when the tempo is too fast, the shuffle hi-hat pattern (see Figures 7-5 and 7-6) is either too busy or too difficult to play. In this case, you can try a couple of different hi-hat rhythms (check out Figure 7-8).

You can also use the hi-hat patterns from Figure 7-8 for slower tempos if you choose. They give the song a slightly different feel. You should be able to play these rhythms with each of the different bass drum patterns from Figures 7-3 through 7-6.

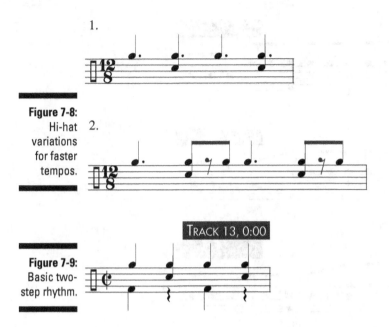

Figure 7-8:
Hi-hat
variations
for faster
tempos.

Figure 7-9:
Basic two-
step rhythm.

For very fast blues, a *two-step rhythm* works best. Figure 7-9 is a basic two-step rhythm, which you can use in blues, gospel, and country music (see the sidebar "When the blues meets country" to find out more about the two-step). A two-step rhythm would be very easy to play, except it's often played very fast. When playing this rhythm, make sure that the backbeats on the second and fourth beats are solid. In fact, an accent should mark the backbeats of this rhythm. The two-step rhythm is common, not only in the blues, but in gospel and country music as well.

Filling in . . . or not

Because the drums are very much a support instrument for most blues songs, fills aren't too important. You can get by just knowing a few basic ones (see Chapter 13 for more fill ideas). The key, as in all styles of music, is to try to match your fill to the overall tune. Figure 7-10 has a couple of the most common and basic fills for the blues. Try these fills with each of the rhythms in this chapter. After you get comfortable playing them, try putting the fills in a four-bar phrase. Figure 7-11 shows you an example.

Figure 7-10: Basic blues fills.

Figure 7-11: Four-bar blues phrase.

Understanding Blues Song Structure

Most blues music is in a twelve-bar form — called, what else but *twelve-bar blues*. If you end up jamming with other musicians and they say, "let's play some blues" or "how 'bout some twelve-bar blues," this form is what they're talking about.

The twelve-bar structure consists of three four-bar phrases. These four bars are generally divided into two two-bar phrases in a call and response format. The singer sings a line over the first two bars (the call) and then he or she follows it with a repeat of that phrase (or something similar), or the guitar player plays a phrase to reinforce the singer's line (the response). Figure 7-12 shows the twelve-bar blues song structure.

When the blues meets country

Traditional country music, which you don't hear much of today on country music stations, has a lot in common with the blues. They have similar origins consisting of folk music inherited from the ancestors of people from many different areas. And both utilize some of the same types of rhythms (one of which is shown in Figure 7-9 — commonly called the "Texas two-step" because of its association with a particular dance step). Another common country music rhythm is a 3/4 waltz feel. The following figure shows you how to play this rhythm. (To play contemporary country-rock music, check out Chapters 6 and 11.)

TRACK 13, 0:05

Figure 7-12:
Twelve-bar
blues song
structure.

Chapter 8

Rallying Around R&B and Funk

. . . .

In This Chapter

▶ Playing a drumset in the funk and R&B styles

▶ Working on basic grooves

▶ Developing the "feel" of these styles

. . . .

Do you like the music of James Brown, Aretha Franklin, or Marvin Gaye? Maybe your tastes run more toward Janet Jackson, Mariah Carey, or Usher. Either way, you obviously have an appreciation for music with an emphasis on drumming that has a solid groove and a smooth feel, which is the essence of R&B drumming. It's about grooving (playing the rhythm solidly) and keeping time. It's also about rhythm and syncopation. So, if you're ready to bring on the funk, this chapter is for you.

This chapter introduces you to the many ways of approaching R&B music on the drums, including how R&B is different from rock music and how it's the same. You can try your hands (and feet) at playing a variety of grooves that fit this style. You can also get funky and explore some of the more intricate rhythms of funk and R&B music.

Playing R&B Grooves

R&B (Rhythm and Blues) is basically a blending of blues, rock, jazz, and gospel music and is very groove oriented. Fills (see Chapter 13) are used sparingly, and solos are almost unheard of. Your main concern when playing R&B music is to make the rhythm flow and fit the rest of the music as well as possible. R&B is much like rock music in this aspect; the differences between these two styles lie in the complexity of the rhythms that you use and the way that you interpret the rhythms.

Keeping time

Because basic R&B grooves are much like those in rock music, the rhythms in this section are similar to the rhythms in Chapter 6. In fact, you can use any of the rhythms from this section and the "Mastering the Basic Beats" section of Chapter 6 in either rock or R&B music. The biggest differences, however, are that you play these rhythms with a little more laid-back feel in R&B than you do in rock, and most often, you don't have any accents on the hi-hats — all beats get the same volume. You treat the backbeat much the same way as you do in blues and rock — you need to play it with conviction. (Figure 8-1 contains a few basic R&B grooves with an eighth-note feel.)

Figure 8-2 shows a few rhythms that you find more often in R&B drumming, but that also work in rock drumming. All these rhythms contain snare drum strokes on all the downbeats, giving the grooves a hard-driving feel.

Sixteenth-note feel rhythms are also common in R&B drumming. In fact, they're more common in R&B than in rock. Figure 8-3 shows a few to get you started. The rhythms in Figure 8-3 are written with a *right-hand lead* (that means that your right hand plays the hi-hat), but you can also play them with alternating (right, left, right, left) strokes (see Figure 8-4). You can find more basic rhythms in Chapters 6 and 9.

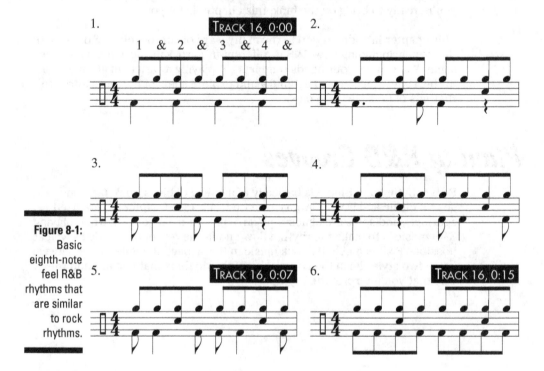

Figure 8-1:
Basic eighth-note feel R&B rhythms that are similar to rock rhythms.

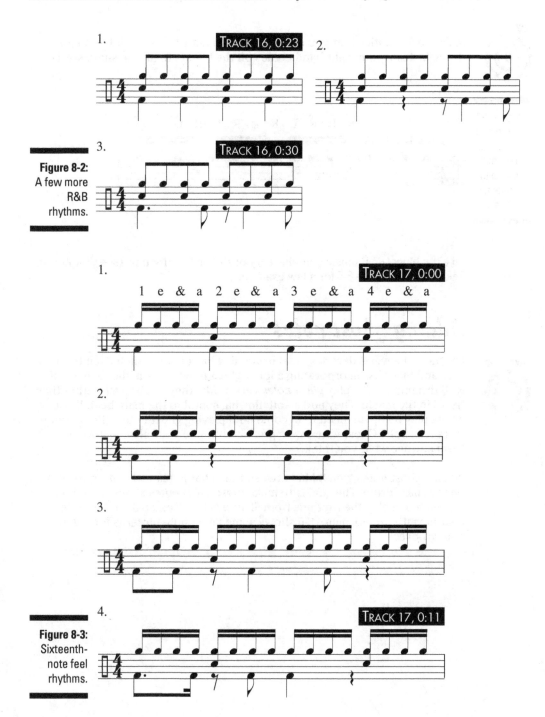

Figure 8-2:
A few more
R&B
rhythms.

Figure 8-3:
Sixteenth-
note feel
rhythms.

In Figure 8-4, notice that you don't play the hi-hat when you hit the snare drum. Instead, your right hand comes off the hi-hats to hit the snare stroke.

Figure 8-4:
Alternating
stroke
pattern for
sixteenth-
note feel
rhythms.

Like the blues, R&B music contains a lot of shuffle-feel rhythms (see Chapter 6). Take a look at Figure 8-5 for a few examples.

Adding ghost notes

For the last several decades, R&B drumming has distinguished itself from rock and blues by incorporating a lot of ghost notes. This is the essence of R&B drumming. You play *ghost notes* very softly; they're often *felt* rather than heard in the music. They add a soft, flowing sound to the main beat. If you're gonna play R&B, you need to become fluid playing ghost notes. (Rock drummers take note: Ghost notes are a great addition to your playing, too. Try them and see what you think.)

To play ghost notes, you fill in between the hi-hat notes with very quiet notes on the snare drum. The goal is to make these quiet notes almost inaudible. (Listen to me play the rhythms from Figures 8-6, 8-7, and 8-8 on the CD to hear how it's done.) Figure 8-6 shows some ghost note patterns for eighth-note grooves.

Figure 8-5:
Some R&B
shuffles.

1 & 2 & 3 & 4 &

1.

2. TRACK 19, 0:00

3.

4.

5. TRACK 19, 0:08

Figure 8-6:
Ghost note
patterns for
eighth-note
grooves.

TIP

Want to make your R&B and rock shuffles really shine? Add some ghost notes. Not only does this addition help you keep your right-hand rhythm solid, it also sounds great, especially with the half-time shuffles. Figure 8-7 shows a few. Rhythms 5 and 6 are half-time shuffles and are written in cut time, which means you count them half as fast. For example, instead of counting rhythm 6 in Figure 8-7 "1–tu–tu–2–tu–tu–3–tu–tu–4–tu–tu," you count it "1–tu–tu–&–tu–tu–2–tu–tu–&–tu–tu."

Figure 8-7:
Ghost notes
for shuffle
feels.

Opening and closing the hi-hat

No self-respecting R&B groove is complete without an open hi-hat or two. The contrast between open and closed hi-hats creates a texture and flow that fit particularly well into R&B music. Figure 8-8 shows you a few to help you get used to playing ghost notes with open and closed hi-hat combinations.

Don't open the hi-hat too much — you want a tight "tsst" sound.

Figure 8-8:
Opening
and closing
the hi-hats.

Getting Funky: Exploring Funk Drumming

Funk drumming is kind of a cross between R&B and the more contemporary jazz-fusion drumming (for more on jazz-fusion, check out Chapter 9). Funk and fusion developed around the same time in the 1960s and 1970s, so you can find many similarities between the two. Each of these styles uses more complex rhythms within its grooves and often incorporates a lot of *syncopation* (the emphasis of the rhythm is on the "e" and "a" of the beat; see Chapter 2 to get a handle on counting out the beat).

The rhythms in Figures 8-9 through 8-12 are very challenging and may take you a while to get the hang of — just start out slowly, take your time, and practice to a metronome.

Incorporating syncopation

Funk grooves tend to syncopate the bass drum the most. You find both single strokes played on the "e" or "a" of the beat as well as double strokes that start or end on the "e" or "a" (for more on how to play double bass drum strokes, check out Chapter 5). Take a look at Figure 8-9 for some basic funk patterns that use syncopated bass drum beats. (You can find more syncopated bass drum grooves in Chapter 6.)

Rhythms 1 and 2 in Figure 8-9 have quarter notes on the hi-hats. The hi-hats create a strong quarter note pulse that contrasts nicely with the syncopated bass drum patterns. This approach is very common in funk drumming.

Most people tend to rush the notes in rhythms 1 and 2 because of the amount of open space (rests) in these grooves. When practicing these rhythms, set your metronome to play sixteenth notes slowly so that you can get the proper placement of the notes. Doing so keeps you from rushing the notes and speeding up as you play.

Rhythms 3 and 4 utilize eighth notes on the hi-hat. Rhythm 3 includes a double bass drum stroke (the "a" of two and beat three). At first, playing this double stroke will be challenging. Take your time and remember that most funk music is played at a moderate (not too fast) tempo of about 90 to 100 beats per minute (see Chapter 2 for more on tempo). You can hear this tempo range on the CD (track 21).

Figure 8-9:
Some basic funk rhythms using syncopated bass drum beats.

Rhythms 5 and 6 use a sixteenth-note feel. These rhythms are played using alternating strokes on the hi-hat (right, left, right, left). Rhythm 6 has a double bass drum stroke on the "&" and "a" of beat two. Notice when you play this rhythm that the bass drum stroke on the "a" of two is accompanied by your left hand on the hi-hat. Playing this rhythm takes some time to get used to, so go slowly and be patient.

Syncopating the snare drum beats

Here's where funk drumming starts getting interesting. Take a look at Figure 8-10 and notice how the snare drum rhythms move away from the two and four. No standard backbeats here. Instead, you play syncopated rhythms on the snare drum to give the groove an unusual feel. The most common placement for the snare drum beats (when you don't play them on the two and four, that is) is on either the "a" of one or the "a" of three. This placement creates some anticipation in the groove and makes the rhythm particularly "funky."

Figure 8-10:
Some funk rhythms with syncopated snare drum beats.

Rhythms 1 and 2 have a straight eighth-note hi-hat pattern while rhythms 3 and 4 incorporate the sixteenth-note pattern (alternating strokes). You play the syncopated snare drum beat on rhythms 3 and 4 with your left hand.

Including ghost notes

Like R&B drumming, funk tends to include a healthy dose of ghost notes. This time, however, the ghost notes occur in addition to syncopated bass drum and snare drum beats. You can include ghost notes with syncopated patterns on the bass and snare drums in a couple of ways: You can play the ghost notes at the same time as the syncopated bass drum beats or not. Figure 8-11 illustrates these two approaches.

Figure 8-11:
Adding ghost notes to the rhythms from Figure 8-10.

Rhythms 1 and 2 have ghost notes that you play *underneath* (at the same time as) the syncopated bass drum pattern. Rhythm 2 also includes a snare drum beat played on the "a" of one. Rhythm 3 has a double bass drum stroke that you play at the same time as both a hi-hat beat (right hand) and a ghost note (left hand). The coordination that you use to play this rhythm is similar to the sixteenth-note pattern from Figure 8-9 (see rhythm 5). The only difference is that your left hand plays on the snare drum instead of the hi-hat.

The combination of a ghost note and double bass drum stroke is one of the most difficult techniques to master in funk drumming. In fact, try to play rhythm 4 in Figure 8-11. Rhythm 4 is the same as rhythm 3 without the ghost note/syncopated bass drum combination, except this time you don't play the ghost note when you play the bass drum on the "a" of two. Both approaches are common, but by not playing the ghost note when the bass drum plays its syncopation, you allow the bass drum beat to be heard better because its sound doesn't compete with that of the ghost note.

Opening and closing the hi-hat

Funk drumming uses a lot of opened–closed hi-hat combinations within the groove (see Figure 8-12). These combinations often occur along with the syncopated snare drum and bass drum beats. Rhythms 1 and 3 in Figure 8-12 each have an open hi-hat stroke on the "&" of four, which lasts for one eighth note (1/2 beat). For rhythm 3, you can choose to play the hi-hat on the "a" of four or not. Each has its own feel. Rhythms 1 and 3 are very common funk grooves.

Rhythms 2 and 4 both have open hi-hats that you play on the syncopation itself and that stay open for only one sixteenth note. In rhythm 2, the open hi-hat occurs on the "a" of two and is supported by the bass drum, which you play at the same time. In this rhythm, you don't play the hi-hat on beat three; instead, you rest. Rhythm 4 has its open hi-hat on the "a" of four. You don't play it at the same time as a bass drum beat; instead you play the bass drum when you close the hi-hat (on beat one). Both of these approaches are very common.

Take your time with rhythms 2 and 4 in Figure 8-12; they're very difficult. It takes some practice to open the hi-hat on the syncopation. The key to a good sound is to close the hi-hat immediately after hitting it. Look for a tight "tsst" sound that lasts only one sixteenth note (if you listen to Track 22 on the CD, you can hear how it's supposed to sound).

TRACK 22, 0:34

TRACK 22, 0:42

Figure 8-12:
Hi-hat
embellish-
ments for
funk
rhythms.

Embracing the machine

Most new R&B and hip-hop drum rhythms are created on a *drum machine*. A drum machine is a device (not unlike an elaborate metronome) that creates the sound of a drumset or other percussion instrument without a musician actually playing it. This isn't so bad in itself, except most of the people programming these machines aren't drummers and they don't know what's really possible to play on the drums.

Therefore, many of the drum parts are unusual and somewhat awkward (read: very difficult) to play.

If you end up playing contemporary R&B or hip-hop, you'll encounter some of these bizarre drum machine parts that you'll have to interpret onto the drumset. The easiest way to do so is to choose the most important rhythms in the music.

Chapter 9

Swinging into Jazz

. . . .

. . . .

*J*azz. Improvisation. These two words are inextricably linked in this style of music. Jazz is all about being in the moment and creating something new. It's said that jazz music mirrors society: It's a balance between individual expression and community responsibility. I don't know about that, but I do know that jazz is a whole lotta fun to play. It's one of the few styles of music where you get to improvise, experiment, and create something new.

In this chapter, I introduce you to the fundamental rhythm of this truly American art form so that you can develop the skills to play jazz rhythms and make your music swing. I also show you how jazz has blended with other styles of music to form what is called jazz-fusion. In addition, I give you some tips for playing well with others.

Getting Into the Swing of It

Most traditional jazz music, like ragtime, swing, or bebop, relies on a fairly simple rhythm consisting of a ride cymbal (played with your right hand) and the hi-hats (played with your left foot). This rhythm (see Figure 9-1) uses a triplet feel and is the precursor to the many shuffle rhythms that you find in rock, blues, and R&B music. Check out Chapter 2 for help reading drum notation and playing triplets and shuffle feel.

Jazz started out having a backbeat on the snare drum (not played nearly as loudly as the rock backbeat discussed in Chapter 6) and a constant bass drum beat played on all four beats of the measure. You can hear this beat in early ragtime music from the turn of the century (the last century, that is).

As jazz developed, the snare drum and bass drum parts slowly changed, and musicians began to use these instruments for accents and embellishments (I discuss these later in this chapter). So for most jazz music, the rhythm in Figure 9-1 can get you started.

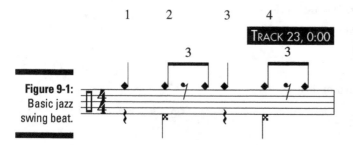

Figure 9-1:
Basic jazz
swing beat.

Occasionally, you may encounter a jazz rhythm written as sixteenth notes. You'll almost always play these notes as triplets. See Figure 9-2 for the difference between the way the jazz feel is written and the way it's played.

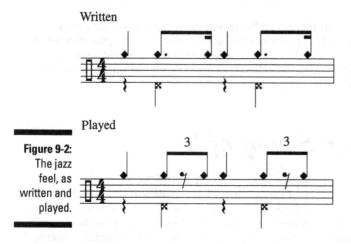

Figure 9-2:
The jazz
feel, as
written and
played.

Swing is all about creating anticipation and forward movement in your drumming no matter how fast or slow you play. You create the swing feel two ways:

- **Concentrate on the third note of the triplet (check out Figure 9-1 to see it on beats 2 and 4).** This note is called the *pick-up beat* because it leads into the next downbeat (the beats that mark the pulse of the music. In this case, the one, two, three, and four are all downbeats). The pick-up beat is without a doubt the most important note in jazz.

  Playing or accenting this note gives the rhythm the edge and drive that people most often associate with swing music. Whether you play this note or not, just thinking about it and being aware of where it should be played allows you to *feel* it. This *feeling* then transfers to how the rest of the band and the audience hear this note.

- **Try to play just slightly on top of the beat.** This rule basically means that you anticipate the downbeat by playing each note a tiny bit before a metronome would play it. The tricky part is doing this without speeding up or getting out of time with the other musicians.

  This trick isn't as difficult as it sounds because the rest of the musicians will also be playing on top of the beat. So all you have to do is make sure that you don't speed up as you play (you can guard against speeding up by practicing to a metronome. For more on metronomes, go to Chapter 20). An easy way to understand what it means to play on top of the beat is to listen to any jazz swing or bebop music.

If you use these two tips, you can play the rhythm in Figure 9-3 and make it swing.

Figure 9-3:
You can really make this rhythm swing.

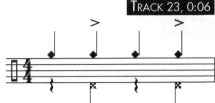

Varying the tempo

You play the basic swing rhythm slightly differently when you play at the extremes of possible tempos. Take a look at Figure 9-4 to see how to interpret the basic swing rhythm at three different tempos. Notice how the pick-up beat (which is notated in Figure 9-4 as a dotted eighth note and a sixteenth note) is played closer to the downbeat as the tempo decreases. At very fast tempos, you play the pick-up beat closer to the center between the two downbeats (notated as two quarter notes in Figure 9-4). These subtle shifts will automatically become a part of your playing as you listen to and play this style of music. Most of your playing will be in the middle tempo range where the triplet rules.

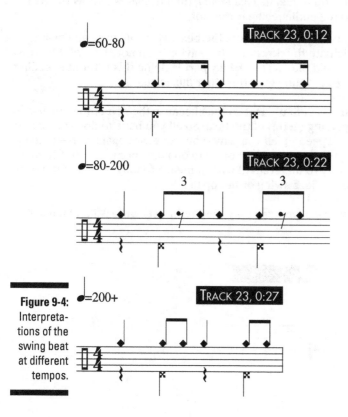

Figure 9-4:
Interpretations of the swing beat at different tempos.

Tackling different textures

Musicians often play jazz using brushes instead of sticks (for more on brushes, check out Chapter 3). Depending on the tempo, you can play a couple of different ways to create a softer, quieter sound for songs or sections where sticks are just too loud.

Figure 9-5 shows a basic slow-tempo brush groove that's a must for quiet ballads (songs with tempos under 100 or so beats per minute). The ties on the notes refer to a circular motion that you do with the brushes on the snare drum head. This motion (shown in Figure 9-5) is reflected by the stems going both up and down on the snare drum line of the figure. Both hands are moving in opposite directions (left hand clockwise and right hand counterclockwise). In this groove, you play the hi-hat on beats 2 and 4 with your left foot, and you may play the bass drum on beats 1, 2, 3, and 4 very quietly.

For faster tempos (over 100 or so beats per minute), the rhythm in Figure 9-6 is the standard. In this groove you play the basic jazz ride cymbal pattern on the snare drum with your right hand while your left hand moves in a clockwise circle around the head. At the same time, your left foot plays the hi-hat on beats 2 and 4. This combination creates a softer, mellower version of the basic jazz groove that I describe in Figure 9-4 (the medium- and fast-tempo versions).

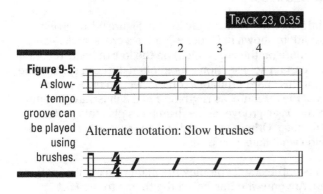

TRACK 23, 0:35

Figure 9-5: A slow-tempo groove can be played using brushes.

Alternate notation: Slow brushes

TRACK 23, 0:58

Brushes

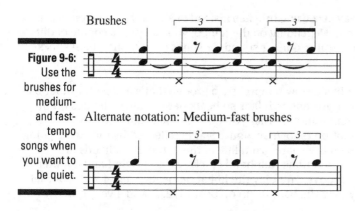

Figure 9-6:
Use the
brushes for
medium-
and fast-
tempo
songs when
you want to
be quiet.

Alternate notation: Medium-fast brushes

Brush technique is an art that you could spend a lifetime exploring. The two grooves I describe in this section are just scratching the surface of what you can do with brushes. If you want to know more about brush technique, check out Chapter 3 for some great resources.

Adding to the beat

You can make some additions to the basic swing beat in Figure 9-1 to give it some variety. The first addition, shown in Figure 9-7, adds a cross-stick snare drum beat (Chapter 3 has more on the cross-stick) on the fourth beat. You can use this technique during certain solo sections, most often during a saxophone solo. Likewise, you can put this snare drum beat on the second or both the second and fourth beats of the measure, as rhythms 2 and 3 illustrate. Rhythm 4 adds the bass drum to the basic groove. Some drummers play this pattern very softly throughout the song. Others use it only when the music calls for a four-beat pulse. You decide what suits you best.

During very quiet sections of the song, you play the main ride cymbal pattern on the hi-hat (Figure 9-8). Anyone who has heard the theme to the *Pink Panther* by Henry Mancini can recognize this very common pattern. It also works well during solos — especially bass solos. Rhythms 2, 3, and 4 in Figure 9-8 add a cross-stick snare drum beat.

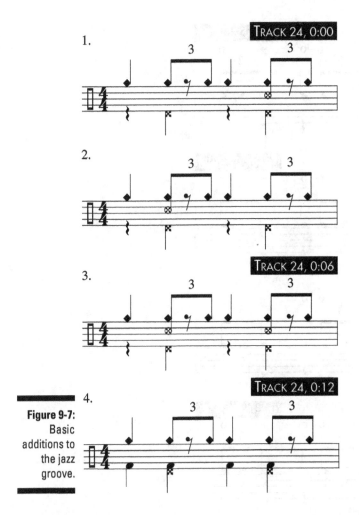

Figure 9-7:
Basic
additions to
the jazz
groove.

Expanding Your Horizons

Much of the art in playing jazz is varying the basic groove (as I touch on a little in the previous section). The exercises in this section can help you develop some more skills to add to the interest in your jazz playing. The ability to smoothly interject a snare beat here or a bass drum accent there makes playing the swing beat much more interesting for you and the other members of the band.

Figure 9-8:
The hi-hat
rhythm
swing beat.

Practice each rhythm in the following section until it becomes fluid. Then add three bars of the basic swing rhythm (see Figure 9-1) to the front of the exercise.

When you play with others, use the rhythms in this section with an ear toward how they fit with the rhythms of the other instruments. The greatest jazz drummers listen intently to the other instrumentalists, and they can anticipate the next rhythmic phrase. They then add the embellishment that complements that rhythmic phrase. Anticipating the next rhythmic phrase isn't as difficult as it sounds. As you gain experience by playing with others and listening to other drummers, you also gain the ability to use these fills (or embellishments) appropriately.

Riding the cymbal

Have some fun with the basic swing beat by making occasional, minor alterations to the ride cymbal's rhythm. These minor changes allow you to play more musically and to complement the rhythms of the other instruments. Figure 9-9 shows you some ride cymbal variations. Remember to play the hi-hat solidly and think ahead to what you're going to play next to keep the rhythm swinging.

You can use the variations in Figure 9-9 to create phrases that travel across several measures. Figure 9-10 is a four-bar phrase with the ride cymbal pattern that uses a three-beat phrase. This pattern is great if you use it sparingly.

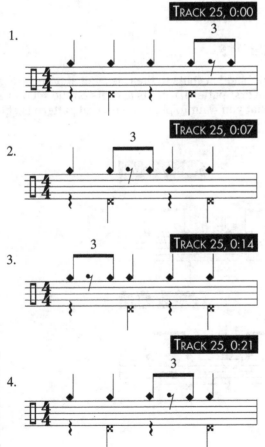

Figure 9-9:
Ride cymbal variations for the swing beat.

Figure 9-10:
Four-bar
ride cymbal
phrase.

Adding accents

Sometimes you want to add accents to the ride cymbal pattern. Figure 9-11 shows you a few. The first pattern, with its accents on the second and fourth beats, is typically what you want to play. The second pattern is effective if you use it occasionally.

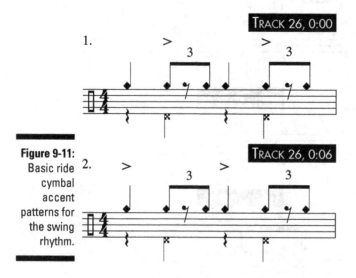

Figure 9-11:
Basic ride
cymbal
accent
patterns for
the swing
rhythm.

You play swinging accents on the third beat of the triplet, as you can see in the rhythms in Figure 9-12. Notice that all the rhythms in Figure 9-12 have a *tie* (see Chapter 2 for more on ties) attached to the accented note. The tie indicates that you don't play the second of the two tied notes. On rhythms 3 and 4, you can either play the note in parentheses or not.

When a composer puts a note in parentheses, she leaves it up to the musician to decide whether it's necessary or not. As you can imagine, you won't find parentheses in music very often, because most composers are very explicit about what they want you to play. Sometimes, depending on the tempo of the song, not playing them may be most effective. Faster tempos get cluttered if you add the extra note.

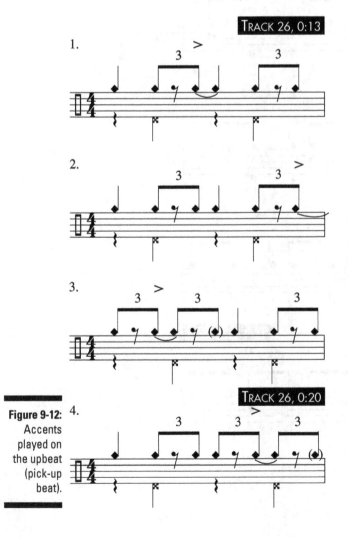

Figure 9-12: Accents played on the upbeat (pick-up beat).

Incorporating the snare drum

The snare drum, with its crisp, cutting sound is a great complement to the main jazz groove. The rhythms in Figure 9-13 use single snare drum accents to add punch and to create anticipation. Notice how all the snare drum accents are played on the third triplet beat. This technique helps the rhythm to swing.

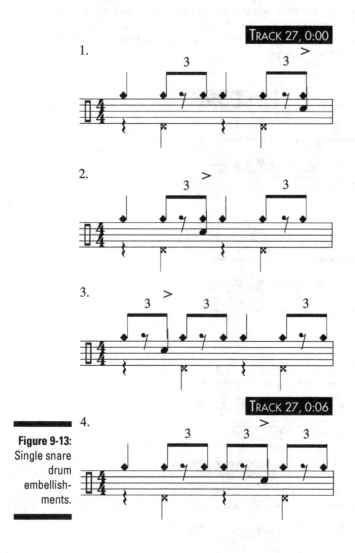

Figure 9-13:
Single snare drum embellishments.

When you get used to these rhythms, try adding a little accent on the cymbal to the snare drum accent (this addition further accents the accented note). For example, on rhythms 1 and 2, you can hit the ride cymbal with the shoulder of your stick or hit the crash cymbal at the same time that you hit the snare drum accent. Although the music doesn't indicate that you play a ride cymbal at the same time as the snare drum accent on rhythms 3 and 4, you can still add a cymbal beat. Just drop the next beat. Figure 9-14 shows how you can do this.

Figure 9-14:
Adding cymbal accents to the snare notes.

Sometimes you want to play more than one snare drum accent in a measure. Figure 9-15 contains a few examples. With each of these rhythms, you want to accent the pick-up beat harder than the other notes in order to keep it swinging.

Rhythms 3 and 4 in Figure 9-15 contain a snare drum beat on the second note of the triplet. Make sure that you play this beat in its correct place. These rhythms are best played with a *crescendo* (a gradual increase in the volume of the snare drum that makes the last note the loudest).

You can also add a cymbal accent to each of these rhythms on the last note to create even more intensity.

Figure 9-15: Multiple snare drum accents.

Including the bass drum

Most of the time in jazz music, the bass drum isn't played or else it's played very quietly. Bass drum accents can add a needed low-end push to the rhythm and add more variety and interest to your drumming. Figure 9-16 has some basic upbeat accents for the bass drum. When playing these rhythms, you may add an accent on the ride cymbal with the shoulder of your stick. Or, you can also add an accent on the crash cymbal. Either of these techniques can add more impact to the bass drum accents.

TRACK 28, 0:00

1.

2.

3.

TRACK 28, 0:07

4.

Figure 9-16:
Single bass
drum
accents.

Figure 9-17 adds a second bass drum beat to the first two rhythms in Figure 9-16. If you play the second beat louder with the cymbal accent, you can create a nice feel of forward movement.

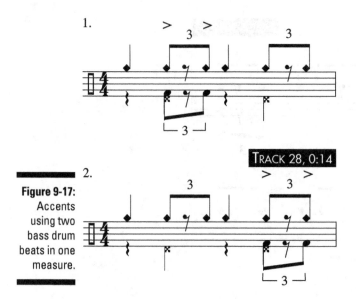

Figure 9-17:
Accents
using two
bass drum
beats in one
measure.

Mixing up your accents

If you feel like you have the hang of adding some snare drum and bass drum accents (see the previous sections), you can combine them to create additional textural interest to your drumming. Figure 9-18 has a few rhythms with which you can practice.

The next set of rhythms (see Figure 9-19) uses more complex snare drum rhythms. You play the double notes on the snare drum very softly.

If you end up playing in a situation where you read *jazz charts,* you'll often see accents marked on the music for the whole band. These accents look different than the basic "greater than" accents because they aren't part of the actual rhythm that you play. Instead, they're written for several members of the band, so they allow you to interpret the rhythm in the ways that you choose. These accents are noted in one of two ways: above the staff lines or within the staff (see Figure 9-20). Each is treated differently.

As a general rule, you play accent markings set above the staff lines as individual accents while you keep time (the basic swing rhythm). These marks above the staff lines are called section figures and are generally played by only a few instruments in the band. You can play these accent figures by adding a snare drum, bass drum, or combination snare drum/cymbal or bass drum/cymbal to the basic groove. Figure 9-21 shows some common accent figures and one way to play each of them.

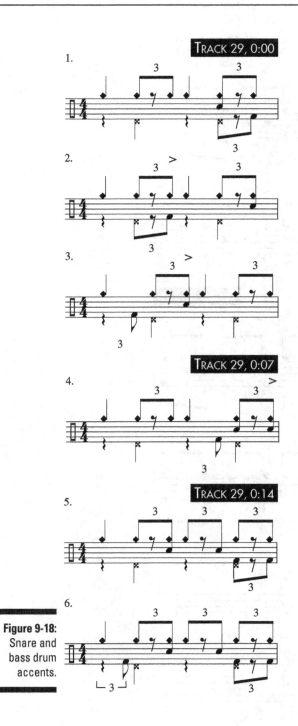

Figure 9-18:
Snare and
bass drum
accents.

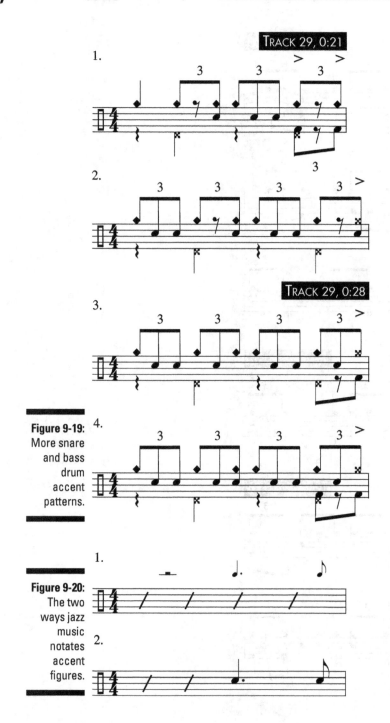

Figure 9-19: More snare and bass drum accent patterns.

Figure 9-20: The two ways jazz music notates accent figures.

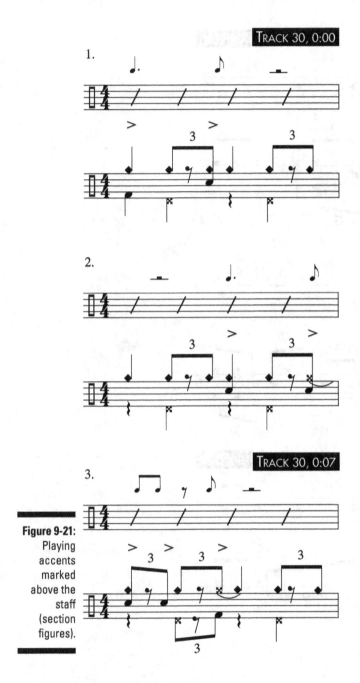

Figure 9-21:
Playing accents marked above the staff (section figures).

Whenever accents are written within the staff lines, you play them within the entire ensemble (band). You'll almost always stop playing time and set up the figure with a fill. Figure 9-22 shows how you do this.

1.

TRACK 30, 0:15

2.

3.

TRACK 30, 0:24

Figure 9-22:
Ensemble
accent
figures.

Telling Your Story: Soloing

Because jazz is an improvisational art, you have many opportunities to stretch your creative muscles and exhibit your chops (technical skills). The *solo* is your time to tell your story and have some real fun. An effective solo can add a lot to the music, but a poorly executed one only disrupts the flow of the song.

The two most important things to remember when soloing are

- **Keep it swinging.** If you can keep the swing, it doesn't matter if you just keep time with a few accents during your solo or if you pull out all the stops and play like Buddy Rich. In either case, the audience and other musicians will respect and appreciate you (of course, the more cool licks and rolls you can add musically, the more appreciation you'll get).

- **Play musically.** The best way to do this is to match your rhythmic phrasing to the song and to the solos of the other musicians. Get to know the song structure and listen carefully to the other musicians as you play and you can choose the licks, fills, and rolls that complement them.

Making two-bar phrases

Solos typically come in two- or four-bar phrases (a phrase is just a musical idea). Many times in a two-bar phrase solo, you *trade bars* with the bass player or other instruments (in other words, you play two bars of a solo, and then the other instrument plays two bars, and so on).

The possibilities for what you can play are endless. Figure 9-23 contains some two-bar phrases to use as a starting point. After you learn the rhythm, practice by playing two bars of the basic swing beat before it.

As you get comfortable with these rhythms, try creating your own variations by combining elements from one rhythm to another.

Creating four-bar phrases

Another common solo configuration is the four-bar phrase. Figure 9-24 has a few to get you started. After you get comfortable with each of the phrases, practice them with four bars of time in between. You can combine groups of two to make eight-bar phrases.

Figure 9-23:
Some two-bar solo phrases.

Figure 9-24:
Four-bar
solo
phrases.

Blending Styles: Jazz-Fusion

Fusion represents a blending of different styles of music. Fusion music developed out of the free-form jazz music of the 1950s and 1960s. As rock music became more and more popular, jazz musicians started incorporating some of the instruments (mostly electric guitar) and sounds used in rock into their own music. The result was both very popular and extremely radical compared to acoustic jazz music.

Traditional jazz musicians dismissed this new style as nonmusical and a corruption of their art. Despite that backlash, fusion caught on. Over the last 30 years, fusion music has taken many forms. The two most popular are as follows:

- **Jazz-fusion,** a blending of jazz with rock and Latin
- **Rock fusion,** a louder blend incorporating more of the hard edge of rock with the improvisation and experimentation of jazz

Drumming for both of these styles is very similar. The only real difference is in the way the grooves are interpreted (you hit the backbeat harder for the rock versions).

Fusion drumming can be an awful lot of fun to play. This is one style of music where you're actually encouraged to play a lot of notes, fills, and even solos! Can you imagine? At last a style of music where the drummer gets to let loose along with the other guys and gals. Sure you gotta keep the groove happening, but your wings aren't clipped — you get to soar if you want.

Playing Fusion Rhythms

Fusion drumming isn't for the timid. You need to be comfortable playing all styles of music, especially Latin and funk, and be able to play a lot of notes. You also need to be able to play the rudiments fluidly in order to handle the often bizarre sticking patterns used in fusion drumming (for more on the rudiments, check out Chapter 3 or the Cheat Sheet in the front of the book).

With fusion music, the emphasis is on rhythmic intensity. Generally, you play lots of notes in a short amount of time. The measure is filled up with densely layered orchestrations (the different drums and cymbals), often using the whole drumset within a groove.

Take your time with the rhythms in this section. They're very challenging, but if you can play the rhythms in the other chapters, you can get a handle on these as well. Even if you don't want to play fusion music, the skills that you can gain from practicing these rhythms easily translate to any other style of music.

Knowing that more (not less) is more

Filling in the spaces within the rhythm is the main idea in jazz-fusion drumming. Ghost notes are an essential component of fusion drumming. *Ghost notes* are very quiet (almost inaudible) notes played on the snare drum that add a smooth texture to the rhythm. Figure 9-25 has a ghost note pattern for you to try out (for more on ghost notes, check out Chapter 8).

To play ghost notes effectively, barely lift your stick off the head and tap it lightly. The softer you can play these notes, the better.

Figure 9-25:
A ghost note
pattern.

Forgetting swing (at least for now)

With its emphasis on incorporating rock and Latin rhythms, jazz-fusion drumming rarely uses a swing-type groove. In fact, you can easily connect many fusion grooves to some traditional Latin feels. Check out Figure 9-26 to see how a samba and a nanigo (see Chapter 10 for more on these patterns) translate into fusion grooves.

Another common rhythmic structure for fusion grooves comes from unusual sticking patterns. Here's where the rudiments (see Chapter 3 for the basics on rudiments) can come in handy. Check out Figure 9-27 to see how you can use a paradiddle to create a fusion groove. Notice how the bass drum and ride cymbal (right hand) patterns are closely related. This technique is common in fusion drumming.

Figure 9-26: Latin samba and nanigo fusion grooves.

Figure 9-27: Using paradiddles to create a fusion groove.

TRACK 32, 0:08

TRACK 32, 0:16

TRACK 32, 0:22

Dealing with odd meter

Fusion drumming allows you to really explore odd meters (see Chapter 2 to discover more about the meter or time signature) and unusual rhythmic phrasing. Being able to play comfortably in time signatures other than 4/4 is another important part of fusion drumming and one that makes this style of music more difficult to play than many others. Don't worry, after a while, these odd meters become almost as natural as 4/4 for most people.

To get your feet wet in a few odd meter grooves, check out Figure 9-28. These grooves introduce you to the most common odd meters: 5/8, 5/4, 7/8, and 7/4. Practice these rhythms slowly and count out loud until you get the feel of them.

1.

TRACK 32, 0:30

3.

TRACK 32, 0:35

4.

Figure 9-28:
A few odd
meter
grooves.

Chapter 10

Looking at Latin and Caribbean Styles

• •

In This Chapter

▶ Playing Afro-Cuban, Brazilian, and Caribbean rhythms on the drumset

▶ Developing the feel of Latin styles

▶ Interpreting traditional rhythms on the drumset

• •

*L*atin and Caribbean music are some of the most popular styles of music today. You can find the Latin influence in pop music (Shakira and Jennifer Lopez), rock (Santana), and jazz (Chic Corea). Likewise, you can find Caribbean music in many forms, from the traditional Ziggy Marley and the Melody Makers to the reggae-influenced sounds of The Police and No Doubt. Whether you want to play in a salsa band or just integrate some Latin or Caribbean rhythm into your rock or jazz playing, this chapter is for you.

Here, I introduce you to the exciting world of Latin drumset playing. You can explore many styles of Latin rhythm, from Afro-Cuban to Brazilian to the lesser-known Caribbean approach. You can discover how to interpret traditional percussion parts and apply them to the drumset. *Note:* Some of the rhythm styles that I mention in this chapter are also in Chapter 15, but those involve a variety of hand drums rather than the drumset.

Building On Traditions

The drumset is a relatively new instrument in Latin music, going back only about 50 years. The drumset parts in Latin rhythms developed out of the traditional instrumentation (congas, bongos, cowbells, and so on). You generally play the cowbell, shaker, or triangle pattern on the cymbal or hi-hat. You play the conga parts on the snare drum (with the snares turned off, which creates a high-pitched sound and gives the music a more authentic sound), tom-toms, or bass drum. As a result, you can find many interpretations of these rhythms and a variety of possible sounds.

When Latin musicians first used the drumset, they added it to the percussion instruments in the band. Today, you may find only a drumset player and maybe an additional percussionist in a band. The drumset's role has evolved from being used to complement the traditional percussion instruments to replacing them in some cases.

The way that you approach Latin rhythms is determined to some extent by the instrumentation in the band. Most of the rhythms in this chapter work well in situations where you're the only drummer *and* where the band has another percussionist or two. As you get used to playing these rhythms with other musicians, you find ways to make them fit your situation.

Many of these rhythms have been used in Latin-jazz music, beginning in the 1950s. In many cases, they were used in their original form. However, recently, some of the more traditional rhythms have developed into their own unique styles of playing (you notice this new development most in the case of the samba, which I describe later in this chapter).

Playing Afro-Cuban Rhythms

Afro-Cuban drumming is probably the most defined style of Latin music. Because of Cuba's restrictive political climate as well as the Cubans' emphasis on education and tradition, Afro-Cuban rhythms have remained almost constant since the 1950s.

If you find yourself playing in an authentic Afro-Cuban group, you want to stick pretty much to the rhythms that this section presents. Otherwise, the rest of the musicians in the band may not appreciate your playing.

Bolero

The *bolero* is the Latin ballad. Slow-paced and romantic, the drumset part is subdued and relatively easy to play. Figure 10-1 shows some basic bolero patterns. These rhythms are orchestrated with the snare drum (second space from the top), with the snares turned off, and the tom-tom (first space from the top) covering what is traditionally the conga part. Rhythm 1 uses a simple bass drum (first space from the bottom) pattern on the one and three with the hi-hat (top of the first line) playing the traditional afuche/shaker part. Rhythm 2 is a little more complex, adding a more syncopated bass drum pattern, implying the clavé rhythm (see Chapter 17 for more on the clavé). (For a complete breakdown of reading drum notation, see Chapter 2.)

"What? You want me to play fewer fills?!"

Years ago, I played with a reggae band that didn't have a percussionist. My rhythms were designed to fill out the sound of the band, so I played a lot of fills and bell patterns on my drumset. When I joined another reggae band that had a percussionist playing congas, guiro, cowbell, and timbales, I found that I had to alter my playing so that I didn't infringe on his parts. I ended up playing much simpler rhythms with a lot fewer fills. Needless to say, it took me a while to get used to the change (I admit that I was a little put-off by not being able to "express" myself the way I had when I played alone, but I got over it).

Figure 10-1:
Basic bolero rhythms.

Cha-cha

The *cha-cha* was very popular in the 1950s and, to the untrained ear, is pretty much a faster bolero. Okay, even to the trained ear the percussion parts are virtually the same. You can play the rhythms in Figure 10-1 a little bit faster to make them fit into most cha-cha songs. If you're interested in some different rhythms, Figure 10-2 shows some common cha-cha drumset rhythms (you can also play these patterns for the bolero if you choose).

Rhythm 2 in Figure 10-2 is a little busier than the rhythms shown for the bolero. You won't really want to use this rhythm if you're in a band with a full percussion setup because it will conflict with the rhythms of the congas and other percussion instruments. This rhythm is best situated for groups with a drumset player only. Again, turn off the snare drum's snares.

Figure 10-2: Cha-cha drumset patterns.

Mambo

This fast rhythm is very common not only in traditional Afro-Cuban music, but also in the jazz-Latin scene of the 1950s and 1960s. The mambo rhythms in Figure 10-3 are traditional in their orchestration. The only real difference among these rhythms is in the bass drum and cymbal parts. The snare drum and tom-tom parts remain the same. Rhythm 2 has a bass drum part that skips the downbeat of two (just like some of the bolero and cha-cha patterns). Getting used to not playing the bass drum on a downbeat can take some time. Start out slowly and take your time when learning this technique.

Figure 10-3: The mambo.

Notice that the rhythms in Figure 10-3 are written in cut time (2/2 time). You count them "1 e & a," rather than "1 & 2 &." You play the snare drum with a cross-stick (see Chapter 3 for details on the cross-stick) with the snares turned on.

Nanigo

The *nanigo* is a 6/8 pattern that's quite common in jazz-Latin music and is often the only 6/8 Latin rhythm used. Afro-Cuban music, however, has many 6/8 patterns. Take the rumba Columbia, the bembé, the guiro, and the abakua, for example. Each of these styles has its own feel and traditional approach. The difference, as they say, is in the details. In nearly all these rhythms, the traditional clavé pattern is the same and is played on the ride cymbal (many people play on the bell of the cymbal to give the pattern a more authentic sound).

You can use the rhythms in Figure 10-4 with many of the 6/8 styles of Afro-Cuban music (for a jazz-fusion version of this rhythm, check out Chapter 9).

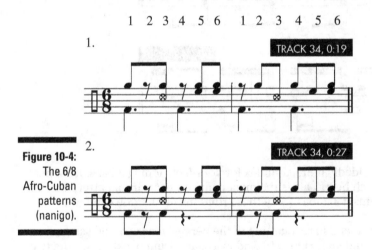

Figure 10-4:
The 6/8
Afro-Cuban
patterns
(nanigo).

Playing Brazilian Rhythms

Brazilian rhythms for the drumset became wildly popular in the 1960s. Samba and bossa nova songs were part of every jazz or Latin band's repertoire. The sultry, syncopated sound was entrancing and lent itself well to *improvisation* (making alternations to the rhythms if you choose).

Samba

The *samba* is one of the most popular Latin styles, and the samba drumset pattern is arguably one of the most used and improvised-upon rhythms in the world. This rhythm has been incorporated into rock, jazz, and R&B drumming. With its driving bass drum and syncopated cymbal pattern, all that you need is a backbeat to make the samba fit with these other styles.

Figure 10-5 offers some pretty traditional samba patterns. Rhythm 1 is the most basic, with the cymbal playing straight eighth notes and the bass drum playing quarter notes. The snare drum plays a syncopated pattern as a rim-shot or as a rim-tap. If you play the rim-shot, the sound that you want is light and high-pitched. Hitting the drum two or three inches from the rim gives you the best sound.

Figure 10-5: The samba.

Rhythm 2 is decidedly more complex for your feet, adding a bass drum beat on the "a" of each beat. This is the most common bass drum pattern for contemporary drumset sambas (play these rhythms on the ride cymbal).

As an added treat and in recognition of the pervasiveness of the samba rhythm in rock and jazz, Figure 10-6 adds a snare drum backbeat on the two and four and creates a "rock samba" pattern (see Chapter 11 for another variation of this groove, and check out Chapter 6 for general information on playing a backbeat).

1 e & a 2 e & a 3 e & a 4 e & a

TRACK 35, 0:14

Figure 10-6:
The rock
samba.

Bossa nova

The *bossa nova* developed out of the samba style of Brazilian music but it has a much mellower feel. The drumset part is very subdued and the basic groove usually doesn't have many variations. Figure 10-7 contains the quintessential bossa nova rhythm. In it, the bass drum plays a pattern very similar to the samba (only at half the speed), and the hi-hat plays straight eighth notes. The snare drum plays the traditional clavé pattern with a cross-stick.

1 & 2 & 3 & 4 & 1 & 2 & 3 & 4 &

TRACK 35, 0:23

Figure 10-7:
The bossa
nova.

The rhythm in Figure 10-7 will get you through almost every situation where you're asked to play a bossa nova rhythm. In case you get tired of playing the same rhythm over and over again, Figure 10-8 gives you a cool variation.

TRACK 35, 0:34

Figure 10-8:
A bossa
nova
variation.

The snare drum pattern in Figure 10-8 has been altered to reflect the rhythms of the bells rather than the clavé. Be careful not to overdo the use of this variation, though. Some musicians have a low tolerance toward drummers messing with their familiar rhythm by eliminating the clavé pattern.

Playing Caribbean Rhythms

The drumming styles of the Caribbean have been a lot less celebrated among Latin America's exports, but the sounds of reggae and calypso are some of the most familiar around. For many, reggae and calypso is the music of a laid-back lifestyle, sun-drenched beaches, and drinks with umbrellas.

The lyrics in Caribbean music are often very political in nature (reggae) and, like the rhythms from Cuba and Brazil, can be based on African celebrations (calypso). Either way, the drumset parts are rhythmically interesting and a lot of fun to play. If you're lucky enough to find a reggae or calypso band in which to play, these rhythms will help you fit right in. Of course, you can always use these rhythms with a rock or jazz band to create some variety or a unique sound (like the band The Police did in the 1970s and 1980s).

Reggae

Most people are familiar with the reggae music of Bob Marley, the laid-back, funky, almost aromatic sound of Jamaica. Reggae and its recent incarnations, particularly ska (which I talk about shortly), have been successfully integrated into rock music with the songs of The Police, UB40, and most recently, the rhythms of the band No Doubt.

The reggae style of drumming actually encompasses several different feels and musical movements. You have *one drop,* the most characteristic of reggae, the hard-driving *ska,* and *rockers,* which is more pulsating than the one drop or ska. Each of these styles has a place under the umbrella of reggae.

One drop

The rhythms in Figures 10-9 and 10-10 represent the most widely-used and familiar reggae rhythm, the one drop. The term *one drop* simply refers to the way you play the bass drum. You have one *drop* or stroke/accent on the second and fourth beats. In each of these rhythms, the bass drum plays the *backbeat* along with a cross-stick on the snare drum. Figure 10-9 uses a sixteenth-note feel, while Figure 10-10 offers a half-time shuffle feel (for more information on sixteenth-note, half-time, and shuffle feels, see Chapter 6).

Figure 10-9: The sixteenth-note one-drop feel.

Figure 10-10: The half-time shuffle one-drop feel.

In both Figures 10-9 and 10-10, rhythm 1 is the basic one-drop rhythm. Rhythm 2 contains an added snare drum beat to add more interest to the main groove.

After you get comfortable with the rhythms in Figures 10-9 and 10-10, try using one of the hi-hat patterns shown in Figure 10-11.

As you play these rhythms, you can occasionally add a syncopated accent beat on the snare drum using a rim-shot. This addition usually occurs on the "a" of beat four. Figure 10-12 shows you how to add this accent (Figure 10-12 is written with straight sixteenth notes but you can play with a shuffle feel as well).

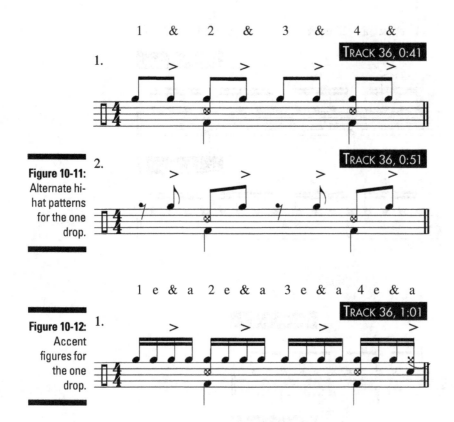

Figure 10-11: Alternate hi-hat patterns for the one drop.

Figure 10-12: Accent figures for the one drop.

Ska

The ska rhythm includes a lot of R&B influence. The ska basically adds an open snare backbeat to the rhythm with a slightly faster tempo. Much of the music of The Police uses a ska-type rhythm. Figure 10-13 shows you a few ska rhythms. Play them with a solid rock-like backbeat and you have the basic feel of ska.

Rockers or funk

The *rockers* style of reggae is said to have developed out of the ska rhythm. What distinguishes this feel from the other types of reggae drumming is a heavy (pounding) bass drum. Figures 10-14 and 10-15 show you a few rockers grooves. Notice how the bass drum plays steady eighth notes. The tempo of the rockers style is slower than the ska groove and sometimes even slower than the laid-back one drop. The rhythms in Figure 10-14 use a sixteenth-note feel, while the rhythms in Figure 10-15 have a shuffle feel. You can play these rhythms with either a cross-stick on the snare drum (as written) or with a strong backbeat (like the ska rhythms in Figures 10-12 and 10-13). You can also play these rhythms using the alternate hi-hat patterns in Figure 10-11.

Figure 10-13: Some ska rhythms.

Figure 10-14: Rockers-style rhythms using a sixteenth-note feel.

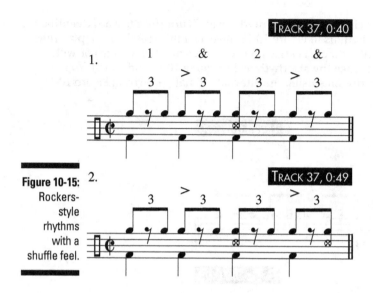

Figure 10-15: Rockers-style rhythms with a shuffle feel.

Calypso

The *calypso* is high-energy dance music. This style of music originated in Trinidad and is an integral part of the yearly Carnaval celebration.

Figure 10-16 shows the basic calypso rhythm written in cut (2/2) time. You play the hi-hat pattern with alternating strokes (see Chapter 6). The tempo is pretty fast, and you have to keep the groove moving and make sure the bass drum beat on the "a" of the first beat is solid. Accomplishing this rhythm can be somewhat difficult with the hi-hat accent pattern playing its accent on the "and" of the beat, so practice it slowly until you get it.

Figure 10-16: The basic calypso rhythm.

After you get the feel of the basic groove, you can start adding some accents on the tom-tom and snare drum. Figure 10-17 shows you a few. Keep in mind that you want to maintain the momentum of the rhythm while you add these accents. Rhythm 1 has a snare drum beat on the "and" of beat 2. Play this beat with your right hand. Notice that the bass drum's second beat moved to the two instead of the "a" of beat one. Rhythm 2 hits its snare accent on the "a" of beat two in the second measure. Play this one with your left hand.

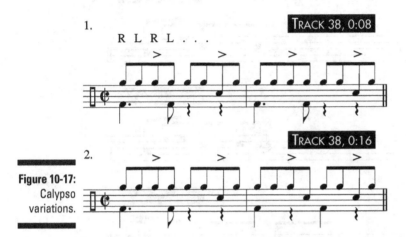

Figure 10-17:
Calypso
variations.

After you get comfortable playing the rhythms in Figures 10-16 and 10-17, you can add an open hi-hat pattern. This rhythm, shown in Figure 10-18, is one of the things that characterize calypso music. Becoming fluid with this rhythm takes some practice. Open your hi-hat on the "&" of beat 1 (marked with an "o"), keep it open during the bass drum beat on the "a" of beat 1, and close it on beat 2 (marked with a "=").

Figure 10-18:
The
quintessen-
tial calypso
hi-hat
pattern.

Filling It Out

Often, the fills for Latin music are syncopated. To get you started, Figure 10-19 has a few fill patterns that fit into most of the rhythms in this chapter.

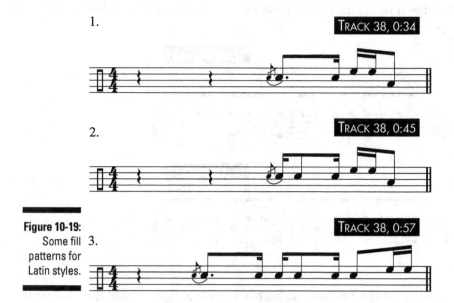

1.   TRACK 38, 0:34

2.   TRACK 38, 0:45

Figure 10-19:
Some fill patterns for Latin styles.

3.   TRACK 38, 0:57

After you get them down, try playing each fill with each of the main grooves in this chapter. Some work better than others, but they all introduce you to playing Latin music. If you're interested in more fill ideas, go to Chapter 13.

Chapter 11

Ratcheting up Your Rock Drumming

. . . .

In This Chapter

▶ Expanding on your rock drumming skills

▶ Exploring grooves from great drummers

▶ Examining real world fills

. . . .

*I*n Chapter 6 I introduce you to the basics of rock drumming. But rock drumming is often more than just the basics. In fact, rock drumming encompasses almost every style of music. This diversity leaves you open to try new things and to build a style all your own.

In this chapter I break the world of rock drumming open to show you the many ways that you can stretch the bounds of what it can be. I introduce you to some of the best rock drumming that has been recorded and let you try some of the grooves out for yourself. Here, you can find many ways to add a little (or a lot of) technical and emotional mojo to your rock sound.

I chose the drummers in this chapter from a long list of great players whose one-of-a-kind styles illustrate how you can play rock music and still impart your own unique personality. These are the drummers who *other* drummers are talking about. After reading this chapter, you'll see why.

Check out the rest of the chapters on the drumset (oh, heck, add the traditional drum chapters to your list as well) to find pretty much all the styles and types of grooves in rock music. For example, in music from the early days of rock, you can hear the traditional jazz rhythm laying down the groove for the song. And in 1960s music, you can hear a lot of Latin styles being used in popular rock tunes (listen to Santana for an example of this style).

Building on a Solid Foundation

The point of this chapter is to expand the boundaries of what you may think of as rock drumming and to give you a glimpse into what is known as *feel*. The key word here is *expand*. To be able to groove on the drumming patterns that I describe in this chapter you first need to be able to do the following things:

- ✔ **Play all the rhythms in Chapter 6 with a solid feel.** The snare drum should "crack" when you hit it, your hi-hat pattern should be steady and consistent, and you should play the bass drum at the exact same time as the hi-hat note that occupies the same beat of the measure.

- ✔ **Play a fill without losing (or gaining) time.** Your tempo should be consistent enough that you can go into and out of a fill without stopping, speeding up, or slowing down. To master this technique, I recommend that you play to a metronome or a recorded song so that you can internalize the pulse of the music. Check out Chapter 13 for in-depth fill instructions.

- ✔ **Comfortably play double strokes on the kick drum.** You play double kick-drum strokes only one sixteenth note apart. Playing double strokes on the kick drum requires mastery over your right foot and is essential if you want to play like a pro. I cover the basics on creating double-kick strokes in Chapter 5.

- ✔ **Comfortably play ghost notes on the snare drum.** Ghost notes are very quiet notes that add a flavor of movement to the rhythm. Chapter 6 introduces the concept of ghost notes and has some simple rhythms to help you get comfortable with them. Many of the rhythms in this chapter employ ghost notes, which give the grooves their awesome feel.

After you have a handle on the skills in this list, you're ready to tackle the techniques and rhythms in this chapter. To help you along, you can find the rhythms played on the CD that accompanies this book. I also highly recommend that you listen to the tunes that I mention in this chapter so you can hear for yourself how these grooves are played in the song. I offer my interpretation of them on the CD in this book, but I can't do justice to the feel that these grooves have when played by the guys who created them.

For most styles of rock music, the drums are the foundation of the song, so you aren't necessarily able to get away with playing a lot of fancy stuff. You're there to serve the song, not your need to show your *chops* (technical skills). So even though you may be able to play with complexity and flash, you may not be appreciated for it if it gets in the way of the story the song is telling.

More than just another rock drummer

The drummers I present in this chapter play on rock records, but many of them are also in demand beyond the rock world and play all the other styles of music (and many of the different drums I present in this book) just as well as they play rock. The bottom line is that a good drummer is a good drummer regardless of the style of music he or she plays. And while all these styles may not currently be burning up the charts, if the future is anything like the past (and it usually is), then many of these approaches will find their way into the spotlight again some-day.

Exploring Some Great Drummers and Their Grooves

With the sheer amount of music in the world, you shouldn't be surprised to find that a ton of decent drummers are out there. But, as in every field, some really rock. In this section I present a bunch of these guys and the rhythms that exemplify why they have risen to the top of a very competitive field. If you want to watch these drummers, check out www.drummerworld.com to see them play.

Peeking into the pop drumming of Kenny Aronoff

Kenny Aronoff is a classically trained drummer who made a place for himself in the straight-ahead (dare I say, pop?) rock world. Starting in 1980 he played for years for John Mellencamp and went on to play with tons of people. When I say tons, I mean tons. In 2005 alone, he recorded with Santana, Trey Anastasio, Alanis Morissette, Iggy Pop, Willie Nelson, and many others. In fact, if you turn on your radio (go ahead, I'll wait . . .), chances are the next rock singer — not a band — that comes on will have Kenny playing the drums.

Kenny's style is relatively simple, but he has the touch (and he beats the heck out of the drums). He's so well respected by drummers that he won Modern Drummer Magazine's annual poll of drummers in the category of "best rock drummer" five years in a row. He also recently won the "best studio drummer" category as well.

He's a good drummer to start this chapter with because his grooves aren't that difficult to play. In fact, you can find almost all the grooves he plays in Chapter 6. What sets him apart is his feel and often his fills. In the sections that follow, I explore the rhythms he played on Melissa Etheridge's "Breathe" (from the *Lucky* live CD). You can find out more about Kenny Aronoff at www.kennyaronoff.com.

Taking a breath into the verse and chorus

During the verse and chorus of Melissa Etheridge's "Breathe," Kenny plays a solid groove with a kick drum that has a syncopated beat on the "a" of 2 (the second beat of the measure). You can see this rhythm in the first groove in Figure 11-1. The chorus uses the same basic rhythm (again the first rhythm in Figure 11-1) but Kenny changes the feel a little bit by opening the hi-hat slightly. Opening the hi-hat increases the intensity (and overall volume) of the rhythm. This opening makes the hi-hat sound longer (legato) as well as louder. This slight variation illustrates how you can change just one simple part of the groove's orchestration and end up with a very different feel. Speaking of variation, in the second rhythm of Figure 11-1, Kenny makes the groove a little funkier by syncopating the hi-hat to accentuate the syncopated kick drum beat on the "a" of 2. He does this only once in a while, which gives this variation more impact within the song.

Figure 11-1: Keeping things simple in the verse and chorus.

Breathing life into the bridge

During the bridge, Kenny plays the hi-hat pattern on a crash cymbal, further increasing the intensity and volume of the groove. He also adds some embellishments to the basic groove. Figure 11-2 shows the pattern. Notice that the snare drum adds a note on the "e" of beat 3 and occasionally has ghost notes at the end of the measure. Often he plays a sixteenth-note triplet on the last half of the fourth beat. This note requires being able to play a quick double stroke where you usually place a single ghost note. This stroke is a common "lick" for rock drummers. (For more on licks, check out Chapter 13.)

If you can't do a double stroke, simply play a single ghost note on the "a" of beat 4 in Figure 11-2.

When you work on playing this rhythm, make sure that the kick drum note that plays on the "a" of beat 2 is placed exactly between the two eighth notes of the hi-hat pattern (the "&" of 2 and beat 3).

To work on this precise placement, play the rhythm really slowly and count in sixteenth notes as you play ("1 e & a 2 e & a," and so on). This count helps you figure out what it feels like physically to play the rhythm right. This way when you speed up to a regular tempo, the placement of this note is perfect.

Figure 11-2:
The bridge section increases in both intensity and complexity.

Building the fill

The fill that Kenny does at the end of the bridge section on "Breathe" is characteristic of his style (see Figure 11-3). At the beginning he plays the dotted eighth note followed by sixteenth notes, and then he intensifies the fill by using sixteenth-note triplets. These triplets start on the second half of the third beat in the measure and go through beat 4 and into the downbeat (the "1") of the nest measure. You can play this sixteenth-note triplet pattern from the snare drum around the tom-toms until you get to the lowest one. Depending on how many tom-toms you have, you may need to stay longer on one or another.

Figure 11-3:
Kenny
Aronoff
plays a nice
fill at the
end of the
bridge
section in
"Breathe."

Bridge fill

TRACK 39, 0:41

1 e & a 2 e & 3 & t t 4 t t & t t

You count sixteenth-note triplets "1 tu tu & tu tu 2 tu tu & tu tu," and so on. This count means that you play the second beat of each triplet (three notes) in the same time as a single sixteenth note. Listen to the CD that accompanies this book to hear how it works.

The only other tricky part of this fill is that you start the sixteenth-note triplets with your left hand. This left-hand start ensures that when to get to the last beat, you hit the cymbal with your right hand.

Checking out punk's Travis Barker

Travis Barker is known for his drumming in the new-punk (often called *pop-punk,* whatever that means) band Blink 182. I have a deep affinity for punk music, having grown up at the birth of punk and being a fan of the original punkers the Sex Pistols and the Dead Kennedys (anyone remember them?). In fact, one of the first bands I played in was a punk band (Jimmy Hoffa and the Gangsters, if you must know). But I digress. Back then the drumming was fast and furious with relatively simplistic rhythms (at that tempo you could hardly do anything else).

Simplistic rhythms aren't the case anymore. Sure, you can find the straight-ahead speed of the old days, but you can also find more funky rhythms being used. Travis' drumming with Blink 182 fits this second category well. In the following sections you can see some of the rhythms he used on the song "Down" (off their self-titled 2000 album).

Groovin' in the verse

The rhythm during the song's verse, pictured in Figure 11-4, is very cool and helps define the song. Heck, I could listen to just this groove without the rest of the band. Wait, I almost can at about two and a half minutes into the song.

Listen to this section and you can clearly hear what Travis is doing. If you can't hear it, check out my interpretation on this book's companion CD.

Travis foregoes the snare drum on beat 2 and moves it earlier (by one sixteenth-note beat) to the "a" of 1. This move gives the rhythm a slanted feel. The other snare drum beat in the measure is on the 4. Travis also plays ghost notes on the "a" of 2 and "a" of 4.

The hi-hat plays steady eighth notes, but if you listen to the recording of the song, you hear a shaker playing sixteenth notes and the afuche/cabasa playing a cool syncopated pattern (for more on these instruments, check out Chapter 17).

The kick drum plays on the 1, the "e" of two (go slowly when working on this beat — it can be tricky), the 3, and the "a" of 3 (this one's tricky too). It may take you a while to get the hang of the snare on the "a" of 1, the kick on the "e" of 2, and "a" of 3, but once you do you'll see how fun it is to play and you won't want to play the snare strictly on 2 and 4 again.

Bringing in the chorus

In a pre-chorus section (a section between a verse and a chorus) of this song, Travis changes it up a bit and plays almost every measure differently. Take a look at Figure 11-5 and you can see one of the rhythms he plays in this section. The basic division of the measure is the same during the verse and chorus rhythms, but the orchestration is different.

In this example, the hi-hat plays eighth notes except for the "&" of 2 where you play a crash cymbal instead. The accented snare drum notes move from the "a" of 1 to the "&" of 2 and from the 4 to the "e" of 4. The kick drum also moves around, replacing the snare drum at both the "a" of 1 and the 4. This groove is very cool.

Figure 11-4: Verse and chorus rhythms on Blink 182's "Down."

Verse and Chorus   TRACK 40, 0:00

1 e & a   2 e & a   3 e & a   4 e & a

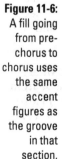

Filling in

In Figure 11-6 you can see a cool fill Travis uses on one of the times he goes from the pre-chorus into the chorus. The accent pattern for this fill is the same as the regular groove (in Figure 11-4) but he uses the snare to push into the cymbal crashes. This approach of picking up into the accent with a snare-hit draws from big band jazz playing in the form of a section figure (a section in the band plays an accent). I'm not saying that's where Travis got this idea, but it's an interesting aside. You can find out more about section figures in Chapter 9.

Figure 11-6:
A fill going
from pre-
chorus to
chorus uses
the same
accent
figures as
the groove
in that
section.

Catching up with the jazz influence of Carter Beauford

Carter Beauford, the drummer for the Dave Matthews Band, successfully brought the progressive rock style of drumming into the forefront again after it spent almost three decades in the closet. Carter brings a jazz sensibility to the band, which makes sense because he cites Buddy Rich as the drummer who influenced him the most growing up. By many, Buddy Rich is considered the greatest jazz drummer of the jazz era. Check out www.buddyrich.com for more information on this jazz legend.

Carter's playing is fairly busy: The grooves are often complex and seem to be ever-changing. That is, the main rhythm changes slightly from measure to measure. This change keeps the music interesting (and makes it really hard to transcribe from the record). His fills are often complex and, because the music he plays with the Dave Matthews Band can handle it, they are also fairly frequent. In this section, I provide some insight into Beauford's work on "Ants Marching" (off the band's 1994 album *Under the Table and Dreaming*).

The rhythms that I present in this section are some of the simplest rhythms Carter plays. If you want to know more about Carter and his drumming, check out www.drummerworld.com/drummers/Carter_Beauford.html. And you can check out www.dmband.com for more on Dave, Carter, and the rest of the group.

Marching along

Check out Figure 11-7. This rhythm includes the basic groove from the verse at the top and a variation beneath it. Notice how the basic rhythm isn't too complicated. It has a sixteenth-note pattern played in the hi-hat with the kick drum on beats 1, 3, and 4. The snare drum plays on beat 2. The only thing remotely difficult here is that Carter plays the hi-hat pattern with both hands instead of the usual right-hand only (this variation is the alternating-stroke version of a sixteenth-note feel that I cover in Chapter 6). What sets rhythm apart from the basic sixteenth-note feel rhythm is that he doesn't play the "e" of each beat. I suggest that you get good at playing this rhythm before you attempt the variation in Figure 11-8.

Figure 11-7:
Carter Beauford plays a sixteenth-note based rhythm in the verses of "Ants Marching."

Keeping it interesting

The variation of the basic rhythm (Figure 11-8) alter not only the hi-hat pattern but also the placement of the kick drum. The kick drum is moved from the 3 and 4 to the "&" of 3 and the "e" of 4.

As far as the hi-hat pattern goes, instead of playing constant sixteenth notes with the "e" of each beat resting, the pattern is more syncopated. In other words, the pattern is more broken. The accents (the ">" above the note) match the rhythmic breakdown of the rest of the instruments in the band, and this pattern is difficult to master. Go slowly, count out loud as you play, and take your time. You'll get the hang of it eventually.

Figure 11-8:
Variations to
the basic
rhythm.

Verse variation

TRACK 41, 0:07

One way to make this hi-hat rhythm easier is to play constant alternating strokes (R, L, R, L, and so on) in the hi-hat and play all the rests (the "e" of 1 and "a" of 2, for instance) very quietly. The sticking patterns in Figures 7-7 and 7-8 show how this is done. Notice how you play the downbeats and the "&" of each beat with the right hand and the "e" and "a" of each beat with the left hand.

From a sticking perspective (which hand plays which note), Figures 7-7 and 7-8 show the way Carter plays the rhythm. Although he doesn't actually play the rests, his sticking pattern acts as though he did. Knowing this fact can help you use Carter's approach to broken-sixteenth-note rhythms on any music that uses a sixteenth-note hi-hat pattern.

Filling in

Earlier I mention that Carter often performs very complex fills, but the fill in "Ants Marching" (Figure 11-9) is used several times in the song and the rhythm is played by everyone in the band. This group effort mirrors jazz musicians' habit of playing together as an ensemble. In fact, if you go to Chapter 9, I describe the use of ensemble figures (musical patterns that everyone plays). In a lot ways the Dave Matthews Band is a jazz band playing a fusion of jazz and rock (progressive rock is also referred to as rock-fusion).

Figure 11-9:
This fill by Carter Beauford is played a few times in the song "Ants Marching."

Discovering rock legend John Bonham

I have two words for you in case you're not familiar with John Bonham. Ready? Led Zeppelin. As part of one of the most influential bands of the rock era, John Bonham was renowned for the huge sound he got from his drums. The interesting thing is that even though he played really loudly on the drums, he hit the cymbals with a degree of finesse that served to make the drums seem even louder. He also created this loud drum sound without whaling on the drums; he just hit them with focused conviction.

Grooving slowly

The groove in Figure 11-10 is probably the most imitated rhythm played on slower rock tunes. If you listen to the original recording of "When the Levee Breaks" you can hear just how huge the drums are. Also if you listen to the whole song along with a lot of other Bonham recordings, you'll notice that he uses fills judiciously — he doesn't overdo it. So when he does play a fill, it has much more impact than if he were to fill every 4 or 8 measures like a lot of his contemporaries did (Keith Moon of The Who comes immediately to mind).

This restraint is the sign of a drummer who is comfortable with himself and his place in the band. That isn't to say that John didn't play awesome fills and didn't have the chops to play difficult ones. He did. If you get a chance, listen to his performance on any of the recordings of the band's "Moby Dick." He does a solo that will blow your mind (and if you turn up your stereo too high, probably your speakers too).

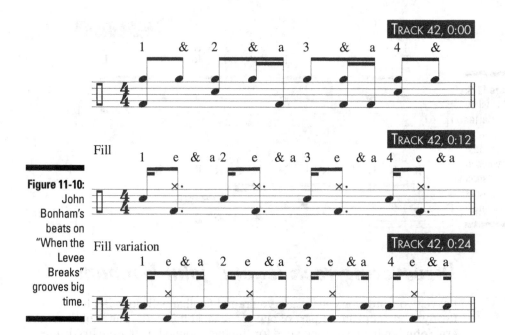

Figure 11-10:
John
Bonham's
beats on
"When the
Levee
Breaks"
grooves big
time.

The fill that I put in Figure 11-10, like the one in the Carter Beauford section earlier in this chapter, is a rhythm played by everyone in the band. I have two versions — a bare-bones version and a variation that adds another snare drum note on the "a" of each beat to give the fill more momentum going into the cymbal crash on the "e" of each beat.

Shuffling Bonham-style

The last tune of John Bonham's I want to explore is a half-time shuffle. Later in this chapter I talk about Jeff Porcaro and his legendary half-time shuffle. John's performance on "Fool in the Rain" comes in a close second as the best half-time shuffle ever recorded (some people would disagree with me on the order of the two best half-time shuffles but, hey, it's my book so you get to read my opinion). Figure 11-11 shows this groove.

Figure 11-11:
John
Bonham's
half-time
shuffle also
rocks.

We can all agree that Led Zeppelin was a rock band and that John Bonham was arguably the consummate rock drummer, right? Take another look at the groove in Figure 11-11. Now flip to the end of Chapter 9 and look at the groove in Figure 9-24. This rhythm is a jazz-fusion groove that derives from the Latin nanigo groove (which is in Chapter 10). As long as you're flipping through the book, take a look at the rhythm John plays in Figure 11-12 and compare it to the sambas in Chapter 15. Listen to the samba groove on the accompanying CD, and you hear a groove similar to what happens in the bridge of "Fool in the Rain."

Figure 11-12:
John
Bonham's
rhythms
have a Latin
feel.

TRACK 42, 0:45

John obviously understood Latin and Jazz styles enough to use some common rhythms in his rock drumming. To learn more about John Bonham, check out www.led-zeppelin.com/johnbonham/.

Looking at Dave Grohl's alternative drumming

In 1991 the band Nirvana turned the music world on its ear. When their debut album *Nevermind* came out, rock music had hit its low point. The hair bands of the 1980s were pretty washed up and the void they left needed to be filled. Nirvana filled it and ushered in a new genre of rock music. Dave Grohl was the drummer for Nirvana and his way of playing was emulated by countless drummers.

Because Dave was at the forefront of this new world of rock music, it makes sense to look to his playing as a way to pigeonhole the style of drumming in alternative rock music. One of the overriding characteristics is a lot of syncopated notes (see Chapter 6) on the snare drum. Many drummers over the years used this approach, but what differentiated Dave Grohl's use of these syncopations is that he almost always played them loudly instead of using them as ghost notes in the background, and he used them as part of the groove rather than as occasional accents. This technique was new in a wildly popular rock band, so lots of other drummers started doing it.

Now if you listen to an alternative band, almost invariably you hear the syncopated drumming happening. This style has also spilled over to other types of rock drumming. An example of this crossover is Travis Barker's drumming in Blink 182 that I talk about earlier in this chapter. In the sections that follow, I deconstruct Grohl's work on one of Nirvana's most popular songs, "Smells Like Teen Spirit" (from *Nevermind*). (You can find out more about Grohl at www.foofighters.com.)

Digging into the verse

Take a look at Figure 11-13. The rhythm for the verse is a pretty straightforward rock beat. The hi-hat plays a steady eighth-note pattern and the snare plays the backbeat on beats 2 and 4. The kick drum plays on the 1, "&" of 1, 3, and the "&" of 3. The only embellishment is the open hi-hat note on the "&" of 4.

Checking out the chorus

During the chorus the rhythm changes a lot; Figure 11-14 shows this groove. First Dave opens the hi-hat slightly to create a loose, trashy sound. Instead of playing an unaccented eighth-note rhythm, he still plays eighth notes on the hi-hat but places accents on the downbeats (beats 1, 2, 3, and 4). The snare drum adds syncopated beats on the "a" of 2 and the "e" of 3. He plays these syncopated beats as loudly as the backbeats on 2 and 4. The kick drum, ahem, kicks it up a notch and adds a beat on the "a" of 3 — creating a double-kick drum pattern — and the "&" of 4. This groove just feels like you're banging your head against the wall (and this is a good thing).

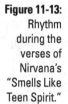

Figure 11-13: Rhythm during the verses of Nirvana's "Smells Like Teen Spirit."

Figure 11-14: The groove during the chorus steps it up a notch or two.

Introducing the intro

You can also get a feel for the types of fills Dave uses in this song. The third rhythm in Figure 11-15 shows the fill that he uses to enter the song. The snare plays on each downbeat (the 1, 2, 3, and 4) while the kick plays on the syncopations ("e" and "a") of beats 1, 2, and 3. The hi-hat is also active with a steady eighth-note pattern. This intro is a classic rock fill that sets the tone for the song really well.

Figure 11-15:
This classic rock fill sets the tone of the song right from the start.

TRACK 43, 0:19

Jamming with a drummer's drummer: Jeff Porcaro

Jeff Porcaro is a drummer's drummer and is often credited with playing the best half-time shuffle ever recorded on Toto's "Rosanna" (his regular-time shuffle is pretty good too). The son of jazz and session drummer Joe Porcaro (whom I studied with at the Musician's Institute), Jeff's shuffle has a definite jazz influence, which explains why it sounds as good as it does. Jeff has played with a ton a of great musicians but he's best known for his work with Steely Dan and Toto, of which he was a founding member and where he played with his two brothers (Mike on bass and Steve on keyboard).

Exploring what legends are made of

The key to Jeff's shuffles is the liberal use of ghost notes that fill in the triplet. Figure 11-16 shows the hand pattern that he often uses. Figure 11-17 shows another way that I've heard him play. This second pattern is one that his father is known for and is an integral part of the techniques Joe has in his book *Joe Porcaro's Drumset Method* (JoPo Productions).

If you want to become adept at playing a half-time shuffle, I can't recommend highly enough that you spend a little (or a lot of) time working on the hand patterns in Figures 11-16 and 11-17.

Figure 11-16:
One of Jeff Porcaro's trademarks is using ghost notes to fill in the triplets.

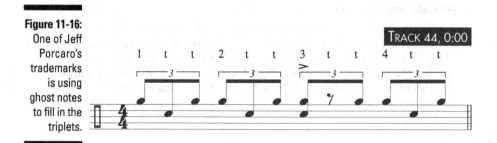

Figure 11-17:
Sometimes Jeff Porcaro adds another ghost note right after the backbeat.

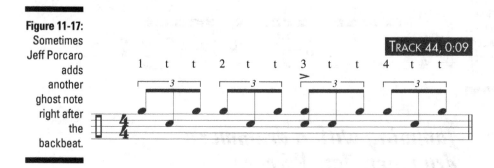

Feeling out "Rosanna"

Now on to the groove that I talk about a couple of times in this book. I had the pleasure of learning this rhythm directly from Jeff when I first met him in 1983, and listening to him play it by itself really drives the point home that he's a master at this type of groove. The shuffles in Toto's "Rosanna" are written in Figure 11-18.

As you can see in Figure 11-18, aside from the hand pattern, the rhythms are pretty straightforward — no double-kick drum beats here. What makes this groove difficult is the hand pattern and creating the right feel. The basic beat is the intro and verse of the tune. The variation (the second rhythm in the figure) shows a way Jeff often, ahem, varied the rhythm during the verses. The difference is on the last triplet of the pattern. Instead of playing just one ghost note, he plays two and drops the hi-hat beat on the last triplet beat of the measure. This variation allows him to get to the crash cymbal and still keep the rolling feel that the shuffle creates. He often does this variation without hitting a crash at the beginning of next measure.

Verse

TRACK 44, 0:18

TRACK 44, 0:28

Variation

Figure 11-18:
Jeff
Porcaro's
groove on
Toto's
"Rosanna"
is arguably
the best
half-time
shuffle ever
recorded.

Making sense of the chorus

The third rhythm in Figure 11-19 is the groove for the chorus. Your hand patterns stay the same, but the kick drum changes. Here the kick plays on a pattern that takes four measures to complete and follows the bass guitar pretty well (for more on the relationship between the kick drum and bass guitar, check out Chapter 12). It may take you a while to get the hang of it, but when you do, you'll probably be addicted to playing it.

Chorus (4 bars long)

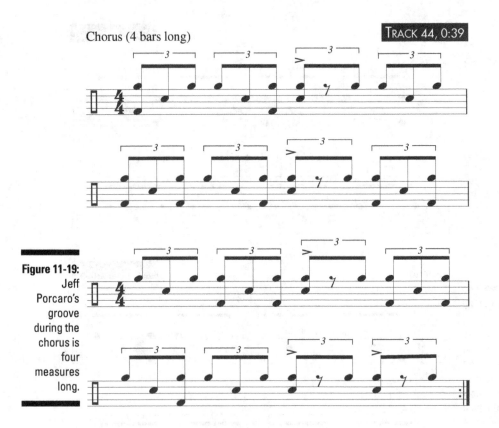

Figure 11-19:
Jeff
Porcaro's
groove
during the
chorus is
four
measures
long.

Examining Spüg's heavy rock style

A rock chapter wouldn't be complete without looking at one of the many heavy rock drummers gracing the planet. In this section I explore some of the grooves that Spüg (whose real name is Matt McDonough) plays with the band Mudvayne.

His style is hard hitting and includes a liberal dose of double-bass drumming. Using two bass drums became wildly popular in the hard rock genre of the 1970s (think Deep Purple, Black Sabbath, and Ozzy Osborne) and continues to be popular in the heavier styles of rock today (of which there are many). In this section I look at grooves that Spüg plays on the song "Dig" from Mudvayne's *L.D. 50* album from 2000. (If you're young, please listen to the "clean" version of their songs if you want to hear Spüg play.)

Pounding out the verse

As is typical in this general style of music, the double bass-drum patterns take center stage and the hi-hat creates a simple quarter note groove (that is, it plays on the downbeats 1, 2, 3, and 4) in Figure 11-20. The snare is on 2 and 4. During the verse, Spüg mostly plays the first rhythm in Figure 11-20. Occasionally he throws in the quintessential hard rock bass drum groove of all sixteenth notes in the quarter note hi-hat and 2 and 4 snare pattern. If you learn no hard rock groove other than this one, you're at least able to play the essentials.

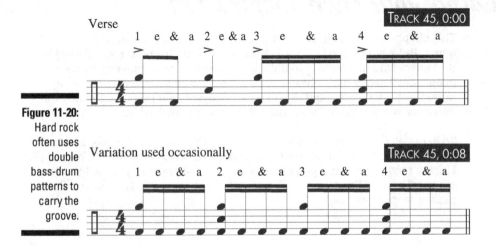

Figure 11-20: Hard rock often uses double bass-drum patterns to carry the groove.

Slamming through a fill

"Dig" has some cool fills. One I particularly like is shown in Figure 11-21. The reason I like this one is that it has a lot of power behind it and leaves some space to simply act as an accent. A lot of hard rock fills with double bass drums tend to scream "listen to me, I'm filling now!" Nothing's wrong with that approach, but I prefer what Spüg does here.

This fill, located about 1:48 into the song, repeats a rhythmic phrase four times over two measures, matching the tension that the section has in it. The first time through the phrase, the snare drum and the cymbals play a simplified version, the second time the kick drum and floor tom-tom play, the third time you're back to the cymbal and snare drum accents, and the last time it's back again to the kick and floor tom.

Figure 11-21:
This fill matches the tension created by the song.

Finding Your Own Inspiration

This chapter provides only a tiny peek into the ways you can dress up rock music. But what I hope to do is inspire you to look (or better yet, listen) for drummers who inspire you to dig a little deeper in your playing. By hearing people challenge what's always been done, your mind opens to the many possibilities that exist. And, who knows, you may end up using the inspiration to create something new that others can be inspired by.

To help you find drummers who can get you thinking, I offer some great resources and ideas for continuing on your drumming journey in Chapter 21. I highly recommend that you check it out. Also, if you find yourself wanting to study with a real live teacher, Chapter 22 offers some tips to help you find the perfect teacher for you.

Part III

Dressing up Your Drumset Skills

The 5th Wave   By Rich Tennant

Of all the drum players that worked with pianist, Bill Evans, the strangest was "Gil" Montgomery, who also doubled on carp.

In this part . . .

*P*art III steps up your drumset playing and shows you
how to impart your own personality into your playing. In Chapter 12 you discover the secrets to creating a
great groove and develop the skills to compose your own
rhythms. Chapter 13 leads you into the fabulous world of
fills — the drummer's musical signature. And in Chapter
14, you get to nurture the exhibitionist in you by exploring
ways to play a drum solo.

Chapter 12

Getting Into the Groove

. . . .

In This Chapter

▶ Making your rhythms sound great

▶ Fitting your rhythms to the song

▶ Adding your own touch to your drumming

. . . .

*R*egardless of what musical style they choose to play, all great drummers have one very important thing in common: They can play their rhythms with a solid, pleasing feel. In other words, they know how to get inside the rhythms and make them complement the music they're playing. Ultimately, it doesn't matter whether you can play a fill or a solo. If you can solidly play a basic time-keeping rhythm with heart and conviction, you'll be successful as a drummer.

In this chapter, you can discover how to really *get in the pocket of a rhythm* (play a rhythm solidly and simply) and make it groove. You can also find out what questions to ask yourself in order to choose the best rhythms that fit with the music of the other guys and/or gals in the band. In addition, this chapter helps you examine what makes a groove work and what to listen for in the other instruments' rhythms. And, you can take the first steps toward creating rhythms that you infuse with your own unique style and personality.

Getting the Feel of the Music

Good drumming is all about *feel* — how you play the rhythm and how it relates to the music going on around you. You don't have to be the fastest drummer in the world or be able to play an impressive 30-minute drum solo as long as you can play the groove with a solid feel.

Here are four things that you can do to make your drumming groove:

- **Practice the basics.** Work on getting your rhythms tight by keeping them simple and striving for limb synchronization. You need to lock in the hi-hat or ride pattern with the bass drum and snare drum rhythms. When two or more instruments are notated for you to play them together, they should play at exactly the same time. You shouldn't experience any flam-type sounds. (For more on flams, see Chapter 3.)

- **Work on developing steady time.** You absolutely must be able to play a rhythm without speeding up or slowing down. The best way to develop great time is to practice to a *metronome* (a device used to help musicians keep time). If you can, get a metronome that plays the subdivsions of a measure, such as eighth notes, triplets, or sixteenth notes. (For resources on metronomes, check out Chapter 19.) When you practice, set the metronome to play the subdivisions of the measure that match the rhythms of the groove. For example, in an eighth note straight-feel rhythm, set the metronome to play eighth notes. Doing so helps you keep the rhythms between the main pulses accurate.

- **Listen to the style of music you intend to play.** Every style of music interprets rhythm differently. The triplets in swing music, for instance, are played differently than the triplets in a rock shuffle. Even if they're played at the same tempo, they *sound* vastly different. The rock shuffle has a more laid-back feel while the swing beat seems to jump forward. The only way to fully understand these subtleties is to listen to the music and get used to its sound.

- **Play along to your favorite music.** Playing along helps you get used to switching from one rhythm to another and makes you think about song structure. Playing along to others' music is an important step in learning how to *play the drum musically* (a topic that I cover in the next section). To begin, try matching what you play to the drummer on the CD that you're listening to — fills and all. After you get the hang of that, you can start putting in some of your own fills.

Playing Musically

With a little practice, just about anyone can bang the drums and jam on a couple of fills, but the true art in playing any type of music on drums is being able to *apply your skills musically* (in other words, being sensitive to the music and the other musicians with what you choose to play). Being able to play musically is what separates the men from the boys, so to speak. This aspect of drumming is often overlooked and, at times, has given drummers of all musical styles a bad name. Your mission (if you choose to accept it) is to overcome the stereotypical view of the drummer as an insensitive show-off.

Hey, don't make this mistake

When I was 16, I was on the roster of the local musician's referral service and was pretty busy playing your typical fill-in jobs: weddings, parties, a few bars (I had to leave the bar during breaks because I was underage). By this time I'd been playing professionally for about two years and was getting pretty comfortable playing the types of music I was called to do (mostly light rock, swing, and country). And, I was starting to get pretty regular work.

So what do I do? Well, I do what any cocky teenager does when he starts feeling "successful." I forget that I'm just a hired hand and a dime-a-dozen musician, and I start overplaying to suit my fancy. Okay, to be quite honest, I was beginning to feel like I wasn't able to stretch my musical muscles at these gigs, but that's no excuse for what happened one night in a bowling-alley bar.

On this particular gig, I was playing with a country band and I got bored so I started throwing in rolls and turning the beat around. I'm embarrassed to admit this, but at one point I think I played one continuous 32nd note roll between the snare drum and bass drum during an entire second verse, drowning out the singer and throwing off the bass player. Needless to say, I never got called to work with that band again. In fact, I mysteriously lost a lot of my regular gigs after that. The funny thing is that I didn't even know what I'd done until years later.

The best way to apply your skills musically is to think of playing the song rather than the drums. Sure, you still play your drums, but your mindset changes to putting the need of the song and the support of the other musicians in the band above your own desire to showcase your *chops* (chops is musician-speak for skills or technique).

Understanding song structure

In order to play musically, you need to understand basic song structure. Generally, almost all styles of songs have between two and four different sections. These sections include the following:

- ✔ **The intro.** The intro, or introduction, is a short phrase, usually between two and eight measures long, at the very beginning of the song. The intro can suggest a melody from within the song or be entirely different than the rest of the song.

- ✔ **The verse.** The verse is the section that tells the song's story. The verse is usually fairly quiet and is eight to sixteen measures long. A song generally has three or four verses.

✔ **The chorus.** The chorus section is louder than the verse and contains the hook of the song. The *hook* (if it works) is the melodic phrase that you sing and can't get out of your head. The chorus is between eight and sixteen bars long and follows the verse. The end of the song may repeat the chorus a few times.

✔ **The bridge.** The bridge is another loud section that's often between four and sixteen bars long. This section usually follows the second or third chorus and can contain either a vocal phrase or a solo. Not all songs have a bridge section.

Most rock tunes have an intro followed by a verse and then a chorus. Next comes another verse followed by another chorus. This second chorus may be repeated, and then followed by a bridge, which goes into a third verse. After this verse comes a few repeats of the chorus to end the song.

Fitting your playing style to the song

For most songs, you can get away with playing one or two rhythms — one for the verse and another for the chorus. The difference between these two rhythms can be slight. For example, you can go from a tightly closed hi-hat during the verse to a more open hi-hat, or maybe the ride cymbal, during the chorus. Most often though, the bass drum pattern changes from the verse to the chorus along with the volume change created by the change in the hi-hat or ride cymbal part.

A fill usually marks the transition from verse to chorus and chorus to verse (see Chapter 13). Likewise, a *crescendo* (playing gradually louder) marks the transition from the verse to chorus and a *decrescendo* (gradually softer volume) marks the transition when going from the chorus back into a verse. Choose your fills and dynamics (crescendo or decrescendo) to fit the section into which you're going. For example, when transitioning from a verse to the chorus, choose a fill that builds intensity. When going from the chorus back to the verse, your fill should reflect the decreasing volume and intensity that this transition makes.

During the verses and choruses, you can add fills and embellishments that complement the rhythmic and dynamic textures of the other instruments. These fills are usually at the end of two- or four-bar phrases. A well-placed fill can add a lot to a song, whereas a misplaced fill can destroy the feeling of that section. When you're not sure whether to add a fill or not, you're better off not playing one. (To further explore fills, go to Chapter 13.)

The best way to learn how to use fills and embellishments effectively is to listen to a really good drummer play. The song and style of music that you're playing largely determines the number and complexity of the fills that you use. If you're in a jazz-fusion band, you can get away with many more fills than if you're backing a pop singer such as Celine Dion.

Choosing the Perfect Rhythm

Okay, if you've read the last few chapters of this book, you've spent some time getting comfortable behind your drums and gotten pretty good at playing some basic grooves. You can go in and out of fills smoothly; maybe you can even play along to your favorite CDs. Now you want to play with other musicians. Great! Here's where drumming gets really fun. But, it also poses some challenges, most notably, being able to pick the right rhythm to play.

When you get together with other musicians, you need to be able to choose the correct rhythm for each song. If you end up reading music, this task is easy because the style of the music and basic groove pattern are notated on the chart (sheet music), but if you play without music, you have to figure out what to play. To do so, you need to listen to what the other musicians are playing and immediately choose a rhythm that fits.

Getting hints from other musicians

Often, somebody tells you the basic style of the tune by saying "straight-ahead rock" or "blues feel." This hint gives you some idea of the genre of the music, but, depending on the person's knowledge and skill level, it may or may not really help you figure out what to play. Just nod your head knowingly and listen very carefully (asking for clarification if you don't understand is often okay).

If the person counts the song in (for example, "one, two, three, four — play") without playing an intro, you may have to fake it until you can actually hear what the other musicians are playing. The best thing to do is play the rhythm in Figure 12-1 until you can figure out what's going on. This rhythm works well in these situations because it contains the core instruments (hi-hat, snare drum, bass drum), and it won't conflict with the rhythms of the other instruments, no matter what they're playing.

Figure 12-1:
A great
rhythm to
use if you're
not sure
what to
play.

Using the music as a guide

The most important factor that will guide you in determining which rhythm to use is the overall feel of the music (the section or song). To figure out the overall feel, start asking yourself the following questions:

1. **Does the song have a straight or triplet feel?** You need to listen carefully to the music to answer this question. Depending on the song and the abilities of the other musicians, the feel is pretty easy to determine. In some cases, though, hearing it will prove to be more difficult. Fast songs in a shuffle feel, for instance, can sound surprisingly like a straight feel. For more information on feel, see Chapter 6.

   If you're unsure whether the song has a straight or triplet feel, asking is generally okay. However, if you're in a situation where asking isn't possible or desirable, the best thing to do is keep it really simple until you can figure it out (try starting with the rhythm in Figure 12-1).

2. **What subdivisions are being used?** Whether eighth or sixteenth notes are the basis of the main rhythm determines what type of rhythm you choose. If the guitar or keyboard player uses sixteenth notes, for example, you'll probably find that playing sixteenth notes on the hi-hat fits well.

3. **Is the feel regular or half-time?** To answer this question, listen for the basic pulse and watch other musicians as they play their parts (they often give this information away by the way they tap or sway as they play). It's often pretty easy to tell the feel: One style fits much better than the other.

4. **What is the length of the rhythmic phrase?** After you know the overall feel of the music, start listening for the rhythmic phrasing of the other instruments. The length of the rhythmic phrase can help you decide how long you want your rhythm to be. The most common lengths for rhythms are either one or two bars, although a groove that's four bars long isn't unheard of. Listen to the bass player. His or her rhythms are your cue for what to play on the bass drum.

   Unless you're playing in a free-form jazz-fusion band using bizarre odd meters or you're into experimental music where no distinguishable pulse exists, the style of the song gives you an immediate sense of what to play. In most cases, you draw from a handful of established grooves.

Figure 12-2 shows you an example of how a drum part relates to the rhythms of the guitar and bass players' parts. Notice how the hi-hat pattern and the bass player's notes on the 1 and "&" of 2 (played on the bass drum) match the guitar player's eighth-note rhythm. Because this is a rock tune, the snare drum plays on the 2 and 4.

Guitar rhythm

Bass guitar rhythm

Figure 12-2:
The way a
drum
rhythm fits
with the
other
instruments
in a band.

Drumset part

Adding Your Personality

If you're like most drummers, you want to make your own personal statement with your drumming (it's okay — go ahead and admit it). Even if you play a common groove, you can make it your own by playing solidly in the pocket and in the way that you interpret or orchestrate the rhythm. How you orchestrate your rhythms also helps determine what type of feel the song ends up having, so be careful not to get too carried away.

Orchestration simply refers to the sounds that you choose to use. As a drumset player, you choose between the bass drum, snare drum, cymbals, and tom-toms. With hand drums, you choose between the various hand strokes. For example, on a conga drum, you can choose from an open tone, muted tone, slap, heel-tip stroke, palm stroke, bass tone, drone tone, and so forth. (See Chapter 4 for more on the hand drum strokes.)

With the drumset, you have a pretty large palate from which to draw. You have the bass drum, snare drum, tom-toms, hi-hats, ride cymbal, and any other accent instruments that you've incorporated into your ultimate drum kit (for more on the drumset, check out Chapter 5). You probably want to stick pretty close to some conventions of orchestration in order to best fit the style of music that you're playing. The descriptions in this section apply to most music, but you'll find some exceptions when playing traditional jazz (swing). For example, the bass drum in jazz doesn't generally relate to the bass player's rhythm — it's used for accents and embellishments.

Choosing the bass drum part

Most often, the bass drum plays a rhythm that supports the rhythm of the bass player. To do this, match your rhythms to the bass player's, play the bass player's accented notes, or play a complementary rhythm. If the bass guitar part is busy (with lots of notes), you may want to play a straight 1 and 3 beat or 1, 2, 3, 4 pattern on the kick (bass drum).

Selecting the snare drum part

In most popular music, the snare drum plays the *backbeat*, which means beats 2 and 4 of the measure (see Chapter 6 for more on the backbeat). You're not limited to this pattern, however, as long as you understand that the snare drum's beat greatly affects the overall feel of the music.

Picking the cymbals

Your first choice is whether to play a ride cymbal or the hi-hats. For most situations, you use the hi-hats during verses and other quieter sections of the song, while reserving the ride cymbal for the chorus or solos. Other times, a slightly loose hi-hat during the chorus works well. You can also choose to use a ride cymbal during a verse and switch to the bell for the louder sections. Which instrument you choose depends on how full of a sound you want.

For example, if the verse is filled with long, sustaining chords on the guitar and pulsating eighth notes on the bass guitar, using a ride cymbal isn't out of the question. On the other hand, if the verse consists of *staccato* (short notes without sustain) passages and a simple, defined melody, the tightly closed hi-hats are a better choice.

The hi-hat or ride pattern should relate to the subdivisions present in the music. You don't want to play a sixteenth-note rhythm if the song has a strong eighth-note feel.

Electing embellishments

Ghost notes, accents, cymbal crashes, and splashes can all be part of your rhythms. Some drummers, such as Terry Bozzio (check out `www.terry bozzio.com`), incorporate a lot of these embellishments into the main groove. Because embellishments have the ability to add another melody to the song, you should choose them with care. If you overdo embellishments, you end up cluttering the song.

Figure 12-3 shows how orchestration has a huge impact on the way a rhythm sounds. The first rhythm is a basic rock beat, while rhythms 2 through 4 use the same basic rhythmic structure to create some unusual grooves. The purpose of these rhythms is to, hopefully, open your mind to what's possible as well as give you permission to stretch your creative muscles.

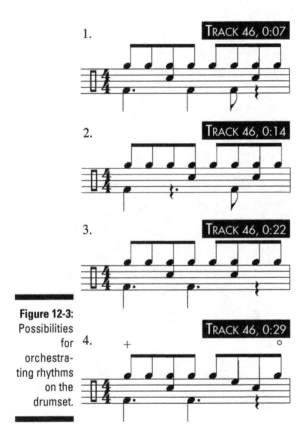

Figure 12-3:
Possibilities for orchestrating rhythms on the drumset.

Chapter 13

Expressing Yourself with Fills and Licks

*F*ills and licks are a chance for you to put your musical signature on a tune. Playing a groove can be fun but playing a fill can be *really* fun. And playing a lick or a fill can add some increased percussion presence and some spice to an otherwise simple rhythm. Fills and licks are very similar; when used correctly, they both add to the music and invoke a certain feeling. The difference between them lies in how each relates to the main groove.

 A *lick* is simply an embellishment (a note or two) added to the main rhythm. To play a lick, keep the time (groove) going and add your lick to it. A *fill*, on the other hand, breaks from the main groove and takes over. To play a fill, *stop* playing time and add your fill. You go back to playing time when you're finished. Filling allows you to get creative and increase your impact on a song. With the perfect fill, you can effectively direct a song's intensity and dynamics.

In this chapter, I help you develop the skills to determine when to use fills and licks. In addition, you can find out how to add licks to your playing that give your groove an added bit of character that separates good drummers from the truly great ones. You can also examine how fills work so that you can make the greatest impact and add to, rather than detract from, the music. Finally, I help you uncover some tricks to creating your own unique fills.

Enhancing Your Drumming with Licks

Licks can fall almost anywhere in a song as long as they complement what the other musicians are playing. You can find classic examples of adding licks to a song in jazz bebop drumming. You create the basic time with the swing ride pattern and the hi-hat (playing on the 2 and 4). Add the snare drum and bass drum throughout while maintaining the time-keeping (ride cymbal and hi-hat) pattern. Check out Figure 13-1 for an example of a jazz lick (see Chapter 9 for more on jazz drumming).

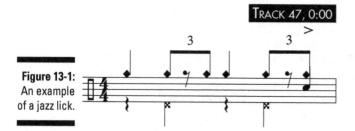

Figure 13-1: An example of a jazz lick.

Another common lick technique involves using syncopated or ghost notes on the snare drum to fill in the holes of the groove. Figure 13-2 contains an example of this type of lick. If you want more, you can find a bunch of examples of syncopated and ghost note licks in Chapters 6 and 11.

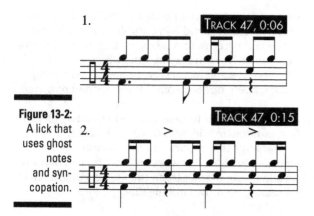

Figure 13-2: A lick that uses ghost notes and syncopation.

The most common type of lick involves an accent that the whole band plays. In jazz, this accent is often called an *ensemble figure,* which generally involves breaking time and setting up the lick with a fill. However, in other styles of music, it's not uncommon for the drummer to incorporate these accents into the groove. Figure 13-3 shows an example of how this technique works.

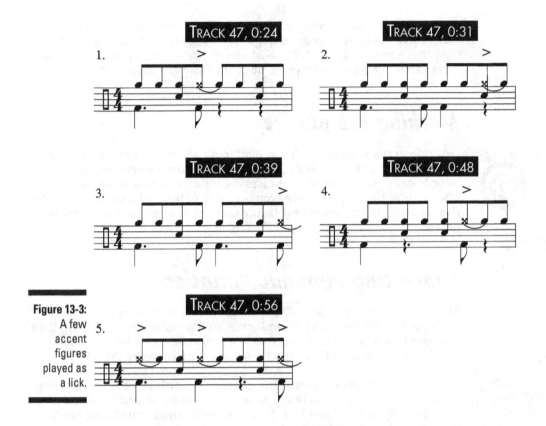

Figure 13-3:
A few accent figures played as a lick.

The cymbal accent figures in Figure 13-3 are very common in rock, R&B, fusion, and Latin styles. Notice that the basic time continues while you play the accents. In each case (except rhythm 4), the backbeat remains steady. This maintains a sense of movement in the song and, by not setting these accents up with a fill, the momentum continues through the accent.

The important thing to remember with these licks is to use sensitivity when adding them to the song by being aware of the rhythmic phrases of other instruments. For example, you can use a syncopated accent that you play on the snare drum on the "a" of beat 2 to match another instrument's accent in the same place or to offset a rest.

Increasing Your Impact with Fills

Fills make a much more powerful impact than licks. Because you have to break away from your main groove to play a fill, you want to make sure that you know how to best incorporate it into the song. The main thing to remember is to use fills with discretion. The more fills you play, the less impact each one has. Of course, this idea is somewhat dependent on the type of music you play — certain styles of music (progressive rock, jazz-fusion) can handle more fills than others (pop rock, R&B). The best way to determine how many and what types of fills fit a particular style of music is to listen to music in that genre.

Marking the phrase

Generally, when you play a fill, you want to do it at the end of a phrase. This technique is called *marking the phrase*. Music almost always consists of 2-, 4-, 8-, or 16-bar phrases. Four-bar phrases are the most common, so you should start to think this way whenever you play. One of the best ways to get used to this is playing three bars of time before each fill measure to create a four-bar phrase.

Supporting dynamic variation

After you know where to put a fill in a song, the next thing to do is make sure that your fill helps set up the dynamic changes that occur within the song. If the song gets louder or more intense, your fill should reflect that by getting louder or fuller. Likewise, when the song's dynamic goes down, yours should too.

Volume is pretty easy to control, but intensity is a little more subtle. *Intensity* lies in the types of rhythms that you use as well as the drums on which you play them. Figures 13-4 and 13-5 show how the rhythms you choose can increase or decrease intensity.

The fill in Figure 13-4 *crescendos* (gets louder) as it gets busier toward the end. The sixteenth notes on beat 4 create a sense of movement into the next bar. This fill ends with a crash cymbal that you play on the downbeat of the next bar, further increasing its impact.

Figure 13-4:
Increasing
intensity
with a fill.

TRACK 48, 0:00

In contrast to the fill in Figure 13-4, the fill in Figure 13-5 opens up rhythmically at the end. This fill creates a sense of space and reserve and almost seems to slow down (this is an illusion though; the tempo remains the same). The tom-tom note on the "and" of beat 4, because of its lower pitch, also reduces the intensity of the fill. You can use this fill as the transition from the chorus of the song back to the verse. You can end it either with a crash cymbal on the one, a splash cymbal (which is slightly softer sounding), or just go right into the hi-hat rhythm, which furthers the intensity-reducing effect.

TRACK 48, 0:09

Figure 13-5:
Decreasing
intensity
with a fill.

Playing Some Fills — From One Beat to Four

You may have experimented with (and even gotten comfortable playing) a few fills in Part III. But, in this section, you have an opportunity to try a bunch of fills in both a straight-time feel and a triplet feel (for more on these feels, check out Chapter 6). Depending on the style of music that you play, some fills work better than others. If a fill fits really well in a particular style, I let you know.

One of the keys to playing fills well is to keep the tempo steady. If you're like most people, your tendency is to speed up as you play the fill. I recommend practicing all the fills in this chapter to a metronome (see Chapter 19 for more on metronomes). Keeping solid time while filling is essential if you want to play with others. You're better off not playing a fill than you are putting in a sloppy one.

The fills in Figures 13-6 and 13-7 are of the one-beat (or fewer) variety. These fills are useful for a large number of occasions where you want to mark the change in a song but don't want to disrupt its flow too much. Figure 13-6 contains fills that fit into straight-feel grooves.

Figure 13-6: One-beat straight-feel fills.

The fills in Figure 13-7 are best suited for grooves with a triplet feel. Fill 3 works best with funkier (Latin, funk, and fusion) grooves. See Chapter 8 for more on funk grooves and Chapter 10 for more on Latin grooves.

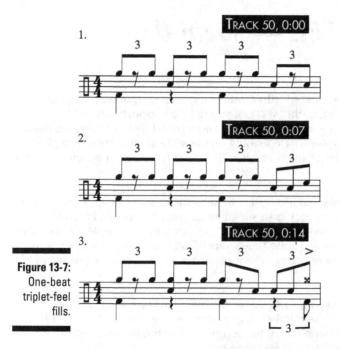

Figure 13-7: One-beat triplet-feel fills.

Two-beat fills are very versatile. They mark the transitions in a song quite well without getting in the way like a longer fill can. Figures 13-8 and 13-9 show a few to get you started.

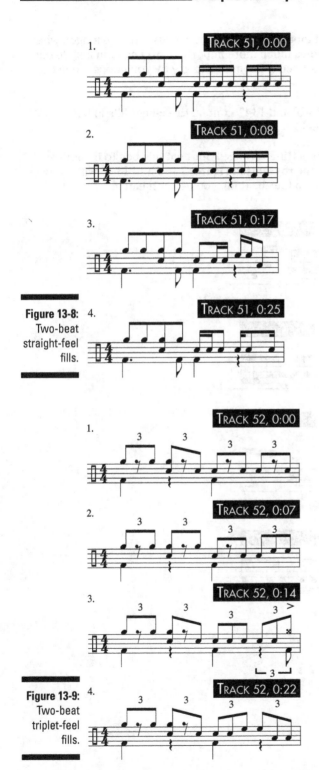

Figure 13-8: Two-beat straight-feel fills.

Figure 13-9: Two-beat triplet-feel fills.

Three-beat fills are much more fun to play, but because they're longer, what you choose to play becomes much more important. You can't just slide one of these fills through unnoticed (of course, that's why you choose to use a three-beat fill, isn't it?).

The rhythms in Figures 13-10 and 13-11 contain three-beat fills in both straight feel and triplet feel.

This is where things start getting serious. Four-beat fills beg to be noticed. Your job, then, is to play the rhythms in Figures 13-12 and 13-13 with conviction. If you're going to play a four-beat fill, you better mean it!

Figure 13-10:
Three-beat
straight-feel
fills.

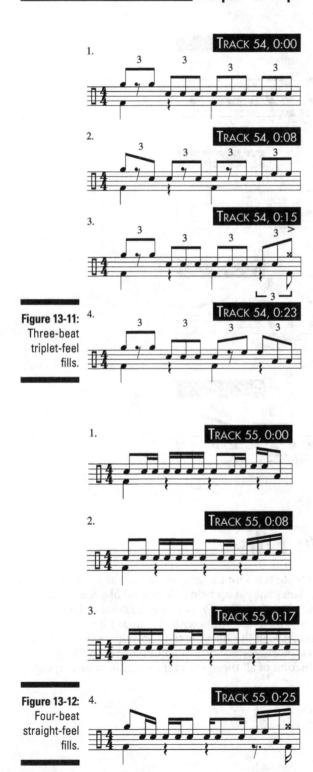

Figure 13-11:
Three-beat
triplet-feel
fills.

Figure 13-12:
Four-beat
straight-feel
fills.

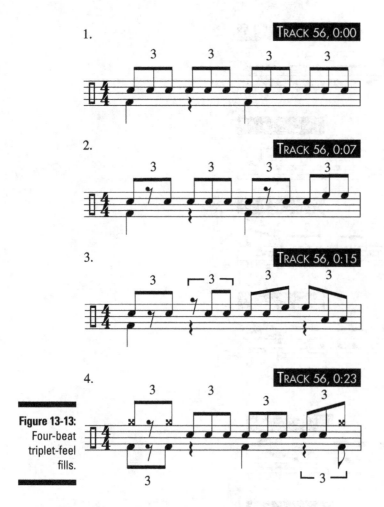

Figure 13-13:
Four-beat
triplet-feel
fills.

Creating Your Own Fills

The types of fills that you create tell a lot about who you are as a musician (and perhaps as a person). You can end up being kinda wild like Keith Moon of The Who with his all-over-the-place fills. Or, you may be reserved in the style of Rolling Stones drummer Charlie Watts with his single fill every few minutes. Likewise, you can reside in the turn-the-beat-around world of Terry Bozzio-style drumming (www.terrybozzio.com). But more than likely, you'll end up with a combination of all these characteristics in your playing.

These examples lead me to make my strongest recommendation yet for listening to other drummers. If all you ever listen to is the straight-ahead drumming of Charlie Watts, for instance, you won't have the necessary ear for Neil Peart-style filling in your drumming that you'd have if you listened to some Rush. So, the number one thing that you can do to become a really good drummer is to become familiar with how different drummers play and how their fills fit into the music and musical style in which they're playing.

Fitting the musical situation

The types of fills that you use will largely depend on the style of music that you play. A 30-second-note roll doesn't work very well in country music, for example (trust me on this one — I found out the hard way). This type of roll may very well work in certain types of jazz or fusion music, however.

Check out Figure 13-14 to see some fills that are characteristic of certain styles of music. (You can also go back into each of the drumset style chapters in Part III to see some more.)

Syncopating

Syncopating essentially means creating some space in your fill (by resting or playing ghost notes) and accentuating the notes on the upbeat. Syncopated fills can be especially interesting because they tend to mask the basic pulse of the music. To get an idea of some syncopated fills, check out Figure 13-15.

Examples 1 and 2 use syncopations with space in between while rhythms 3 and 4 fill those spaces with ghost notes. Depending on the style of the song and your overall playing characteristics, one approach will work better than the other. For example, rhythm 1 works well in straight-ahead rock music while rhythm 3 is better suited for R&B or funk styles.

Figure 13-14:
Fills charac-
teristic of
particular
musical
styles.

Rolling

Okay, here's a touchy one. Playing *rolls* within a contemporary musical setting can be tenuous. You need to be very careful and use them sparingly (or
not at all). One example of how to effectively use a roll is in a slow blues tune
at the very end of a really quiet section to abruptly bring up the volume into
a loud chorus section. Rolls can also work well in jazz music. Check out
Figure 13-16 to see how it's done.

Basically, you want to start out really quiet (*pp*) and play a buzz roll with a
crescendo into the next bar with a huge cymbal crash on the downbeat.

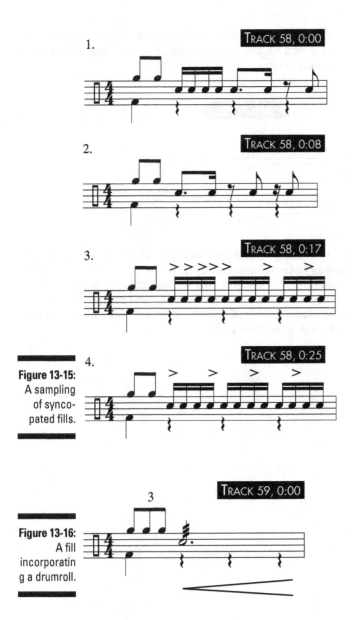

Figure 13-15:
A sampling of syncopated fills.

Figure 13-16:
A fill incorporating a drumroll.

Figure 13-17 shows you another way of using a roll as a fill. This fill is best when used at a point in the song where the volume is really low and you want to mark a vocal or solo phrase. This type of approach is most common in blues and jazz music.

TIP

The key to making the fill in Figure 13-17 work is to start the roll very quietly, build the volume slightly, and hit the accented note solidly. Then go back into the grove at about the same volume as when you left it.

Figure 13-17:
Another fill
using a roll.

No matter what style of music you end up playing or which approach you use in creating your fills, you have an opportunity to infuse a little of your personality into your drumming. That's what fills are about (okay, aside from trying to make the music more musical). So, have fun and remember that your main role in most music is to create the foundation of the band and support the other musicians in what they play.

Chapter 14

Flying Solo

· ·

In This Chapter

▶ Understanding solos

▶ Knowing when to play a solo

▶ Getting used to playing a solo

· ·

*I*f you find yourself going to a concert and eagerly awaiting the drum solo, or if your favorite part of a CD is the few bars where the drummer gets to strut his or her stuff, this chapter is for you. Drum solos can either add to or seriously detract from the music. A beautifully composed and executed solo can make a concert, whereas an ill-conceived, poorly timed solo can ruin the evening. This chapter helps you discern the difference between a well-conceived solo and one that just wastes time. You get a chance to try your hands (and feet) at a few solos in a variety of styles. You also discover some secrets that you can use to make your solos shine.

Soloing is never necessary, and in many styles of music, soloing isn't an option. But knowing that you can do it if you need to is a good thing. The exercises and solos in this chapter will help you develop technical skill and independence. So, if you have even a little interest in soloing within a band, rest assured that any time you spend learning this stuff won't go to waste.

On a technical note, the solos in this chapter can be somewhat challenging. They're intended to illustrate some of the many ways that you can approach a drum solo. Take your time learning them and don't be discouraged if it takes you a while to get the hang of them. And, above all, remember to practice them *very* slowly at first.

Soloing Basics

What you choose to do with a solo depends somewhat on the type of music that you play. In some styles of music, such as straight-ahead rock (a basic eighth-note feel, a la the Rolling Stones) or blues, drum solos are rare or nonexistent. Others require specific techniques, such as the hard rock or heavy metal solos that generally involve as much pyrotechnics as rhythm, or jazz solos that generally fit into the song. Regardless of the style of music, the best solos generally utilize a display of *chops,* which is musician-speak for skills or technique, and a certain musical quality (yes, even metal solos can be musical). In this chapter, I list a few approaches that you can use to make your drum solos interesting for both you and the audience.

Keeping time

No matter what type of solo you play (okay, a metal solo may be the exception), you need to play it within the context of the song and keep the groove happening. Well, not exactly *the* groove — if that's what you're playing, it isn't much of a solo. But whatever you play should be in time and should reflect the main groove of that section of music. One way to do this is to keep part of the groove happening while you solo around it. Check out Figure 14-1 to see an example of this approach. This solo uses a swing feel, and you feel the time by playing the hi-hat in its usual place on the 2 and 4.

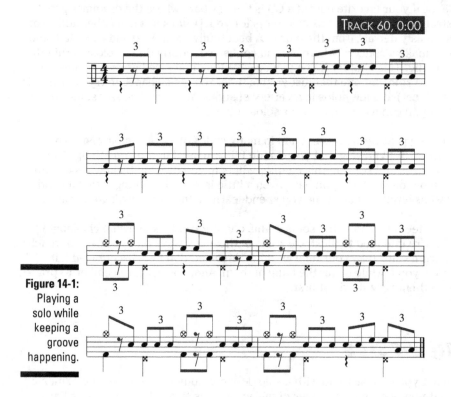

Figure 14-1: Playing a solo while keeping a groove happening.

Figure 14-2 shows you another example of a solo that keeps the time happening. This solo is based on a samba groove and keeps the foot patterns going while your hands play rhythms around the drums.

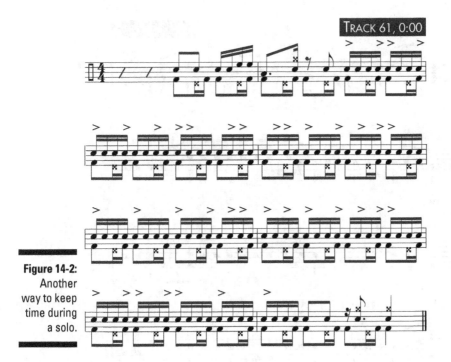

TRACK 61, 0:00

Figure 14-2:
Another
way to keep
time during
a solo.

Playing musically

The best solos have a musical component to them. They follow the structure of the song and occasionally accentuate its rhythmic phrases. Generally, when you're asked to solo, you have a given number of bars to play through and then you need to get back into the groove. An example of this standard is in jazz music when you trade bars or sections with other instruments (Chapter 9 contains a few two- and four-bar solos to get you started on this technique). Having a solo cover one entire time (a verse or chorus) through the song's structure is common. (Go to Chapter 12 for more about song structure.)

The solo in Figure 14-3 gives you an idea about how a solo can fit into a song's progression. This example uses a typical twelve-bar blues form played as a medium tempo swing (jazz) feel. I noted the chord changes (these are the little Roman numerals I, IV, and V that tell the other musicians which chord to play) above the staff so that you can see how the drum part follows the phrasing of the song. An accent is on the downbeat of each of the measures where a new chord is played.

Figure 14-3:
Following the song's phrasing structure while soloing.

Many drum solos that are played through the song also have a few, if not all, other instruments playing the accent figures during your solo. In this case, playing some of those figures along with the other instruments is a good idea. Take a look at Figure 14-4 to see what I mean. This solo has a straight funk feel. Notice that section figures (accents) are marked above the staff. (*Section figures* are notes written on the music that you play by accenting the notes. Check out Chapter 9 if you need a refresher on section figures.) The solo incorporates many of these accents. Not only does this sound great, but it also lets both the audience and the other musicians know that you know where you are within the tune.

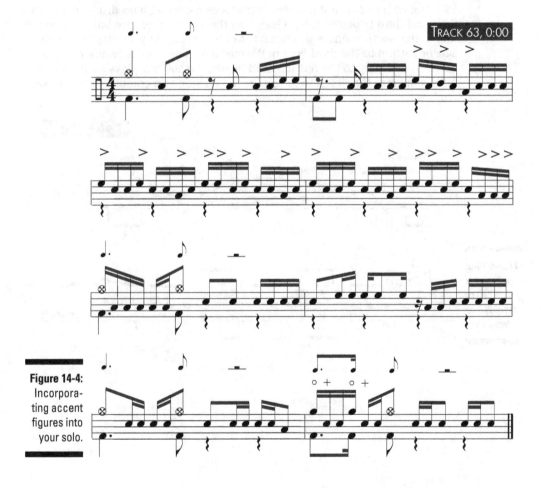

Figure 14-4:
Incorpora-
ting accent
figures into
your solo.

Thinking melodically

Playing a melodic solo doesn't necessarily mean playing the song's melody on the drums, although you can do that if you want. Instead, playing a melodic solo can mean playing your solo with some sensitivity toward its orchestration and phrasing. You can approach the solo in several ways. One is to create a phrase that you can repeat and build upon. The solos in both Figure 14-1 and Figure 14-3 accomplish this.

Take a look at Figure 14-5. I pulled this solo from the last four bars of Figure 14-1. Notice how the first measure introduces a cymbal/bass drum accent on the 1 and third triplet of 1. Next, see how the second measure builds upon that pattern with a single accent on the downbeat and by shifting the original accent pattern to the third beat of the measure. The third measure repeats bar 2, thus adding to the tension. And finally, the last bar plays a rhythm more similar to the first one to resolve the tension and complete the phrase.

TRACK 64, 0:23

Figure 14-5:
Infusing a
sense of
melody into
your solo.

Another way to add a sense of melody to a solo is by using accents on different pitched drums. You can see an example of this technique in Figure 14-6. This phrase is taken from the solo in Figure 14-4. These two measures show how you can build a phrase by adding a slight variation on both the accents and the orchestration. In this example, the first two beats of the first bar create a melody with the accents on the tom-toms. The next two beats play a variation. The next measure repeats this combination but further varies the rhythm by adding two extra floor tom beats at the end.

Figure 14-6:
Another approach to adding melodic feeling to a solo.

TRACK 65, 0:00

Pushing the limits

Now that you have an idea of how to play a solo that fits nicely and neatly into a particular piece of music, you may want to throw caution to the wind and try something a little riskier. The solo in Figure 14-7 is a more free-form type of solo than those that I showcase earlier in the chapter.

Free-form solos disguise the pulse by using broken syncopated notes and by incorporating a variety of note groupings that give the illusion of changing the pulse. For example, take a look at the third and fourth bars in Figure 14-7. Bar three creates the feeling of the tempo speeding up because of the combination of eighth notes, triplets, sixteenth notes, and a grouping of five notes. This type of rhythm is not uncommon in fusion solos. Take your time practicing this and use a metronome (you can also play along with me on the CD).

Figure 14-7:
A solo that
turns the
beat around.

Part IV
Pounding Out the Beat: Traditional Drums and Percussion

The 5th Wave   By Rich Tennant

"How do I know these are real calfskin drumheads?

In this part . . .

There's hardly a place on the planet that doesn't have a drumming tradition. This section opens your mind to the many types of drums and rhythm-makers from around the world. Chapter 15 introduces you to a bunch of hand drums. Chapter 16 lets you check out some stick-played drums, and Chapter 17 has a few percussion instruments that allow to you make even more noise (musically, of course). Chapter 18 shows you how you can put all those instruments together and make music.

Chapter 15

Handling Hand Drums

*H*and drums are the world's most enduring, accessible, and portable musical instruments. You can learn to play one of them musically very quickly. And, unlike the drumset, you can strap a hand drum over your shoulder or throw it in your backpack and play just about anywhere.

In this chapter, I describe some of the most common hand drums used today. Not only will you discover where they're from and what they look like, but you also find out how to play them using proper technique. To top it off, you get to play traditional rhythms on these drums and discover some interesting facts about them.

As you read this chapter, keep in mind that you can explore each one of these instruments for a lifetime. Throughout the world, you can find expert musicians for each of these instruments. In Brazil, for instance, some drummers spend their entire lives playing just the *pandeiro,* and they never run out of rhythms and techniques to explore. I don't say this to discourage you, but rather to open your mind and hopefully instill in you the limitless possibilities of each and every drum. So, choose the drum or drums that resonate with you the most and have fun.

Embracing the Variety in Drums

The selection of drums in this chapter doesn't even come close to covering all the hand drums out there, but what I do provide is a variety of drums that represent some of the most common types and styles. You can use the techniques that you learn for these drums on any other drums that have a similar shape or sound. So, if you already have a drum that I don't describe in this chapter, find one that looks like yours and start there.

You can play most drums in a variety of ways. I list the traditional ways to play these drums, and I also sometimes list another common way. Use these methods as a starting point. The important thing is to produce a quality sound and to play the rhythms fluidly. How you do it doesn't really matter. Just remember that these techniques developed over time, and in most cases, they're simply the most efficient way to play the drum.

You can play all the rhythms in this chapter on any of the drums that I describe, but remember that these rhythms are simply places to begin. Just as each culture's rhythms have evolved over the centuries, you should feel free to experiment and come up with your own variations. Take one rhythm and combine it with another or chop it in half and join it with half of another. You can even cut off or add one note and turn the rhythm into an odd meter. (See Chapter 2 for more details about odd meter.) The possibilities are endless and limited only by your imagination.

Throughout this chapter you may notice phrases such as "tons of playing positions," "limitless hand positions," and "dozens of rhythms." This is drummer code for "anything goes." Play what you want; just look good doing it! I'm just kidding, kinda. Drumming rhythms and styles constantly evolve. Master the basics and you can go anywhere you want with any of these drums. Just make sure that you're sensitive to the musical situation that you're in and to the other musicians that you play with. And above all, listen to those around you as you play.

If you need a refresher on the strokes that I present in this chapter, you can find them in Chapter 4.

Beating the Bongos

When someone mentions *bongos* (like I did just now), you probably can't help thinking of a beatnik poet dressed in black, embellishing his obscure poetry with flourishes on a pair of these little drums wedged between his legs. Though this image may seem somewhat ridiculous, the role of the bongos as an instrument of improvisation and accentuation isn't far from true.

The bongos hail from Cuba and came into being within the Son style of music in the mid-1800s. *Son* is an organic merging of African and Spanish music from the eastern part of Cuba. The bongos were originally the only drums used in Son music and, because of their soft sound and high pitch, were played only during the introduction and verses of the songs. During the louder sections of the songs, the *bongocero* (the name for the bongo player in Cuba) switched his or her playing to a cowbell, traditionally called the *campana*.

Today the bongos (see Figure 15-1) are one of the most recognizable of the Latin drums, and you can find their sound in all styles of music.

Figure 15-1:
The bongo drums come from Cuba.

Playing position

The bongos are a pair of small drums that are connected and played as a unit. Traditionally, you hold the bongos between your legs with the smaller drum on your left. Figure 15-2 illustrates the proper holding technique.

Figure 15-2:
Traditional playing technique for the bongos.

As a *bongocero,* you use four basic strokes (Chapter 4 explains these strokes in more detail):

 ✔ The open tone (O)
 ✔ The slap (S)

✔ The heel-tip movement (H)

✔ The basic muted tones (M)

Traditionally, your left hand does a heel-tip rocking movement, but most modern players choose the basic muted tone instead.

Understanding the rhythms

The Son bongo rhythm, called the *Martillo*, has an improvisational quality to it. Traditional players used this rhythm as the basis for experimentation. Not too much though, because the basic 1, 2 pulse created by this rhythm is important to the overall feel of the song. If you're going to play the Martillo in a Son group, you can't stray too far from its basic 1, 2 pulse or you'll end up getting a few nasty looks. Figure 15-3 shows the Martillo and a few variations on the rhythm. (Check out Chapter 2 to brush up on reading music notation for drums.)

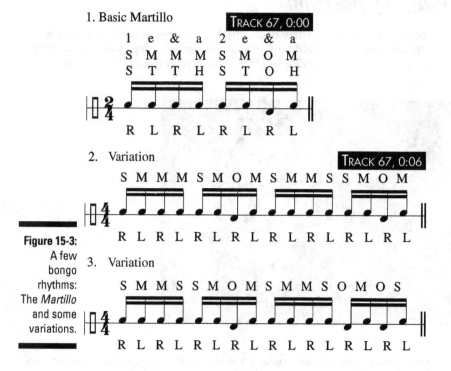

Figure 15-3: A few bongo rhythms: The *Martillo* and some variations.

The basic Martillo in Figure 15-3 includes two *hand patterns* (the hand patterns are the Rs and Ls written below the rhythm; for more info on hand patterns, go to Chapter 2). One is the traditional heel-tip pattern while the other shows the basic muted tone. Try them both to decide which pattern you prefer.

Personally, I switch back and forth depending on what type of rhythm I'm playing. The following variations show only the basic muted stroke, but you can substitute the heel-tip movement instead if you choose.

The first rhythm in Figure 15-3 is a two-beat pattern. Beats 1 and 2 (both played with your right hand) play an accented slap tone at the edge of the smaller drum. On the "&" of beat 2, your right hand plays an open tone on the larger drum. In this rhythm, your left hand plays soft, muted tones to give the rhythm a sense of movement. The second and third rhythms are four-beat variations.

I realize that you may not have much of a calling for playing the Martillo in a Son band, but this rhythm and its variations apply to contemporary music as well. All the rhythms in Figure 15-3 can fit into most pop music situations.

In contemporary music, the bongos are often mounted on a stand next to the conga drums (see the next section) and played as an accent to the main conga beat and as a solo instrument. Because of their high pitch, the bongos work best when playing a *syncopated* beat (a rhythm that accentuates the "e" and "a" of a beat rather than the downbeat — the 1 or 2; see Chapter 2), especially during a solo. Experiment with the Martillo or one of its variations and add more left-hand accents. Doing so gives your rhythm a syncopated feel. For contemporary music, you can even eliminate the right-hand accents once in a while.

Carrying On with the Congas

The *conga drum* is by far the most common hand drum used in popular music. Most people associate the conga drum with Latin music. The conga has its origins in the African Congo, but the barrel-shaped drum that you're used to seeing is a Cuban invention, emerging out of the many varieties of folk music that developed between the Africans and Spaniards around the island. Conga drums came to the U.S. in the 1940s and quickly found a place in nearly every style of music. You can find them in jazz, rock, blues, R&B, and reggae. Even country music uses congas every now and then.

The conga drums are actually three drums, each of which you can check out in Figure 15-4. Here's a quick thumbnail sketch of the three drums:

✔ The **tumba** (sounds like *toom*-bah), or *tumbadora,* is usually about 12½ inches in diameter.

✔ The **quinto** (sounds like *keen*-toe) is 11 inches in diameter and is usually the smallest drum in a conga line-up.

✔ The **conga** (sounds like *kong*-ah) measures 11¾ inches across.

DRUM HISTORY

It takes two to . . . conga

The first drummer to ever play more than one conga at a time was Candido Camero in 1946. Until then, a separate drummer played each drum. This shift all started when Cuban-born Candido was playing the quinto drum with the dance team *Carmen y Rolando* in Cuba. The team arranged a tour to the U.S. but couldn't afford to bring a conga player and quinto player. Because the quinto was a solo drum and so important to the dance numbers, the team asked Candido to go along instead of the conga player. He secretly brought a conga drum on the tour and played both parts at the same time. By 1955 he was playing three congas, a guiro (I talk more about the guiro in Chapter 17), and a cowbell at the same time. At one point he played as many as six congas, but stopped doing that because taking all those instruments on tour became too cumbersome.

Figure 15-4:
The conga drums: tumba, quinto, conga.

All three drums stand between 28 and 30 inches tall and have cowhide heads, although synthetic heads are becoming more common. They can be made of either wood or fiberglass (the fiberglass congas have a louder, brighter sound, while their wood counterparts have a warmer tone). You play the conga drums one at a time, in twos, or in groups of three or even four. (Recently a fourth-sized conga has emerged. This drum is called the *requinto* (pronounced reh-*keen*-toe) and, at 9¾ inches in diameter, is even smaller than the quinto.)

Playing position

There are almost as many playing positions for the congas as there are *congueros* (this is the cool name for a conga drummer; it sounds like kon-*gair*-ohs). Figure 15-5 shows a common playing position for the congas. In this photo, the right hand is in the heel-tip position while the left plays an open tone.

Figure 15-5:
Common
playing
position for
the conga
drum.

A true *conguero* has an almost unlimited variety of hand positions and strokes available, but with four basic strokes, you can play almost any rhythm. The four strokes are

✔ The open tone (O)

✔ The muted heel-tip movement (HT)

✔ The bass tone (B)

✔ The slap (S)

Understanding the rhythms

Because of their wide use, the congas have literally dozens of traditional rhythms associated with them. I tried to choose a few rhythms that represent traditional conga drumming but that also work in a contemporary music setting.

The rhythm in Figure 15-6 is the Tumbáo. This one-bar rhythm is the most basic and most common pattern found within Latin music. You can use the Tumbáo for many of the common styles of Latin music played today, including the cha-cha and the mambo, as well as contemporary music styles, such as pop, rock, and jazz music. If the Tumbáo is the only rhythm you know, you can fit it into most musical situations. The second rhythm is a common bolero Tumbáo pattern using two drums. Rhythm 3 is a common two-bar pattern.

1. Tumbáo

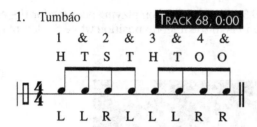

2. Variation

3. Variation

Figure 15-6:
A few
conga
rhythms.

Discovering the Djembe

The *djembe* (also spelled *jembe* — either way it's pronounced *jem*-bay) is a goblet-shaped African drum that is the staple of every drum circle. With its unabashedly tribal look, loud expressive sound, and ease of playing, the djembe has become one of the most popular drums around. In fact, you can hardly walk the streets of San Francisco, Seattle, or Portland and not see some hip young guy or gal with a djembe. This is *the* drum to carry around and be seen with. And if you plan to play with other drummers in a drum circle, the djembe can help you be heard above the crowd. (Of course, every other drummer who wants to be heard over other drummers will have a djembe, so you may want to rethink this strategy.) Figure 15-7 shows the djembe.

Traditionally, the djembe is carved out of one log and has a rope-tuning system, but recent versions consist of glued-up staves with metal hardware (Chapter 19 has more about drum construction methods). Figure 15-7a shows a traditional African rope-tuned djembe, while Figure 15-7b shows its modern counterpart. The djembe's tightly-tuned, thin goatskin head contributes largely to the drum's expressive sound.

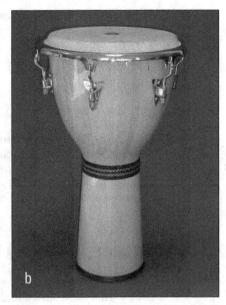

Figure 15-7:
The African
rope-tuned
djembe (a)
and its
modern
counterpart
(b).

a

b

Playing position

Traditionally, when playing the djembe, you hold it between your legs while supporting it with a strap that hangs from your shoulders. Today, you can get stands to hold the djembe, thereby reducing the pressure on your back. Check out Figure 15-8 to see how to play this drum.

Figure 15-8:
Djembe
playing
position.

The djembe utilizes four basic hand strokes:

✔ The open tone (O)

✔ The muted tone (M)

✔ The bass tone (B)

✔ The open slap (S)

Each of the strokes that you use with the djembe has a name (this is how the rhythms are generally taught). The open tone is *Go* for the right hand and *Do* for the left. The slap is *Pa* for the right hand and *Ta* for the left. The bass tone is called *Gun* for the right hand and *Dun* for the left. (Go to Chapter 3 to find out more about saying the rhythms out loud.)

Understanding the rhythms

Great variation exists among today's djembe rhythms. Traditionally, each tribe within West Africa had its own interpretations of the rhythms and, as this drum became popular in the West, many variations also emerged. Check out Figure 15-9 for some basic djembe rhythms.

1. Kakilambe

2. Fanga (Funga)

3. Mandjani (Mandjiani)

Figure 15-9: Basic djembe rhythms.

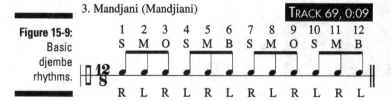

In Figure 15-9, I include a name for each rhythm based upon how I learned them, but you may hear the same rhythm called by a different name or find the rhythm played differently.

The rhythms in Figure 15-9 are written with muted notes that fill in the spaces between the main accented notes. Some drummers choose not to play these notes; instead, they rest. The choice of whether to play them is up to you. (I usually play them because it gives the rhythm a nice flow.) If you do play them, however, you should make the muted notes almost inaudible.

African ensembles use the djembe to cue the other instruments for solos, rhythm changes, and song endings. This cue is referred to as a *call* and consists of an easily recognizable rhythmic *lick* (a short rhythmic phrase). Check out Figure 15-10 for the most common call.

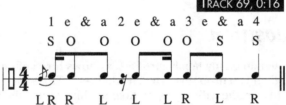

Figure 15-10:
A djembe call for African drum ensembles.

TRACK 69, 0:16

Uncovering the Udu

The udu, a funny-looking drum (see Figure 15-11), is one of the few drums that doesn't have a head that you hit to make a sound. Instead, the entire instrument is tapped, slapped, scraped, or otherwise drummed to create a sound.

The udu comes from Nigeria, and legend says that it developed out of a pot that accidentally had a hole punched in its side, making it useless for holding stuff. As highly rhythmic people, the owners of this pot did what anyone would do: Rather than throw it away, they started drumming on it. It made a really cool sound, so they started making pots with an extra hole in them and thus was the birth of the udu. Interestingly, only women played the udu until recently.

I, for one, am glad that someone broke that pot. The udu is one of my favorite drums. It produces a whole range of unique sounds, from a bell tone to a watery bass tone. You really must play one — I know you'll like it!

Figure 15-11:
A broken
clay pot . . .
er, I mean,
an udu
drum.

Playing position

I prefer playing the udu on my lap. Figure 15-12a shows how I often hold it. (Be careful, though; if you drop this drum, it will break. Trust me — I know firsthand). I create a cradle with my leg to hold it. I like to play the top hole with my left hand and the other hole with my right. Other drummers mount the udu on a snare drum stand using towels and duct tape (see Figure 15-12b), while others rest the drum on its ring on a table or the floor.

The basic strokes for the udu consist of the following:

- The open tone (O)
- The closed tone (C)
- The bass tone (B)
- The slap (S)

Other strokes, such as finger or thumb taps, brushing, scraping, or trilling are also used. Chapter 4 covers the details about some of these unusual strokes.

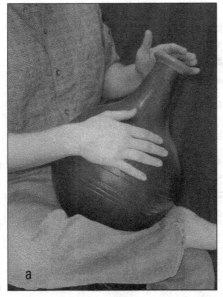 

Figure 15-12:
Udu playing
positions:
Lap position
(a) or duct-
taped to a
stand (b).

Understanding the rhythms

The rhythms in Figure 15-13 use some unusual hand patterns. You may find the double left-hand strokes difficult at first (you can rest during one of them to begin). To create the bass tones, hit over the holes and keep your hand over the hole while it resonates. Slapping over the top hole but not covering it up creates the slap tone. Notice that you can get different sounds depending upon how much you cover the hole and whether you keep your hand over it (like playing a palm stroke) or if you play it like an open tone. Experiment and use the sounds that you like.

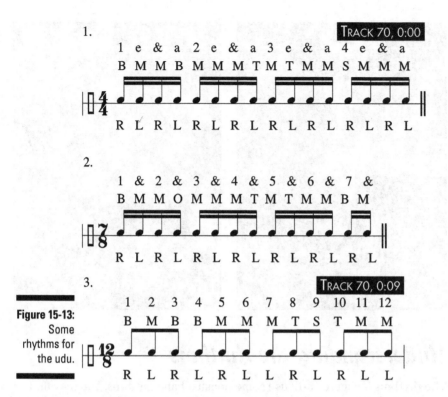

Figure 15-13: Some rhythms for the udu.

Deciphering the Doumbek

The *doumbek* is one of several drums used in Arabic folk music. The doumbek is a goblet-shaped drum, similar to the West African djembe, which also has a very expressive sound. This drum is from the Middle East and can be made of either metal (see Figure 15-14a) or clay (see Figure 15-14b); its head is very thin (traditionally made from fish skin). This drum produces a very bright, sharp sound and, like the djembe, possesses a rich, full bass tone.

Figuring out Middle Eastern drum language

Because the drum has been around so long — longer than the written word — Middle Eastern drumming has its own language. This language describes the sound the drum makes. There are three basic sounds: doum, tek, and a slap. The doum tone is the lowest tone the drum makes. The tek (tak) stroke is like a rim-shot — you play on the edge of the head — and is higher in pitch. The slap is a closed slap, meaning you press you fingers or palm into the head to stop it from ringing. If you study with a traditional teacher, she'll likely teach you the rhythms by singing the sounds.

Figure 15-14: The Middle Eastern doumbek can be made out of metal (a) or ceramic (b).

a

b

Playing position

Hold the doumbek under your left arm and rest it on your left leg. Rest your left hand on the upper rim where your third (ring) finger taps the head. Your right hand plays the drum at about the nine-o'clock position. Figure 15-15 shows this holding technique.

Figure 15-15:
Playing
position
for the
doumbek.

As the drum's name suggests (well, almost), the strokes are

✔ **The bass tone (often called *doum*).** Play this stroke (represented by a D in the rhythms) by striking your fingertips in the center of the head. Make sure your fingers come off the head right after you hit it so that the sound can resonate.

✔ **The open tone (often called *tek*).** Play this stroke (represented by a T in the rhythms) by striking the edge of the head (right at the rim) with your fingers.

✔ **The slap.** You make this stroke by pressing your fingertips into the center of the head. None of the rhythms in Figure 15-18 use this stroke, but it's used in other traditional doumbek rhythms.

The doumbek is a small drum, so adjust your hand positions until you get the best sound.

Understanding the rhythms

Unlike the drumming of West Africa, where layered rhythms from several drums create complex rhythmic combinations, Middle Eastern drumming is largely a solitary venture. As a result, the rhythms played by one drummer are often complex and encompass an almost infinite variety of layers and textures.

The rhythms shown in Figure 15-16 are the basics, incorporating just the three fundamental strokes. Be patient with the third rhythm — it's in an odd meter (for more on odd meter, go to Chapter 2).

Figure 15-16:
A few common doumbek rhythms.

Touting the Tar

The *tar* is a member of the frame drum family that hails from North Africa. (Frame drums are drums with a shell that's shallower than the diameter of its head.) Tars are often 14–20 inches in diameter. Because of its thin head and narrow shell, the tar has a somewhat watery sound that can be very entrancing. You can get a look at this drum in Figure 15-17.

Figure 15-17:
The North African tar.

Playing position

You hold this drum with the head facing away from you. Your left hand holds the drum from the bottom with your thumb through the hole in the shell. Your right thumb rests on the shell at the nine-o'clock position, and your third (ring) finger strikes the head. Figure 15-18 shows you how to hold the tar.

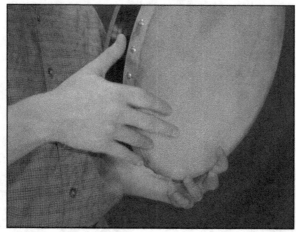

Figure 15-18:
The playing position for the tar.

You have three basic strokes for the tar.

- ✔ **Doum (D):** You play this open tone with the second (middle) finger of your right hand. This finger strikes the drum two to three inches in from the rim by pivoting your hand from your thumb.

- ✔ **Tek (T):** You play this stroke with your third (ring) finger of either hand. Use your ring finger to strike the drum by pivoting your hand from your thumb. However, this time strike the edge of the rim with your finger. You want to create a high-pitched rim-shot type sound. The uppercase "T" in Figure 15-21 is played loud as an accent and the lowercase "t" is played quietly, creating a soft "patter"-type sound on the drum. You can hear how this is supposed to sound on the accompanying CD.

- ✔ **Slap (S):** You use your right hand to play this stroke. Slap your fingertips into the head of the drum several inches in from the rim, pressing into the head to mute the sound.

You can also use other, more elaborate strokes with this drum. They include snaps, rolls, and trills. (Go to Chapter 4 for more on these strokes.)

Understanding the rhythms

The rhythms in Figure 15-19 are traditional Middle Eastern rhythms. The first rhythm, called *Ayyub*, is just two beats long. The second rhythm, called *Jaark*, is a four-beat rhythm. The third rhythm is in an odd meter again and is traditionally played one of two ways: as the groupings 2-2-3 or 3-2-2 (for more on odd groupings such as these, go to Chapter 2). Both groupings use the same rhythm and orchestration; you just start at different points in the pattern.

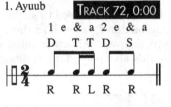

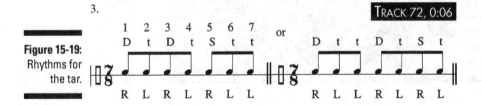

Figure 15-19: Rhythms for the tar.

Tapping the Power of the Tambourine/Riq

Like me, your first encounter with the tambourine is probably the rock singer trying to look cool while shaking it back and forth during the guitar solo. Or maybe your image is of a spaced-out groupie swaying to the music while tapping out the song's pulse (for more on pulse go to Chapter 2). In popular music, the *tambourine* is an often unnecessary prop used only to give the singer something to do when he's not screaming into the mic or trying to woo the audience. Unfortunately, this is a sad image of a fascinating, ancient, and extremely expressive drum.

The tambourine, like the doumbek and the tar, is a Middle Eastern folk instrument. And like the tar, it's a frame drum. What sets the tambourine apart is the jingles attached to the shell. You can find many different types of tambourines throughout the world today, but the instrument's beginnings seem to originate in ancient Mesopotamia. And it's in this region that tambourine playing has become an art. Forget all you know about the tambourine from your rock music experience and take a fresh look at this ancient drum.

Figure 15-20 shows the tambourine you're probably used to seeing (this one has a head while some of the rock versions don't), as well as the *Egyptian riq* (pronounced *rick*). The riq has a slightly deeper shell and is often smaller in diameter than the modern tambourine (it's also played *much* differently).

Figure 15-20:
The tambourine and its Egyptian counterpart, the riq.

Playing position

Hold the modern tambourine in your left hand by its shell (see Figure 15-21a) and shake it back and forth. Your right hand strikes the drum to create accents. Hold the riq in your left hand (see Figure 15-21b) with your thumb inside the drum pressed against one of the jingles (see Figure 15-21c). Your first finger grips the edge of the rim. Likewise, your right thumb lightly touches the drum's shell while your fingers play the drum.

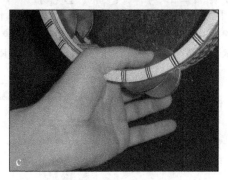

Figure 15-21:
How to
hold the
tambourine
and the riq.

Four basic strokes exist for playing the riq: dom, tak, slap, and tik.

- The *dom* (D) is a low open tone that you play with the index finger of your right hand. It's as close to a bass tone as this drum makes.

- Play the *tak* (T) sound with your third finger (ring finger) of either hand to create a rim-shot sound.

- Cup the fingers of your right hand to play the *slap* (S). It's a muted tone. The rhythms in Figure 15-23 don't use slaps but you will see some in other traditional rhythms for the riq.

- Use the third (ring) fingers of either hand on the jingles at the bottom of the drum to play the *tik* (t) sound.

You can also use the brushing, trilling, snapping, and drone techniques on this drum. (Go to Chapter 4 if you need a refresher on these unusual strokes.) You can also rock the riq back and forth in rhythm while playing it to create a jingle sound with the other tones.

Understanding the rhythms

Rhythms 1 and 2 are four-beat rhythms (see Figure 15-22). Rhythm 3 is in 7/4 (an odd meter). Odd meters aren't uncommon among traditional Middle Eastern drumming. You can also play the patterns from Figures 15-16 and 15-19 on the tambourine or riq.

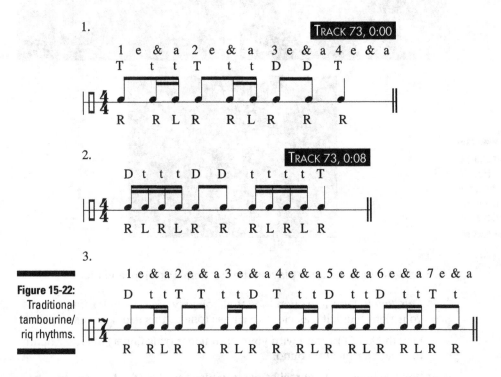

Figure 15-22: Traditional tambourine/riq rhythms.

The rhythm in Figure 15-23 is for rock tambourine players. This rhythm isn't nearly as exciting, but it's something you can show your girlfriend (or boyfriend) when she (or he) insists on sitting in with your band.

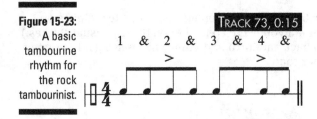

Figure 15-23: A basic tambourine rhythm for the rock tambourinist.

Partying with the Pandeiro

The *pandeiro* (sounds like pan-*dare*-o) is Brazil's answer to the tambourine. By some accounts, this drum is the Brazilian national instrument. It's an indispensable part of the yearly Mardi Gras celebration and is used in all styles of Brazilian music, as well as in pop, funk, and rock music. Check out Figure 15-24 to see the pandeiro.

Figure 15-24: The Brazilian tambourine: the pandeiro.

Playing position

The pandeiro may look like the tambourine or riq, with its thin shell and jingles, but it's played very differently from the other hand drums in this chapter. You must reverse the position of your left hand from the tambourine position: Your fingers go inside the drum while your thumb wraps over the edge of the shell. You play the pandeiro drum with your right hand only (your left fingers sometimes mute the head from behind).

The pandeiro hand positions you need to play the rhythms in this section include the following:

- ✔ **Thumb stroke (T):** This stroke is played with your right thumb on the lower portion of the drumhead. You can see this stroke in Figure 15-25a.

- ✔ **Fingertip stroke (f):** This stroke (which you can see in Figure 15-25b) is made by rocking your hand up and tapping your fingertips into the drum at the upper portion of the head.

✔ **Heel stroke (h):** You play this stroke by pressing the heel of your hand into the drumhead as you tilt your hand back after playing the fingertip stroke. Figure 15-25c shows the position for the heel stroke.

✔ **Slap stroke (S):** The slap stroke is played by pressing your whole hand into the center of the drumhead, which you can see in Figure 15-25d.

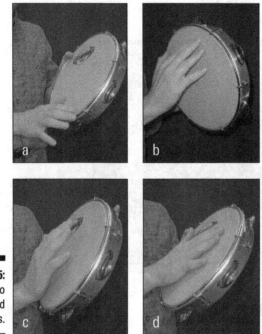

Figure 15-25: Pandeiro hand positions.

Understanding the rhythms

The pandeiro is an essential part of the *samba,* the sound of Carnaval (you can read more about Carnaval in Chapter 10). Every neighborhood within the cities of Brazil has its own samba band and its own variations of the samba rhythms. Figure 15-26 contains basic rhythms for playing the samba. Take your time with the pandeiro. It's one of the hardest techniques to master.

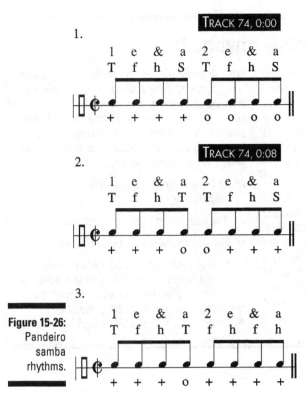

1.

TRACK 74, 0:00

1	e	&	a	2	e	&	a
T	f	h	S	T	f	h	S

\+ \+ \+ \+ o o o o

2.

TRACK 74, 0:08

1	e	&	a	2	e	&	a
T	f	h	T	T	f	h	S

\+ \+ \+ o o \+ \+ \+

3.

1	e	&	a	2	e	&	a
T	f	h	T	f	h	f	h

\+ \+ \+ o \+ \+ \+ \+

Figure 15-26:
Pandeiro
samba
rhythms.

Aside from the basic strokes that the right hand performs, you use your left hand to mute the drum's head. Doing so doubles the number of sounds that the pandeiro can produce. The +s and Os in Figure 15-26 signify this technique. You press your middle finger into the head, muting it, where the +s are and release the head where Os mark the music to let it ring.

Tablas, anyone?

The *tabla* drums are India's most popular drums. The tablas are a pair of drums used in classical as well as folk music, and they're some of the most recognizable drums around (at least their sound is easily recognized). Of course, most people don't know what they're called or how to play them, but if you've seen a movie set in India, you've heard the unmistakable sound of these drums.

The tablas consist of a wood drum, called the *tabla,* meaning "treble," and a metal drum called *dagga,* meaning "bass." Traditionally, you play the tabla (the treble drum) with your right hand and the dagga with your left. The sound that these drums make is very watery with an entrancing, ghostly quality to it. The rhythms are very complex.

Tabla drumming is an art that has a very steep learning curve. Students can spend years just learning the basics. In fact, I don't cover the actual playing technique for the tablas in this book because of the intricacies required to play them. To give you some idea of just how involved playing these drums can be, check this out:

- ✔ The tabla (the drum) has 14 different strokes and sounds.

- ✔ The dagga has 12 strokes and sounds.

- ✔ Six strokes use both drums at the same time.

That's 32 total strokes! The best way to learn how to play these drums is to find a good teacher or instructional video. If you love the sound of these and are interested in studying them, go to my Web site: www.jeffstrong.com.

Chapter 16

Singling Out Stick-Played Drums

In This Chapter

▶ Discovering some drums that use sticks, mallets, or beaters

▶ Developing the skills to play these drums

▶ Exploring traditional rhythms for each drum

*I*f your vision of stick-struck drums consists only of the drumset or classical percussion (snare drums, bass drums, and so on), you'll discover some exciting new drums and approaches to playing them in this chapter. I give you some traditional rhythms for each drum as well as some interesting facts that you can use to impress your friends. The drums in this chapter represent many parts of the world, from Northern Europe to South America. Many of these drums have developed from the influence of more than one culture and their playing techniques are still evolving.

You may notice that you play many of these drums with both sticks and hands. In many cases, your right hand plays the drum with a stick while your left hand plays directly on the head. You also play some of these drums on the rim or shell. This difference gives these drums a variety of sounds and textures.

Even if you're only interested in playing the drumset, the techniques and rhythms in this chapter can open new vistas for you in contemporary music. Use this information as a starting point. If any of these drums pique your interest, they can provide a lifetime of exploration that only enhances your abilities on any drum.

Bopping to the Bodhran

The bodhran (pronounced *bow*-rahn) is an Irish folk drum that is thought to have originated in the Middle East or maybe Asia — nobody knows for sure. But notice how similar it is to the Egyptian tar (see Chapter 15). Unlike the tar though, you play the bodhran with a wooden beater called a *cipin* (pronounced ki-peen). See Figure 16-1 to see what the bodhran looks like.

For centuries, it seems that people didn't know — or maybe they didn't care — how to use the bodhran. The story is that during the Middle Ages, this Irish drum was forgotten, and when it was rediscovered generations later, people used it to sift grain. Not until the middle of the twentieth century did the bodhran make its way back into a musical setting.

Because the bodhran wasn't used in Irish folk music until the 1960s, its place is still somewhat shaky. Fact is, unlike other styles of drumming where the drum's rhythm drives the beat of the music, the bodhran's role is more subtle: Its job is to support, not to solo. (Imagine the reaction of the fiddle player when the first bodhran player comes along and wants to add this *drum* to his already "complete" musical arrangement — the nerve!) The background spot of the bodhran is a hard thing to accept for many drummers. As a result, bodhran players have a bad reputation for not taking their role in music seriously.

Playing position

To play the bodhran, cradle it between your left arm and chest, while holding it perpendicular to the floor. Hold the cipin (the drum's wooden beater) in your right hand (see Figure 16-1a) while pressing your left hand (see Figure 16-1b) against the head to produce variations on pitch and note duration.

Figure 16-1:
Traditional playing technique for the bodhran.

To hold the cipin, grasp it like you would a pen or pencil. Now turn your wrist in so that your fingers point to your chest. Strum your hand up and down (you know, like a guitar player). Make contact against the head on both the down-stroke (see Figure 16-2a) and upstroke (see Figure 16-2b). You use the backside of the cipin for rolls and grace notes (Chapter 2 has more about these strokes).

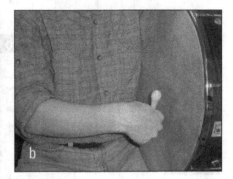

Figure 16-2:
The proper bodhran stroke.

Understanding the rhythms

The basic rhythms for the bodhran are pretty simple (I say this at the risk of offending true bodhran masters). The art of bodhran playing is in the subtleties and variations that you can create within these rhythms. If you can play each of the rhythms that I discuss in this section cleanly and fluidly, you can fit into most situations where the bodhran is used.

Figure 16-3 shows the three basic bodhran rhythms. These rhythms represent the three styles of Irish folk music: the reel, the jig, and the slip jig. The arrows below the rhythm designate an up or downstroke. Rhythms 2 and 3 each have an accent on an upstroke. You may find that the upstroke accent is difficult to play at first, but with some practice, you'll get the hang of it. (Accents, as I discuss in Chapter 2, are simply played louder than the notes surrounding them.) Rhythm 3 is in 9/8 time (see Chapter 2 for more on playing in odd meter). Your sticking pattern actually reverses the second time through the rhythm (all your upstrokes become downstrokes). This reversing pattern occurs every two times through the rhythm. Counting the rhythm out loud as you play it helps you get used to the rhythm's changing pattern.

Aside from the basic rhythms, you can add rolls, accents, and other embellishments to bodhran music. Be careful not to overdo it though, and make sure that you follow the structure of the song, or you'll add to the bad reputation that plagues bodhran drummers.

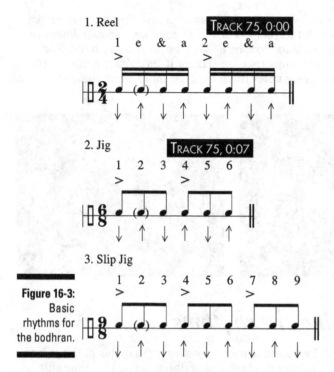

Figure 16-3:
Basic rhythms for the bodhran.

After you get comfortable playing the rhythms in Figure 16-3, you can eliminate the second note in the pattern (these notes are marked with parentheses around them) to create more interest in the rhythms. The way to do this is to play the second upstroke, but don't make contact with the drumhead. Your arm continues the constant down and upstroking even though you don't hit the drum on the second note.

Detailing the Djun Djuns

The *djun djuns* (also spelled *jun jun* or *doun doun* and pronounced either way) are natives of West Africa and consist of three drums.

- ✔ The largest drum, called *dundunba,* is usually about 13–14 inches in diameter.

- ✔ The middle drum is called *sangba* and is often between 10–12 inches in diameter.

- ✔ The smallest drum is called *kankini.* This drum is often about 8 inches in diameter.

These drums are each hollowed out of a log so there are large variations in their size (by as much as 12 inches in some cases). Djun djuns usually sport goatskin heads.

Djun djuns create not only the bass pulse of the African rhythms but also add a little melody. Traditionally, an individual drummer played each size djun djun and the group of drummers interwove the rhythms, but today one person usually plays all three drums. Likewise, the djun djun player often plays the drum rhythm with one hand (the left) and a bell with the other (usually the right). Figure 16-4 shows the djun djuns.

Figure 16-4:
The African bass drums, the djun djuns.

Playing position

Djun djuns are mounted on stands, and you play them with a mallet or stick in each hand. The mallet gives a lower, softer sound than a stick. These drums create the foundational rhythm of the African drum ensemble. You won't hear a djun djun playing a solo.

Understanding the rhythms

Figure 16-5 shows you some rhythms for the djun djuns (I use their traditional names and include the bell patterns in these rhythms). Working on one part at a time when learning them is easiest. After you're comfortable playing the rhythms separately, join them together.

Rhythms 1 and 2 are orchestrated for only one djun djun. If you want to play these rhythms on two drums, play the open tones (O) on the larger drum and the muted tones (M) on the smaller one. There are two rhythms for the Kakilambe even though only one is written in Figure 16-5. This is because the song speeds up and essentially turns into a Fanga. Because of this, rhythm 2 is for the slower section of the kakilambe. Use the Fanga (rhythm 1) pattern during the fast section of the tune. (The middle space on rhythm 3 is for the higher-pitched djun djun while the lower-pitched drum is notated on the bottom space.)

Most of the djun djun parts are orchestrated for only one or two drums. The larger drums are the first ones used. In fact, the smallest drum, the kankini isn't very common in the West.

Figure 16-5:
Rhythms for
the djun
djuns.

Rubbing the Cuica

The *cuica* (see Figure 16-6) is an essential part of Brazilian samba music and can be traced back to Africa where it was often used to lure lions. Because the cuica is such an expressive and unique sounding drum, it has made its way into a lot of contemporary music settings, such as jazz, fusion, funk, and pop music. Its role is usually as a solo or sound effects instrument.

Figure 16-6:
The cuica.

The cuica is in the stick drum section not because you hit it with a stick, but because it has a stick inside of it that you rub to create sound. This is the only drum that I include in this book where you don't strike the head (okay, you don't hit the head of another drum in Chapter 15, but that's because it doesn't have a head to hit). Instead, the sound results from a vibration created by the stick and transferred to the head. This type of drum is called a *friction drum* because the sound is made from friction created between the bamboo stick and your fingers.

Playing position

To play the cuica, hold it with your left hand and hang it from either shoulder with a strap. Your left hand's fingers press against the head about a ¼ inch away from the bamboo stick (see Figure 16-7a). Your right hand holds a damp cloth and *lightly* grips the stick between your thumb and forefinger from inside the drum (see Figure 16-7b). The drum's sound comes from rubbing the stick back and forth. Increasing or decreasing the pressure against the head with your left hand changes pitch.

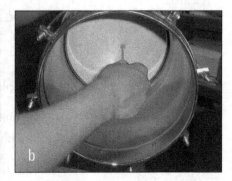

Figure 16-7:
The right way to hold the cuica.

a   b

Understanding the rhythms

The cuica is a very expressive drum. Its sound often resembles grunts, groans, screeches, or moans. A good cuica player can create an almost infinite number of sounds and almost two octaves of pitch changes. Cuica masters can play complete melodies of songs by themselves.

The rhythms in this section are just a starting point to get you used to creating the basic sound on the cuica. These rhythms contain only one pitch, but after you get comfortable with the basic rhythms, experiment with changing the pitch of the drum with your left hand. For a higher pitch sound, press harder against the head; for a lower pitch sound, release the pressure. (I often move my fingers in and out from the center of the head to change pitch. Try both to see which you prefer.) Figure 16-8 offers some basic exercises that you can use in contemporary music.

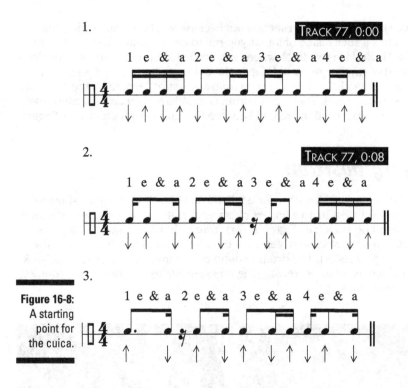

Figure 16-8: A starting point for the cuica.

You'll find two strokes for playing the cuica, and they sound different:

- **Pulling stroke:** The up arrow means that you pull your hand outward.
- **Pushing stroke:** The down arrow tells you to push inward.

As you get accustomed to playing the basic strokes, try altering the pattern. Reverse the stroking pattern or do double strokes or combinations of double and single strokes. Each of these changes gives the rhythm a completely different flavor.

Striking the Surdo

With its driving pulse and deep bass tone, this large drum, the *surdo,* is the heart of the Brazilian samba. The surdo is a bass drum (see Figure 16-9 for a look), and like the djun djuns, it has three sizes, each with its own name.

- ✔ **The largest is the *surdo marcacao* and is 20–24 inches in diameter.** It plays the strongest beat, the 2 (see Chapter 18).

- ✔ **The middle-sized surdo, generally 16–18 inches in diameter, is the *surdo reposta.*** Its rhythm complements that of the marcacao, playing its main rhythm on the downbeat (the 1).

- ✔ **The *surdo cortador,* the smallest drum, is 13–14 inches in diameter.** Its role is to provide variations on the surdo's rhythms.

Figure 16-9:
The Brazilian bass drum, the surdo.

Large samba bands can have as many as a dozen or more of each of these drums while smaller groups may have only a handful of the largest type of surdo. The marcacao is indispensable, while the reposta and cortador are used only when the group has enough drummers. If the marcacao is the only surdo played, its rhythms are more complicated, because it has to fill in for the missing surdos.

Because of its deep, thunderous bass tone, the surdo is making its way into some contemporary music settings and is becoming a favorite in drum circles and jams.

Playing position

Because the samba band is a marching band, the surdo hangs over your shoulder. Figure 16-10 shows the playing position of the surdo. You play this drum using a mallet in the right hand, which alternates between hitting the head and the rim of the drum (notated by the X). You mute the head with your left hand (no sticks). This technique both raises the pitch, giving the drum a variety of sounds, and cuts off the note, making it quieter.

Figure 16-10: Playing position of the Brazilian surdo.

Understanding the rhythms

The surdo is fairly easy and fun to play. Because samba is the most popular music in Brazil (see the "Samba, anyone?" sidebar, later in this chapter), you have an enormous variety of rhythms that you can play. Figure 16-11 shows you some typical rhythms for the marcacao.

Rhythms 2 and 3 require that the left hand (L.H.) play a muted note before the right hand (R.H.) plays its muted note. If you keep your left hand on the drum when your right hand plays, it will mute the sound. You can then just lift your left hand before you use it again. Rhythm 2 is probably the most common samba rhythm today.

As you get comfortable with these rhythms, feel free to experiment. Just remember that the most important beat in samba is the second beat.

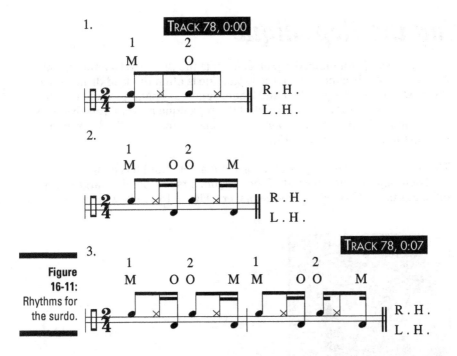

Figure 16-11: Rhythms for the surdo.

Samba, anyone?

Samba is the national music of Brazil and one of the most well-known styles of music around the world. A blend of African, Indian, and European musical traditions, samba developed in the *favelas* of Rio de Janeiro in the early 1900s (the favelas are the slums of Rio that envelop the hillsides and surround the city). You may be familiar with this intoxicating style of music from its association with the yearly Carnaval celebration. Every year in February, hundreds of samba bands crowd the streets and fill the city with their rhythms.

In spite of its perception as party music, samba is taken very seriously in Brazil. You can see competitions for the best samba bands and singers. Samba schools (the different styles of samba and groups around the city) practice year-round and spend enormous amounts of time and money preparing for the competitions.

Samba bands consist of bells and shakers (see Chapter 17), one or more sizes of surdos, tom-toms called repaniques (I talk about the repanique later in this chapter), cuicas, snare drums called caixas (Chapter 18 has some caixa rhythms), and small frame drums called tamborims (see "Tapping the Tambourim," later in this chapter). More than 100 drummers can take part in a typical samba band.

Rapping the Repanique

The *repanique* (pronounced rep-an-*eek*-ay) is the Brazilian tom-tom drum. Also a part of the samba band, the repanique is often the lead drum. In fact, the *mestre de bateria* (samba band leader) plays a repanique and cues the band with his rhythms. For the rest of the repanique players, this drum also has an improvisational role, playing solos and syncopated licks (for more on syncopations, go to Chapter 13).

The repanique is generally 8–14 inches in diameter and has a high tone, easily cutting through the rest of the instruments in a band. A large group often has up to 40 or 50 repanique players. Figure 16-12 shows the repanique.

Figure 16-12: The repanique (Brazilian tom-tom).

Playing position

Because the repanique is also a marching drum, you carry it from a strap over the shoulder. You play the repanique much like the surdo (See "Striking the Surdo," earlier in this chapter), with a stick in your right hand alternating between the head and the rim and your bare left hand playing directly on the head. Figure 16-13 shows you how to play the repanique.

Figure 16-13: Proper playing technique for the repanique.

Understanding the rhythms

This drum can play anything that it wants. Just kidding. Because the repanique is often a solo drum, you can play a wide variety of rhythms within samba music. Figure 16-14 shows you some basic groove-type patterns, and you can build variations on these. Solos consist of syncopated patterns.

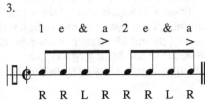

Figure 16-14: Rhythms for the repanique.

Rhythms for the repanique contain those pesky accents on the "a" of the beat. Rhythms 2 and 3 in Figure 16-14 have variations in sticking, which add a slightly different sound to the main groove. After you get comfortable playing each of these, try mixing them up — go from one rhythm to the next to create variety.

Tapping the Tamborim

The *tamborim* (pronounced tam-bor-*eem*) is a tiny drum, which is usually only six inches in diameter. The tamborim, not to be confused with the tambourine, is another staple of samba music. And, like the tambourine (see Chapter 15), the tamborim is a frame drum, except that this drum doesn't have any jingles and you play it with a stick in one hand (usually your right). Figure 16-15 shows the tambourim.

A typical *bateria* (samba band) can contain as many as 70 tamborim players. This high-pitched drum plays syncopations against the main groove of the surdos.

Figure 16-15: The Brazilian tamborim.

Playing position

You hold the tamborim in your hand (either one; it doesn't matter) with your thumb on the front rim and your fingers wrapped around the shell. The middle finger of your drum-holding hand mutes the head as your right hand beats the head with a small stick. Occasionally, the middle finger of your drum-holding hand plays filler notes on the backside of the head as ghost notes (notes played *very* softly). Figure 16-16 shows you the basic tamborim technique.

Figure 16-16: How to hold the tamborim.

Understanding the rhythms

The rhythms for the tamborim are syncopated, occasionally accenting the main beat of the samba (beat 2). Check out Figure 16-17 for some basic tamborim rhythms. Work on these without your drum-holding hand muting the head as you play until you're comfortable playing the syncopated notes. The "+" means you mute the head with the index finger of your drum-holding hand and the "o" means you let the drum ring. Remember, start out slowly and count out loud as you play.

When you get really good at these rhythms, try to fill in the spaces with your left hand. Lightly tap the inside of the drum head with your middle finger between right-handed notes.

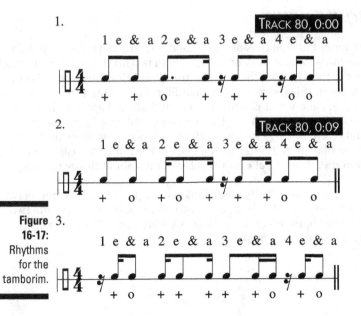

Figure 16-17: Rhythms for the tamborim.

Tinkering with the Timbales

Although you can trace their roots back to the European timpani drums, timbales are two metal-shelled drums from Cuba. Timbales produce a bright, cutting sound that you may recognize from the solos of Tito Puente, the late, great Latin showman, musician, and bandleader. In many ways, Tito was responsible for the timbales becoming as popular as the congas in the West. Today you can find the timbales in most musical situations including jazz, funk, and pop. Check out Figure 16-18 to see the timbales.

Figure 16-18: The timbales.

Playing position

Timbales are mounted side by side on a stand and are played several different ways. The most familiar way of playing them is with the sticks going back and forth on the two drums, making open tones and rim shots (see Chapters 3 and 4 for more on these strokes). This familiar way is how you use the timbales during solos and when playing accents and fills (Chapter 13 has more info about fills). Throughout the rest of the song, timbales keep time, with your left hand often playing directly on the head. However, more and more timbale players play muted notes with a stick in the left hand using a dead-sticking technique. (Check out Chapter 3 for details about dead-sticking.)

Your right hand also uses the dead-sticking technique, except it often plays its rhythm on the shell of the drum or a cowbell mounted between the two drums. Check out Figure 16-19 to see how you play these drums during the time-keeping section of the music.

Tackling taiko

Taiko isn't just one drum; it's a whole class of drums. Actually it's a whole style of drumming. _Taiko_ is a Japanese drumming technique or ensemble that has its roots in fifth-century Asia. The modern taiko that you see today (the groups of drummers synchronized into one rhythm-making whole) developed during the 1960s. This style of drumming is called _kumi-daiko_ and was brought to the U.S. by San Francisco Taiko Dojo founder Seiichi Tanaka in 1968. Since then, groups have been forming all over the U.S. with the largest concentration on the West Coast.

Taiko combines martial arts-type discipline and music. In many _dojos_ (schools), new taiko drummers must go through many hours of physical and mental training before they're even taught how to drum (although learning some basic rhythms takes just a few minutes). Unity is one of the most important elements of taiko drumming — unity with the other drummers, unity with one's self, and unity with the drum and rhythm. In fact, Kodo, one of the world's most popular taiko groups, inhabits a private island in Japan where all the members live and work together as one.

If you find the philosophy and drumming style of taiko appealing, your best bet is to find a dojo in your area with whom you can study. Learning taiko rhythms in a book only diminishes the beauty of this art (go to my Web site at www. jeffstrong.com for some taiko drumming resources).

Figure 16-19: Basic time-keeping technique for the timbales.

Understanding the rhythms

You can break the rhythms for timbales down into two categories: _time-keeping_ and _fills_. Figure 16-20 shows you some basic time-keeping patterns. Rhythm 1 uses open and muted tones on the larger drum with the left hand.

In rhythms 2 and 3, your left hand alternates between the two drums while your right hand plays on the shell of the drum or a cowbell.

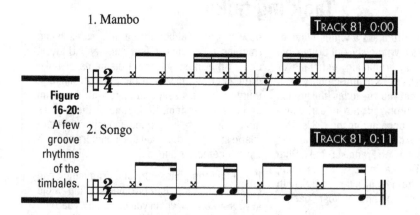

Figure
16-20:
A few
groove
rhythms
of the
timbales.

Figure 16-21 contains rhythms that you can use for solos and fills. Play these very slowly until you get used to them. The most important thing to remember with these rhythms is to play the flams (one of the rudiments; check out Chapter 3 for more info) very open and allow the rhythms to be loose. You can also go to Chapter 13 to see more licks and fills to play on the timbales.

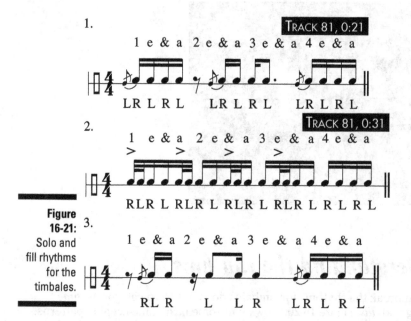

Figure
16-21:
Solo and
fill rhythms
for the
timbales.

Chapter 17

Shake, Rattle, and Roll: Exploring Other Percussion Instruments

In This Chapter

▶ Discovering other percussion instruments (besides drums)

▶ Getting used to playing non-drum percussion instruments

▶ Exploring rhythms for each instrument

Since the beginning of time, innovative — and sometimes bored — drummers have tapped, pounded, shaken, and rattled anything that they could get their hands on in order to express themselves. Many of these makeshift rhythm-makers have evolved into the essential percussion instruments that you see today.

These instruments often require that you use techniques similar to other drums (hands, sticks, and so on) as well as a mastery of rhythm. As a drummer, you find that you almost always tap (or, if you're a rock drummer, pound) on something. These instruments allow you to create some cool sounds while doing what you're going to do anyway.

The instruments in this chapter represent some of the most common and widely used percussion accessories available. They certainly don't cover the entire breadth of rhythm-makers out there, but after being exposed to these instruments, your mind will hopefully open to the possibilities available for rhythmic expression. Just as the rhythm group *Stomp* uses match-boxes, garbage can lids, oil drums, and hubcaps to make music, you can apply any number of the techniques and rhythms in this chapter to the objects that you find in your own environment.

Ringing the Agogo Bells

The *agogos* (pronounced uh-*go*-goes) are Brazilian bells that you play in pairs. (You can also find them played in groups of three or four bells, though these groups are much less common.) These bells are traditionally used to add a high-pitched, almost melodic sound to the rhythms of Carnaval (the Brazilian Mardi Gras celebration). Agogo bells have become very popular in contemporary music and have made their way into jazz, rock, funk, and pop. Figure 17-1 shows you a pair of agogo bells.

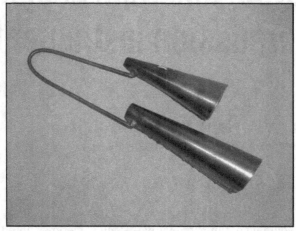

Figure 17-1: The Brazilian agogo bells, a staple in many types of popular music.

Playing position

To play the agogo bells, you hold them in one hand (usually your left) and play them with a stick that you hold in your other hand (see Figure 17-2). Occasionally, you use your left hand to mute the bells (to do so, close your fingers around the bell) as you play them. An agogo player alternates between the bells in the pair, playing each bell in a rhythm. You occasionally see these bells mounted on a stand and added to a drumset or percussion set-up.

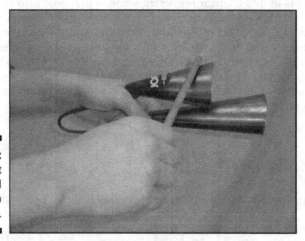

Figure 17-2: A look at how to hold the agogo bells.

Understanding the rhythms

The agogo bells have grown out of Brazilian samba music (see Chapter 10 for more on the samba) and, in many cases, the rhythms have come along as well. These samba rhythms translate well into contemporary music and provide a basis for improvisation. The rhythms in Figure 17-3 alternate between the lower and higher pitched bells (located below and above the X, respectively).

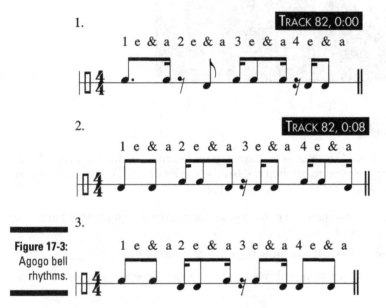

1.   TRACK 82, 0:00

1 e & a 2 e & a 3 e & a 4 e & a

2.   TRACK 82, 0:08

1 e & a 2 e & a 3 e & a 4 e & a

3.

Figure 17-3:
Agogo bell
rhythms.

1 e & a 2 e & a 3 e & a 4 e & a

Twisting and Shaking the Afuche/Cabasa

The *afuche/cabasa* (pronounced aah-foo-*shay* and kah-*bah*-sah) is a recent invention, but it has become one of the most widely used percussion instruments. This instrument is based upon the African cabasa, which was made by carving grooves into a coconut shell and stringing seeds around it, and the Brazilian afuche, which was made from a gourd with a lattice of beads or seeds around it. Figure 17-4 shows the modern afuche/cabasa.

The afuche/cabasa can make a variety of sounds including scraping and shaker-type sounds. This versatile instrument is one that no percussionist should be without.

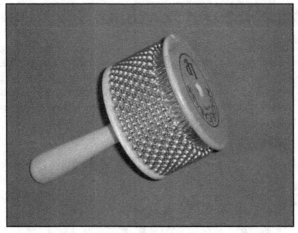

Figure 17-4:
The afuche/
cabasa.

Playing position

You generally hold the afuche/cabasa in your left hand, while your right hand loosely wraps around it, holding the beads (see Figure 17-5). You make sound with the afuche/cabasa in three different ways:

- ✔ By twisting the instrument with your left hand while your right hand holds the beads
- ✔ By shaking the instrument with your right hand free
- ✔ By tapping the beads with your right hand or fingers

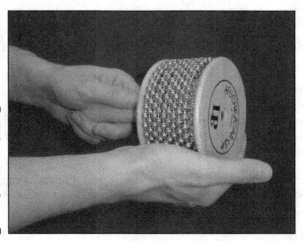

Figure 17-5:
Proper
holding
technique
for the
afuche/
cabasa.

Understanding the rhythms

The rhythms for the afuche/cabasa are as varied as the playing styles. Shaking and tapping techniques can use the rhythms of other instruments, such as shakers and bells. The rhythms in Figure 17-6 use the scraping (twisting) motion. These rhythms work in just about all musical situations that have a similar feel. For example, the first rhythm works well in a basic rock song with an eighth-note feel (see Chapter 2 for more on the eighth-note feel). Notice that each of the rhythms contains a constant pulse with accents. Get comfortable with these accent patterns, and then make up some of your own.

When you play the afuche/cabasa with a group, choose a rhythm that complements the main rhythm of the music and then settle into a groove. Don't vary your rhythm too much or you'll detract from rather than add to the music.

Figure 17-6: Rhythms for the afuche/cabasa.

Keying in to the Clavé

The two little sticks that make up the clavé (pronounced *clah*-vay) are probably the most important instruments in Latin music (see Figure 17-7). Okay, maybe it's not so much the actual sticks, but the rhythm that this instrument plays that's so significant. The word *clavé* means "key" and the clavé pattern is the key to playing the musical styles where it's used (see the following paragraph). All forms of Latin music (Afro-Cuban, Caribbean, and Brazilian) have a clavé pattern in them, and you often hear this rhythm played by other instruments as well. The most common clavé rhythms are associated with Afro-Cuban music, and these rhythms have permeated many of the new styles of Latin music played today.

The *clavé* is a two-bar pattern that repeats throughout the song. One bar, usually the first, includes three clavé hits and the other bar has two. This is called a 3-2 clavé pattern. However, these two bars are reversed in some music, in which case it's called 2-3 clavé. Generally, you play the 3-2 order unless the music (or another band member) tells you that the song is in 2-3.

All musicians must follow the clavé pattern. If you fall out of rhythm with this pattern, you'll get some nasty looks. So, if you intend to play Latin music, you need to memorize the clavé pattern and get very comfortable playing to it.

Most of the time, when people refer to the clavé, they're talking about the rhythm, not the instrument. Of course, if you can play the rhythm on these sticks, go for it. But if you don't have the instrument, you can beat its rhythm on just about anything — a drumshell, a box, a tabletop; heck, you can simply clap it if you want.

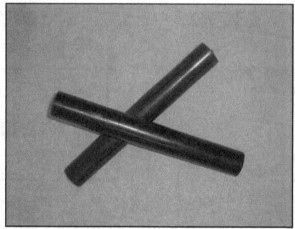

Figure 17-7:
The clavé
instrument.

Playing position

To hold the clavé, cup one of the sticks in the palm of your hand (usually the left) and let it rest without muting the sound with your grip. You want a bright, resonant sound when you hit it with the second stick that your other hand holds. You can experiment with different ways of holding the clavé until you get the clearest tone. Check out Figure 17-8 to see how to hold the clavé.

Figure 17-8:
How to hold
the clavé.

Understanding the rhythms

Drummers have two styles of clavé rhythms — the Son and the Rhumba — and two meters in which they're played — 4/4 and 6/8. Regardless of the style or meter, the clavé rhythm is a two-bar phrase that repeats over and over in the song. All the rhythms of the song relate to this rhythm and everyone (even the singer) must follow it.

The rhythms in Figure 17-9 are the traditional Afro-Cuban clavé rhythms. I present them here in a 3-2 format (the traditional way of playing them). To play them in a 2-3 clavé, start with the second measure. If you plan to play Latin music, particularly Cuban, you need to be fluent in each of these patterns.

Rhythms 1 and 3 are the Son clavé, which is the more common clavé. In fact, if the music says only 2-3 clavé without designating Son or Rhumba, you should play the Son style. As you examine these two styles, notice that the difference between them is very slight. The difference resides with the placement of the third note in the 3-2 configuration.

The tie between the second and third notes in rhythms 1 and 2 in Figure 17-9 mean that you don't play the third note. Your playing of note number two "ties" over to note number three.

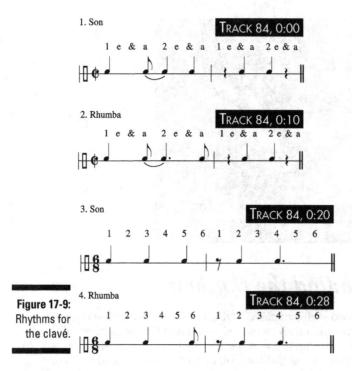

Figure 17-9:
Rhythms for
the clavé.

Clanging the Cowbell

The cowbell isn't just one instrument but a whole class of instruments. Virtually dozens of types of cowbells are in existence. Traditionally, certain cowbells were used only in specific styles of music (the mambo or cha-cha, for instance), but for most people, a cowbell is a cowbell (Figure 17-10 shows you one of these babies). From the dozens of cowbell types, you must choose the pitch and sound quality that you want (bright, dry, lively, loud, fat — well, you get the picture).

Regardless of the type or style, all cowbells have their roots in the fields of Africa. Originally, the cowbell rhythm was played out in the field to accompany the music that kept the farmers working. The predecessor to the modern cowbell is called the *guataca* (pronounced gwah-*tah*-kah), which is literally a hoe blade that you play with a large nail or spike. And like the clavé, the cowbell's rhythm is the essence of African and Afro-Latin music.

Playing position

Like most percussion instruments, you can play the cowbell in a variety of ways. You can hold it in your hand (the traditional way), mount it on a stand and play it with a stick, or even mount it to a bass drum pedal and play it with your foot. Figure 17-10 shows you how to hold a cowbell if you choose to play it the traditional way.

Many musicians often mute the cowbell with their hand while they hold it to give it a softer, quieter tone. This is noted by the "o" (open tone) and "+" (muted tone) in rhythm 2 of Figure 17-11. Each cowbell can create several tones depending on where you hit it. Striking the edge of the open end gives it a bright, loud, open tone while hitting it on the closed end produces a drier, softer sound. Experiment with your cowbell to see the variety of sounds that you can create.

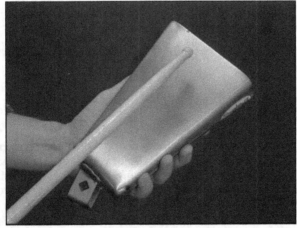

Figure 17-10:
One (of many) ways to play the cowbell.

Understanding the rhythms

Figure 17-11 shows you a few traditional rhythms for the cowbell. Notice that each of these rhythms is fairly *syncopated* (you accent the "e" and "a" of the beat rather than the "one" or "two" — see Chapter 6 for more on syncopation), which is often the case for a cowbell that you play in Latin music. If you listen to rock or funk music, notice that the rhythm often used on the cowbell is simple, usually just pounding out the basic pulse of the music.

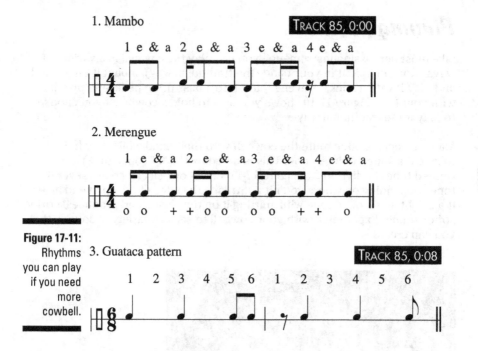

1. Mambo

TRACK 85, 0:00

2. Merengue

Figure 17-11:
Rhythms
you can play
if you need
more
cowbell.

3. Guataca pattern

TRACK 85, 0:08

Scraping the Guiro

You've probably seen the guiro with the guy or gal on stage scraping a stick against a gourd with ridges carved into it. And, you've probably heard the instrument — its distinctive sound comes through in most types of Latin music. But you likely don't know how to pronounce the name of the guiro (pronounced *gweer*-do, with a very soft "d" sound — there, aren't you glad you finally know how to say it?).

The *guiro* was traditionally made from a gourd and has its origins in Cuba where it was an essential part of the Son style of music. Guiros can still be made from gourds, but they're most often made from plastic and sometimes metal today. This instrument's unique scraping sound is indispensable in much of today's popular music. You can see the guiro in Figure 17-12.

Playing position

Hold the guiro in your left hand with your fingers fitting into the holes cut in the back. Your right hand holds a small stick, made of either wood or plastic, and scrapes it across the ridges carved into the instrument. Figure 17-12 shows you how to hold the guiro.

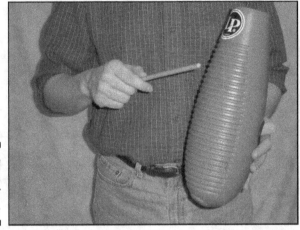

Figure 17-12: Playing position for the guiro.

Understanding the rhythms

Figure 17-13 shows you some common guiro patterns. The key to these rhythms is getting the long stroke right. The long stroke is marked with both a down and up arrow below it. The important thing about this stroke is to have both the up and down stroke sound like one long stroke. This may take some practice — I'll wait here while you try it.

Are you done? Okay. To play these measures in a contemporary setting, choose the rhythm or rhythms that seem(s) to fit best with the type of groove that the rest of the band is playing and stick with it.

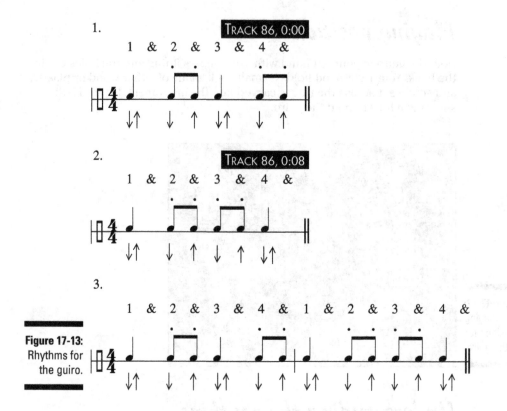

Figure 17-13:
Rhythms for
the guiro.

Movin' to the Maracas

You may think that the maracas (pronounced mah-*rah*-cahs; see Figure 17-14) are just some kitschy souvenir that you see in Mexico or the Caribbean, but in reality, the maracas are an important part of most Latin music. Originally these instruments were made from cowhide formed over a wine bottle and sewn into the shape of a pouch, which was then filled with seeds and attached to a stick. Today maracas are made from wood, plastic, or cowhide. Each method produces a specific type of sound. Traditionally, each of the two maracas in a set has a slightly different pitch, though modern pairs of maracas are often the same pitch. This difference allows the player to create more interesting rhythms.

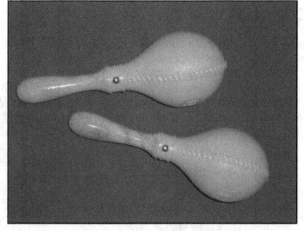

Figure 17-14:
The maracas — same shape, different pitch.

Playing position

Hold one maraca in each hand with the lower toned one on the left (see Figure 17-15). To make the rhythm, gently shake your hand down and stop abruptly. It can help to imagine a table or even drumhead at about waist level that you pretend to strike with the maraca.

Figure 17-15:
Here's a look at how you hold the maracas.

Understanding the rhythms

Rhythms created with the maracas use two pitches, one for each maraca. Figure 17-16 contains some pretty basic, common rhythms for playing the maracas. Rhythm 1 is a bare-bones eighth-note pattern. Rhythm 2 incorporates an embellishment in the form of a double stroke with your left hand. Rhythm 3 introduces a sixteenth-note triplet pattern. Use this sixteenth-note pattern sparingly; otherwise, it loses its impact. You can use any of these rhythms in contemporary music where you want the maraca sound.

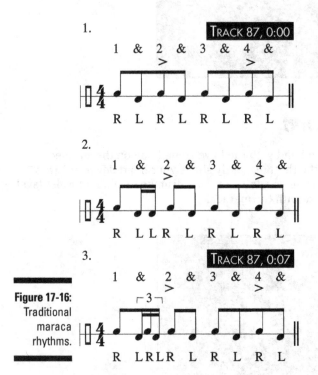

Figure 17-16: Traditional maraca rhythms.

Experimenting with Shakers

Shakers make up a broad category. They can be anything from a large metal tube with steel balls sealed inside to a matchbox with a few matches left over. Figure 17-17 shows a variety of the shakers available, including the universal egg shaker (homemade, of course).

The beauty of shakers is that you can make them yourself. Just partially fill any container (empty vitamin bottles work well) with seeds, dry beans, popcorn (before it's popped), or something similar and shake away. My favorite homemade shaker consists of plastic Easter eggs filled about ¼ to ½ full. Popcorn produces a bright, sharp sound while dried lentils create a softer, mellower tone. Go into your kitchen and experiment until you find combinations that you like. The great thing is that you can change your shaker sounds any time you want.

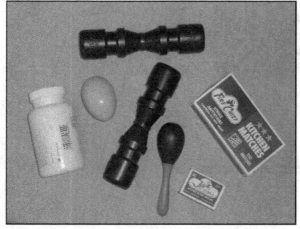

Figure 17-17:
A variety of shakers, and you can make most of them yourself.

Playing position

The best way to play a shaker is to hold it lightly in one hand and rock it back and forth, giving it a slight jerk at the end of the movement. Another way to play it is to tap the shaker against your leg (I know this is cheating, but who cares, right?). Figure 17-18 shows the proper (popular?) way to hold the shaker.

Understanding the rhythms

Rhythms for shakers are pretty simple. The art in shaking is making the accents even and the movement smooth. Doing so may take awhile, so be patient. Shakers are an important and aurally pleasing (pleasing to the ear) addition to many musical situations. Check out Figure 17-19 for a few shaker rhythms. The down arrow means to move the shaker away from you, and the up arrow means to move the shaker towards you. After you get the hang of these rhythms, work on adding some different accents. You may even try doing some rhythms in odd meter.

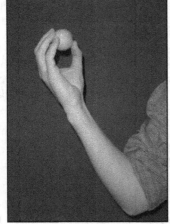

Figure 17-18:
The most common way to hold a shaker.

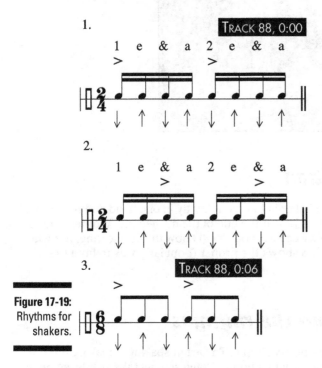

Figure 17-19:
Rhythms for shakers.

Tapping the Triangle

You probably recognize the triangle as a dinner bell from movies set in the Old West. Simply a bent piece of steel, the *triangle* adds a soft, sweet texture to music. Like many of the rhythm-makers in this chapter, the triangle often adds a much-needed high frequency to the drumming.

Playing position

You can position the triangle a bunch of ways — either in your hand or on a stand, but however you hold it, you need to be able to mute it with your free hand. Most drummers prefer to hold the triangle in their left hand from a string so that it rings freely. When they want to mute it, they simply close their fingers around it.

When playing complex or fast patterns, the most efficient way to play the triangle is to go back and forth from the inside between the two sides of the triangle that have an open end. Figure 17-20 shows you this position.

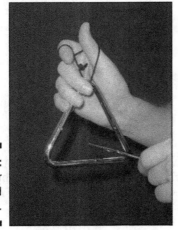

Figure 17-20:
The proper way to hold the triangle.

Understanding the rhythms

The beauty of triangle rhythms is in the play between the open and muted tones (for a great example of this open-muted interplay, check out Peter Gabriel's, "In Your Eyes"). Figure 17-21 has some basic groove patterns for the triangle. Rhythm 1 is a basic pop pattern where you play constant sixteenth notes. The first two beats are muted (marked with a "+") and the last two are open (marked with an "o"). Rhythm 2 is a variation on this pattern, making you wait one sixteenth note to open on the first beat (the "a" of one). Rhythm 3 is a triplet pattern with the open tone on the third note of the triplet.

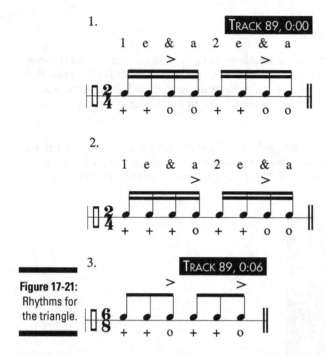

Figure 17-21:
Rhythms for
the triangle.

 The possibilities for improvisation with the triangle are far-reaching. Like all the percussion instruments in this chapter, the key is to create a rhythm one or two bars long and keep grooving on it. The repetitive rhythm, if done right, adds flavor to the song.

Chapter 18

Jamming with World Rhythms

Drumming is most fun when you can groove with other people. You get to play with other drummers on many of the drums that I introduce you to in Chapters 15, 16, and 17. The interplay between similar instruments all digging into cool rhythms can be intoxicating; just ask any drum circle participant.

In this chapter I introduce polyrhythms and present a bunch of traditional grooves from Africa, Brazil, and Cuba where multiple drums and percussion instruments play off one another to create interesting and dynamic musical compositions. These rhythms are extremely fun to play, and even if you consider yourself primarily a drumset player, they can help you develop one of the most important musical skills needed for any style of music: The ability to keep your rhythm going while playing along with other people who are playing opposing rhythms.

The rhythms in this chapter are the core of all Latin-based drumset rhythms. If you look at these rhythms closely and compare them to drumset rhythms, you can see the connection. For example, the clavé or bell part from these rhythms is often played on the drumset's cymbal. As I describe in Chapter 1, the modern day drumset started out as a conglomeration of different drums and percussion instruments that one person wanted to play all at the same time.

Demystifying Polyrhythms

If you're like most people, when you discovered your interest in drumming, you kept hearing this mysterious word: polyrhythms. Maybe you heard stories that so-and-so was a great drummer because he or she could play polyrhythms. Or, maybe you were warned that you'd have to learn how to play a polyrhythm before you'd be any good. Well, just between you and me, polyrhythms aren't that difficult or mysterious. A *polyrhythm* is, simply, more than one rhythm happening at once.

When you get together with your friends to jam, each playing what you feel like, you create a polyrhythm. When you tap your foot while you play your drum, you create a polyrhythm. When you play along to a CD with drumming on it, you create a polyrhythm (unless you play the exact same rhythm as the drummer on the CD). When you count out loud as you play, you create a polyrhythm. So, if you've played along with any music (live or recorded) or if you've tried any of the rhythms in this book, chances are, you've already played a polyrhythm.

It Takes a Village: Using More Rhythms for Better Sound

Drumming takes on an entrancing and invigorating quality when more than one instrument is played at the same time. The different drum sounds and textures of the individual drum parts blend together to become beautiful music (hopefully). To the uninitiated ear, it becomes difficult to discern what each individual instrument is playing when rhythms are layered on top of one another.

For example, many people say that African drumming is highly complex and that it takes years of study to play such intricate rhythms. Not true. African drumming sounds difficult because, taken as a whole, a lot is going on, but taken individually, the parts are often very simple. The difficulty lies in being able to keep your rhythm steady while the other instruments around you play opposing rhythms.

When you first start playing with other people, the different rhythms going on around you may throw you off very easily. At first you need to concentrate very hard on what you're doing. As you concentrate on your rhythm, try to be aware of the sound of the other drums and how they relate to what you're playing. Notice what it feels like when you're in or out of time with them. Eventually you'll be able to play your rhythm without having to concentrate as much.

As you play the rhythms in this chapter, remember that your goal is to blend in as well as possible with the other instruments. Listen carefully, and if you can hear all the other instruments as you play, you're probably playing at the right volume. If yours is the only drum that you hear, you're definitely playing too loudly.

In many parts of the world drumming is a community activity. Cooperation and unity are the goals, and drumming is a means of getting there (not to mention an awful lot of fun).

The Rhythm Nations: Playing Well with Others

The most common world rhythms being played today come from Africa and the places where African music and drumming have influenced local music, such as Cuba and Brazil. Many of these rhythms are constantly evolving (with the exception of the Cuban rhythms, which have stayed pretty true to their roots), and drummers have considerable flexibility in how to play them. As long as you create your variations with sensitivity to the rhythms of the other instruments, you'll be fine.

Exploring African polyrhythms

Considered the heart of polyrhythmic drumming, African rhythms have been developing and evolving for centuries. These rhythms are regional in Africa and their interpretation varies greatly from village to village. I present the rhythms in Figures 18-1 and 18-2 the way that I learned them. You may find them performed differently by different people. After you become adept at playing along with them, try your hand at soloing (for some ideas for your solo, check out Chapter 14).

The rhythms in this section are set up for you to solo over with your own drumming. Each of the rhythms has a *call* in it (a call is a rhythmic phrase used in African drumming to announce a musical change to the rest of the band; check out Chapter 15 for more about the call). On the CD that accompanies this book, each set of rhythms in this chapter starts with a count, followed by the call. The ensemble plays for 31 bars. The call plays again, followed by 8 more bars of the rhythm. The call then plays once more and the music ends.

The djembe (pronounced *jem*-bay) parts in Figures 18-1 and 18-2 are written as bare-bones versions, without the muted notes. To play the muted notes, fill in the rest of the sixteenth notes in the measure. You can also go to the djembe section of Chapter 15 to see how to do this.

Fanga

Fanga, a West African rhythm, uses four instruments: the bell, a set of two djun djuns (one person can play both the bell and the djun djuns), and two djembes. (Check out Chapter 15 for more on the djembe and Chapter 16 for a description of the djun djuns and bell.) Figure 18-1 shows the fanga (pronounced *fahn*-gah) ensemble parts.

Figure 18-1: The West African fanga ensemble parts.

The bottom djembe (djembe 2) part is the lead and is usually the instrument that plays the call. You can play the djun djun part on one drum or two. If you use two drums, play the higher note on the higher pitched drum and ignore the stroke markings — let the drumhead ring free. If you play this part on one drum, follow the stroke markings written above the part: Mute the drum with your stick where you see an "M" and let it ring where you see an "O."

Kakilambe

This rhythm is slightly more complicated than the Fanga. The kakilambe (pronounced kah-kuh-*lahm*-bay; see Figure 18-2) adds a third djembe part. The rhythms for djembes 2 and 3 play off each other. In many cases, you want two different pitched djembes playing these parts in order to make them sound as interesting as possible. But, if you don't have three djembes, one drummer can play all these parts. In that case, you can play slap tones (go to Chapter 4 if you need a refresher on this stroke) instead of open tones for the third djembe's rhythm to keep the groove from sounding overly repetitive.

Figure 18-2:
The
kakilambe
ensemble
parts.

The kakilambe often speeds up as you play it. At the faster tempos, the djun djun and bell parts change. You want to play the djun djun and bell rhythms from the fanga during the faster section.

Checking out Cuban polyrhythms

Cuba has a rich drumming tradition. Because slaves were taken to this tiny island and intermingled with other people, a very definite style of music has emerged. Until very recently, this music remained relatively unchanged by Western popular music because of political factors. But, Cuban music continues to gain popularity.

At the risk of oversimplifying Cuban drumming (not to mention begging for a citation from the rhythm police), you can interchange many of the rhythm parts in the following styles of music. In many cases, the only thing that changes is the song's tempo. As you become familiar with these styles of music, you can determine which parts to move around. (The best way to do this is to listen to music played by really good musicians. Go to my Web site at www.jeffstrong.com for some resources.)

Bolero

Played at a slow tempo, the bolero is considered the Cuban ballad style of music. The tempo for the bolero can vary quite a bit, even within one song (solo sections can speed up). Figure 18-3 shows you the instrumentation of the bolero.

Figure 18-3: The Cuban bolero parts.

The bolero is written in 3-2 clavé, so if you want to play it in 2-3 clavé, start on the second bar. As you listen to the bolero rhythm on the CD, try to hear how the clavé pattern relates to the rhythms of the other instruments (Chapter 17 has more about the clavé).

In the rhythms in Figures 18-3 and 18-4 you play the timbales with your right hand on the rim of the larger drum (the top line, marked with an "x"), and your left hand plays on the heads of the two drums (the second and fourth spaces).

Mambo

The mambo is one of the fastest Cuban musical styles. As you look at Figure 18-4, notice that it's written in *cut time* (cut time basically means to play the rhythm in 2/2 time). Also, notice how similar the parts are to the bolero. In fact, many songs have a mambo section in them. The mambo section is an intense section of the song that usually separates solo sections.

Figure 18-4: The mambo — king of the song.

After you get comfortable with playing the parts of the mambo and bolero, you can try switching back and forth between them. For example, play eight bars of the bolero, eight bars of the mambo, and then back again. Doing so can help you get used to changing rhythms.

Banging out Brazilian polyrhythms

With its blend of African and European influences, Brazilian music is unique. In Brazil, music is an essential part of the culture, and Brazilian musicians receive the same kind of treatment that movie stars do in the U.S.

Bossa nova

The bossa nova (pronounced *boss*-ah *no*-vah) is a style of music that evolved out of the samba in the 1940s. As samba musicians were exposed to jazz, this new style of music developed. Figure 18-5 shows the rhythms for the bossa nova.

Keep in mind that the percussion parts are often more subtle in the bossa nova than in many other styles of music. The focus of this music style is song writing and lyrics.

TRACK 94, 0:00

Figure 18-5:
The
Brazilian
bossa nova.

Samba

The samba is probably the best-known style of Brazilian music and the most played in Brazil. As a result, you can play the samba in many ways. The rhythms in Figure 18-6 represent the type of samba that you hear during Carnaval. This pattern is a hard-driving rhythm meant to make people dance and party.

The samba rhythm (see Figure 18-6) is written in cut time (2/2 time) and should be counted "1 e & a 2 e & a". You play the top line of the surdo/zabumba rhythm (notated with an "x") with your left hand and the notes in the second space of the staff with your right hand (notated with the regular note).

This rhythm also includes a drum called *caixa*. The caixa (pronounced *kay-shah*) is a Brazilian snare drum that's played with sticks just like the rudimental snare drum (you can find out more about this drum in Chapter 3). You play the caixa part with alternating strokes (right, left, right, left), and you can choose whether to play the rolls (on the "a" of "1") or not.

Soloing in a drum circle

Okay, you're grooving on your djembe (or conga or whatever hand drum you prefer) and you have the rest of the drummers behind you. You're feeling pretty good about yourself, and you want to let loose when your turn to solo comes around the circle. Now's your chance. What do you do? You solo, of course!

Whoa! Hold on a minute there, pardner. Soloing is serious business. And one reality of every drum jam is that you will be tempted to solo. So, to keep from embarrassing yourself and being exiled into the "no solo" zone of the drum circle, ask yourself these questions:

- ✔ Can I play the basic rhythm without getting out of sync with the other drummers?

- ✔ Do I have the internal pulse of the rhythm within my body?

- ✔ Can I hear all the other parts as I play my own rhythm?

- ✔ Am I comfortable with this rhythm?

- ✔ Can I think of any licks or rhythms that would complement the main groove?

If you can answer yes to these questions, go ahead and solo. If not, you may want to sit it out and listen to the other soloists so you're ready the next time. *Remember:* There is no shame in passing on a solo.

TRACK 95, 0:00

Figure 18-6:
The samba:
It'll make
you feel like
dancing!

Part V
Choosing, Tuning, and Caring for Your Drums

The 5th Wave   By Rich Tennant

In this part . . .

One of the great things about drums is that so many are available to try. But this is also one of the challenges of playing drums. Chapter 19 guides you through the myriad of options for drums and helps you hone your vision to the drums that fit your needs. You also find out the best ways to tune and take care of your drums in Chapter 20.

Chapter 19

Decision Time: Selecting a Drum of Your Own

So you're ready to buy a drum or a drumset and you're not sure which one is best for you. No problem. You have a couple of ways to find the right drum. One way is to go into a drum shop, play a bunch of drums, and buy the one that you like. Another way is to decide what kind of drumming you want to do and choose a drum that fits that situation. If you're like most drummers, you'll use both approaches and end up with a whole room full of drums.

If you've decided on playing a drumset, the hardest part of choosing is behind you. A drumset is a drumset, at least in its basic sound and how you use it. You basically need some drums, cymbals, and stands, and if you plan on haul-ing your drums around, you need some cases. (Cases are a tough thing to fork over money for. I mean, guitars come with cases, so why not drums?) If you're into other drums, your options quickly explode. There are almost as many types of drums as there are drummers. Well, maybe not quite that many, but certainly enough to make the drum-buying decision a difficult one.

But whether you want to play a hand drum or a drumset, you want a drum that sounds (and looks) good. This chapter helps you sort out the many dif-ferent options. First, I walk you through all the drumset decisions you need to make. Then, I move onto other drums, helping you determine your needs and desires. In addition, I explain the different ways that drums are made and how the different construction techniques and materials relate to the sound, durability, and price of the instrument.

Choosing a Drumset

In order to determine what kind of drumset to buy, you don't really need to know what kind of music you intend to play — I refer you to my "a drumset is a drumset" comment earlier in the chapter. But, you do need to know what your goals are. If you're not sure how much you really want to play the drums or how long you're likely to stick with it, you're best not buying a professional kit, but rather opting for a less expensive student or semiprofessional model. You can always trade up if you find yourself seriously bitten by the drumming bug.

In this section, I try to lay out the different options so that you can make an informed choice for both your first kit *and* a professional one, if you get around to it.

If you're like most people, your final choice of drumsets largely depends on how much money you have to spend. A complete professional drumset setup can cost almost as much as a decent car, so unless you want to forgo driving, you'll probably need to make some tough choices. The good news is that you can find some great-sounding drumsets that won't cost you every penny you'll ever earn. If you do your homework, even a budget-minded person can end up with a drumset that sounds great and is a pleasure to play.

So how much do you need to spend to get a decent drumset? Well, that depends, but plan on at least $500 to $1,000 for a complete beginner set with hardware and cymbals (without the cases). Keep in mind: You always get what you pay for. A more expensive kit has more options and sounds better than a less expensive set. On the other hand, unless you really know what you're doing, playing on a better set won't necessarily make you sound better.

Unless you're on a really tight budget, I recommend buying a set made by a major manufacturer. This way, if anything ever happens to the drums, you can get them repaired. You'll also find that selling them — if and when the time comes — is easier. If even the least expensive set from one of the major manufacturers is still too much for you, I suggest considering a used kit. If you shop around and educate yourself (reading this chapter is a good start), you can end up with a top quality set of used drums for about the same price as a piece-of-junk new kit.

The drums

Drumsets are sold as, well, sets and they're described as having so many pieces (each drum in a set is one piece). The most common drumset sold has five pieces: a snare drum, a bass drum, and three tom-toms. Likewise, most drumsets, except the higher-end professional models, also come with some hardware. This hardware can vary, but for the most part, student and some semiprofessional models have tom-tom mounting hardware along with a hi-hat stand, a snare stand, and one or more cymbal stands. Some may include a bass drum pedal as well. Not included in a drumset are cymbals, a bass drum pedal, a throne (seat), and any additional cymbal stands that you may want.

Sizes

The sizes of the drums in the set are listed in inches with the depth of the *shell* (the body of the drum) first and the diameter second. For example, a snare drum is listed as 5 x 14. This means that the drum is 5 inches deep and 14 inches across. Most five-piece drumsets consist of the following:

- 5 x 14 snare drum
- 14 x 22 bass drum
- 8 x 12 mounted tom
- 9 x 13 mounted tom
- 14 x 14 or 16 x 16 floor tom

Shells

All drumset shells are made by layering thin sheets of wood (called *plys*) 1 to 1.5 millimeters thick and gluing them together to get a certain thickness, usually between 6 and 9 plys total. They are then stained, lacquered, or wrapped with a covering to give them their visual appearance. Lugs are mounted on the shells to hold the rims and heads to the drum.

Much debate surrounds what the best wood and number of plys is for a drum. For the most part, after you get into the semiprofessional level and above, shell composition becomes a matter of personal preference. Ultimately, you choose based upon the type of sound you want.

The types of wood that you can find include maple, birch, beech, mahogany, gum, and the undisclosed "all wood" variety. Each type has its own timbral characteristics. For instance, maple has a louder, brighter sound than birch, while birch has a mellower tone that has a *wetter* (thicker) quality to it. Each can sound great if tuned properly.

In middle price-range kits, how you tune the drums has more impact on how good they sound than what kind of wood they're made out of or what kind of mounting hardware they have. (To really understand how to tune your drums, go to Chapter 20.)

Tom-tom mounting hardware

Your drums (the tom-toms, that is) have to be mounted on some type of hardware in order for you to play them. The mounting hardware allows you to attach your drums to a stand. Most kits (except some of the high-end professional ones where you get to choose the hardware that you prefer) come with mounting hardware already attached.

Two basic types of mounting hardware are around nowadays: those that mount directly on the drum's shell and those that use some sort of suspension system. A beginner kit generally has the hardware attached directly to the shell while the higher-end drumsets use a mounting system that takes the weight of the drum off the shell so that it can resonate more freely.

Additional hardware

Many times when you buy a drumset, except for the top-of-the-line professional models, you get some hardware too. This already-included hardware is a good starting point. Unfortunately, you'll probably get only tom-tom mounting hardware, a hi-hat stand, a snare drum stand, sometimes a bass drum pedal, and one cymbal stand, and you'll have more hardware left to buy.

Other hardware you have to buy separately

As with the rest of the stuff that goes with a drumset, you have a lot of hardware options. And to get your life as a drummer off the ground, you need a bass drum pedal and a throne to sit on.

The bass drum pedal

Bass drum pedals come in a variety of styles. Some have leather or nylon straps, while others use chains to transfer the movement from the pedal to the beater. You can choose from single or double pedals, and every company uses a whole host of innovations in order to distinguish its pedal. Because bass drum pedals can range in price from under $100 to as much as $500, your best bet is to go into your local drum shop and try out a few pedals in your price range to determine which one works best for you. My experience is that even if your complete drumset comes with a bass drum pedal, you should check out some others to see whether you like one of them better. The bass drum pedals that are included with drumsets often aren't the best quality anyway.

The throne

The drum throne is one of the most important and most overlooked parts of a drumset. Most young drummers prefer to spend their money getting a better drumset or some more cymbals rather than buying a decent throne. As someone who suffered through a tour with a terrible case of hemorrhoids (ouch!) because of a hard, uncomfortable, vinyl-covered throne (this was before drum thrones were really padded), I highly recommend that you treat yourself to a decent throne. Even if you can't afford a really good one, any throne is better than a chair or stool, which can cause back problems and make playing that much more difficult. (You wouldn't believe how often I see a chair or stool used as a drum throne!)

When choosing a throne, remember that you will spend an awful lot of time sitting on it. Therefore, it should be solid, comfortable, and have a seat cover that can breathe (some sort of cloth works best). A decent drum throne can cost from about $75 up to around $250.

The cymbals

It used to be that a cymbal was a cymbal, but today you can find a staggering variety of choices — bright and loud, mellow, crisp, warm, and cutting. And that's just the ride cymbals! They can range in price from about $50 all the way up to $500 or more. So, again, where you start in choosing your cymbals depends largely on how much you can spend and what your ultimate goals are in playing.

If you're an absolute beginner and you're not yet sure just how committed you are to drumming, you want to choose a beginner-grade cymbal. The good news is that each of the major cymbal manufacturers makes a line of introductory cymbals that sounds good and costs relatively little.

For the basic drumset you need a set of hi-hats, a ride cymbal, and a crash cymbal. If you're really short on cash, you can get away with a crash/ride (a cymbal that functions both as a crash and a ride cymbal) instead of both a crash and a ride. When buying cymbals, I recommend staying with one of the major cymbal makers. You may pay a little more for them (although not much more in most cases), but they sound better and last longer.

Your best bet in starter cymbals is to buy a cymbal set. These are prepackaged sets of basic cymbals that the manufacturer chooses and matches. They usually contain a set of 13- or 14-inch hi-hats, a 16-inch crash, and a 20-inch ride or a set of hi-hats with an 18-inch crash/ride (some even come with a cymbal bag!). These sets start at about $250 retail, but expect to pay 20 to 40 percent less through most dealers.

The sticks

Drumsticks are sized according to the diameter of the stick and the shape of the tip. The smaller the number, the larger the diameter. An "A" tip is more slender and pointed than a "B" tip, which is rounder. Although sticks are a personal item, if you're like most people, a size between 2B and 5A is a good starting point. Your best bet is to go into a store and try a bunch to see which size you prefer. If you're a rock drummer, try to resist the temptation to get the heaviest sticks. You'll have a hard time playing anything other than loud, straight-ahead rock music.

Using wood or nylon tipped sticks is really a personal preference. Nylon tips produce a crisper, brighter sound on the cymbal while the wooden tip variety has a mellower sound.

Choosing a Traditional Drum

If you're in the market for a *traditional* drum, hand or stick-played, you'll find a lot of options. Luckily, many of the hand drums available don't cost that much. You can buy a top quality frame drum for around $100 and a basic beginner for under $20. On the other hand, a pair of professional congas can cost you more than $1,000. So before forking over your hard-earned money, you need some idea about what type of drum you want.

Your best bet is to read Chapters 15 and 16 and think about which of the drums interests you. Chances are you'll discover a couple types of drums that you want to play. Next, you may want to ask what type of playing situations you see yourself in.

The following are a few questions to get you started.

- ✔ **Do you plan to play with a band or by yourself?** Some drums, like a conga or a djembe, lend themselves much better to group situations than a doumbek or frame drum. Of course, even that idea's changing: Today you can find doumbeks in rock bands and frame drums in jazz bands.

- ✔ **Are you interested in *drum circles* (see Chapter 21) or structured ensembles?** In most drum circles, almost anything goes, but a structured ensemble may have restrictions on what types of drums it allows.

- ✔ **Do you see yourself playing rock, Latin, African, or jazz music?** Do you intend to use a more traditional drum in these contexts or do you want to try something more experimental? If you choose the more experimental route, the *timbre* (the drum's tonal qualities) may play a role in what you choose. Try to choose a drum that sounds good with the other instruments.

✔ **How much money do you have to spend?** Because you can buy many traditional drums for just a couple hundred dollars or less, chances are you can afford more than one.

✔ **Do you just want to make some noise (musically, of course)?** In this case, simply choose the loudest drum!

If, after all this evaluation, you still find yourself walking out of the drum shop with a few drums that you just plain love the sound of but that weren't exactly on your list, that's okay. You can always find a place to play them (and with this book, you can at least learn *how* to play them).

Whether you're interested in a djembe, conga, or any number of other hand drums, you'll likely encounter a few different construction methods/ compositions. Each of these affects the price and sound of the instrument. The following sections give you some background on each method.

Natural or synthetic drumheads

Drumheads are a sticky issue for many people. Natural skin proponents claim that natural heads feel more, err, natural and produce a warmer sound, while synthetic head proponents extol the advantages of consistent sound and durability. In truth, both are right, but you need to look at the pluses and minuses for each:

✔ **Natural hide:** Natural hide heads traditionally have a warmer sound and feel good to the touch. On the other hand, natural heads are greatly affected by temperature and humidity and change pitch with even the slightest change in either. Really extreme changes in temperature can cause a natural hide head to split, requiring you to replace it.

✔ **Synthetic:** Synthetic heads are much more able to handle temperature and humidity fluctuations without affecting the sound of the instrument. However, they tend to be less comfortable for some people to play because they don't feel like natural hide. They also tend to sound *flatter* (less expressive) than a natural head. Of course, synthetic heads are getting better and better every day, so this idea is slowly changing.

Because the price differences between drums with natural and synthetic drumheads aren't significant, you should base the type of head that you choose on how and where you intend to play. If, for example, you plan to take your drum everywhere with you and subject it to constant changes in temperature or humidity, then you're best off getting a drum with a synthetic head. That situation would put too much stress on a natural skin, and you'd have to constantly tune and re-tune it. On the other hand, if you see yourself playing mostly in one place or transporting your drum in a case that can protect it from changes, you can probably get by with a natural head.

Your best bet when choosing a traditional drum is to play each drum and pick the one that you like best while taking into account how you expect to use it and the conditions you're likely to subject it to.

In my opinion, some drums sound better with one type of head rather than the other. For instance, I have yet to hear a synthetic conga drum head that sounds as good as a natural skin, and I prefer the sound of a tar (or any high-pitched frame drum, for that matter) with a synthetic head over a natural one.

Shell type

The shells of traditional drums can be made from a carved log, glued-up *staves* (narrow strips of wood), molded and pounded or cast metal, kiln-fired ceramic, or resin-impregnated wood fiber. Each of these construction methods affects the price, the timbre, and the durability of the drum.

Carved shells

Traditional African drums and most of the more primitive looking djembes are carved out of logs. The advantage of carved drums lies mainly in their visual appeal. Not only is the shell carved out of a log, but the artisan who carves the drum usually carves some designs on the outside as well. Most of the available carved drums come from Africa or Japan, so they tend to be djembes, ashikos, djun djuns, or any of the Taiko drums. (See Chapters 15 and 16 for more on these drums.)

The disadvantage with carved drums is that they have a tendency to crack. These cracks can be small or, in some cases, they can split the drum open. Sometimes you can glue the cracks back together, but don't count on that method always working. If you end up getting a carved drum, I highly recommend buying some sort of case to minimize the stress from temperature and humidity changes that can weaken the structure.

Carved drums can be more expensive than their glued-up counterparts by as much as several hundred dollars. This increase in price is largely related to the intricacy of the designs and the shrinking availability of logs that are large enough to make a good-sized drum.

Glued-up shells

Gluing up narrow strips of wood into a round shell is the construction method of choice for most modern drum manufacturers. Drums made this way tend to be strong and sound great. Manufacturers make them with wood grown in a sustainable way (rather than depleting a rainforest), and you can have them stained, varnished, or wrapped for a variety of looks.

The first glued-up drums were congas and bongos. More recently, you could find all the African-style drums this way as well. You can find glued-up drums that look very similar to carved drums (read: primitive) if you're searching for that look. You can also find them with high-tech hardware if such accessories suit your taste.

Fiberglass shells

Fiberglass is a fairly common hand drum construction method that compares favorably to the glued-up varieties. The most common fiberglass drums are congas and bongos, but today you can find some djembes, doumbeks, and other world drums that are made this way.

Fiberglass drums are louder and brighter sounding than their wood counterparts. They cost about as much, so you pick one over the other based upon your particular tastes. If you play in a rock band, you may find that the fiberglass drum projects better, but if you play in a jazz band, the wooden drum blends in much better.

Metal shells

The only metal drums you're likely to find (not including drumset drums) are doumbeks and timbales. Metal drums can be made from brass, stainless steel, or aluminum. Most are made from sheet stock that's molded and pounded, but you can find cast metal (aluminum, mostly) from a few doumbek makers. Doumbeks are made in the Middle East and are somewhat hard to find outside that region. Metal-shelled drums have a brighter sound than wooden drums. In most cases, you won't have to choose between a wooden or metal drum; rather your choice is more difficult — between brass and stainless steel, for instance. (Hint: Brass is slightly warmer-sounding than stainless steel.)

Ceramic shells

In addition to an udu drum (the clay pot from Chapter 15), some other drums are made from ceramic. The most common ceramic drum is the doumbek. Ceramic is its traditional construction method and by many people's opinions, the best way to make a doumbek.

The only disadvantage of ceramic drums is that they're extremely fragile. Just hit it the wrong way once and you're out of luck. They can sound great (I'm not sure that their sound is any better than a perfectly tuned metal drum, but that's my opinion), but you need to be extra careful with them. In regard to cost, they're about the same as a metal drum of similar quality.

Wood fiber and resin shells

One major drum manufacturer uses a wood fiber and resin method to construct its drums. This method has some advantages, such as sustainability (made from recycled wood pulp) and extreme durability. The downside is that you can't get a wood fiber and resin drum without a synthetic head. The cost of this type of drum is comparable to similar drums of the same quality, and they come in a variety of shapes, sizes, and finishes.

Hardware style

In addition to different shell construction methods, traditional drums can have a variety of hardware styles as well. You can find ropes, tacks and nails, wooden pegs, metal lugs, and cables. Each of these things can be effective, and with the possible exception of the tacks and nails, all are tunable (for more on tuning, see Chapter 20).

Without a doubt, lug-tuned drums are the easiest to tune, and you can tune them to more precise pitches. However, your choice will more often than not revolve around the aesthetic appeal of a particular drum rather than how easy it is to tune.

Pegs are the only tuning method where you can be at a disadvantage when it comes to actually tuning the drum. If you end up considering a peg-tuned drum, make sure that the pegs function well before you buy it. They should hold their grip and be able to maintain the drum's pitch when played. If you play it and the pitch takes a dive, the pegs aren't working properly and you should probably pass on that drum.

Branching Out: The Extras

You can get into a huge variety of additions to your drumset or hand drum setup (for example, percussion instruments like those found in Chapter 17). Aside from the drums, you'll find some accessories that can help you with your drumming. In this section, I describe the two most important additions to the drumset — the metronome and drum cases.

Keeping time with the metronome

The metronome is probably the most useful non-drum item that a drummer can own. After all, you need to learn to play good time, and a metronome can help you do that. A *metronome* is simply a device that produces a click at regular intervals so that you know where the pulse is. Metronomes used to be mechanical, keeping time with a pendulum that rocked back and forth. Now they're electronic and come in a variety of styles that can range in price from about $10 to as much as $175 (retail). They all keep good time but vary in the amenities such as headphone jacks (a must-have for drummers) and the ability to subdivide the measure.

I recommend getting a metronome that has a headphone jack. If you can afford it, I also recommend getting a metronome that can subdivide the measure into eighth notes, triplets, and sixteenth notes, as well as being able to produce a different tone on the first beat of a measure. I've been using a Boss Dr. Beat for 25 years and it still works perfectly, so a good metronome lasts a long time if you take care of it.

Carrying it all in cases

If you intend to haul your drums around, even a little bit, I recommend that you invest in a set of cases. Like everything else, cases come in a variety of styles. Here's a list of the most common case styles:

- **Nylon or cloth bag.** Bags come with or without padding and are great for light travel. They protect drums from some temperature changes as well as scratches and the occasional light bang.

- **Fiber cases.** These cases used to be the standard. Fiber cases are made from wood pulp and resin. They can be padded inside (or not) and work reasonably well, unless they get wet. Water damages the case and sometimes the drum.

- **Molded plastic cases.** Molded plastic is the newer version of the workhorse drum case. Like the bags and fiber cases, they can come with or without padding on the inside, and they've replaced fiber cases in most applications because they're waterproof. Well, maybe not totally waterproof — you wouldn't want to submerge them underwater — but they will keep most moisture out.

- **Flight cases.** These are the hardcore cases designed for air travel and intense road travel. You can push these off a truck and bang them around without ever damaging the case's contents. Flight cases are overkill for the average drummer (and even for most professionals). You need some of these cases only if you intend to embark on that world tour; otherwise, any of the other types of cases should meet your needs.

Knowing Where to Find Drums

You can find good quality drums at a variety of outlets. The first place you're likely to start is your local music store or drum shop. These stores generally offer you great service and the opportunity to play the drums before you buy them. The disadvantage is that you're likely to pay a little more for your drums than if you went through a mail order or Internet retailer. I recommend the local drum shops first because they can help you find what you're looking for, but if you don't have a local drum shop or if you really want to save a few bucks, you may want to consider an alternative.

Wherever you end up buying your drums, make sure you check on the return policy of the store. If something goes wrong or you just plain don't like the way your drums sound, you want to be able to return them. Most reputable retailers have a policy that allows you to return the drums if you need to (the policies usually specify that you need to return the drums between 14 and 30 days from the date you purchased them).

If you order from a mail order or Internet company, you're liable for the shipping charges (to and from your house) unless something is wrong with the drums. If you end up sending a drumset back after ordering from one of these retailers, you'll lose any price savings that you gained over the higher price of the local drum shop.

If you're in the market for a drumset, your local drum shop or music store will probably have a few in stock, but if you want a traditional drum, you may not be able to find one in your area (especially if you're in the market for a surdo or another exotic drum). In this case, you need to find an alternative source. Several great mail order and Internet companies sell drums.

Check out my Web site (www.jeffstrong.com) for resources or try these:

- **American Musical Supply:** www.americanmusical.com or 800-458-4076
- **Brazil Drums:** www.brazildrums.com or 877-484-4961
- **Drum World:** www.drumworld.com or 800-335-3445
- **Interstate Music:** www.interstatemusic.com or 877-213-2580
- **Long Island Drum Center:** www.lidrum.com or 800-240-9326
- **Midwest Percussion:** www.midwestpercusion.com or 800-282-DRUM
- **Music123:** www.music123.com or 888-590-9700
- **Musician's Friend:** www.musiciansfriend.com or 800-391-8762
- **Sam Ash:** www.samash.com or 800-4-samash

Chapter 20

Tuning and Maintaining Your Drums

. . . .

In This Chapter

▶ Getting the best sound from your drum

▶ Knowing when and how to replace drumheads

▶ Taking care of your drums

. . . .

*I*f you're like many new drummers, you get home with your drums and feel the way new parents do when they're alone with their child: "Okay, I've got this great thing here, but how do I take care of it?" Fortunately for you, caring for a new drum is a lot easier than caring for a newborn baby. And although it doesn't cry or make a mess, it can be just as loud. In this chapter I offer the basics of taking care of your drums. I start with tuning and move on to the everyday care and cleaning (no dirty diapers here). I finish this chapter with some guidelines on when to change drumheads and how to perform basic maintenance.

Tuning and general mechanical care make your drumming sound its best. Regardless of the quality of your drum, if it's out of tune or the hardware is falling apart, it's not going to sound good. But you can make just about any drum sound really good if you know how to tune it properly and take care of the drums and hardware. With the tips in this chapter, you can get even a beginner-level drum to sound great.

Checking Out Tuning Basics

Whether your drum is 6 inches across with a rawhide skin or 2 feet in diameter with a coated Mylar head, the fundamentals of getting a good sound out of your drum are the same. You need to tune your drum to its sweet spot in order for it to sound its best. The *sweet spot* is simply the pitch where the drum resonates best. This spot varies from drum to drum based upon size, the construction of the shell, and the type of head that you use.

Finding the sweet spot is fairly easy: Just adjust the pitch a little bit at a time until the sound is clear and without a lot of *overtones* (higher pitched sounds that the drum creates, which are usually hidden behind the fundamental tone of the drum). After it's tuned well, you shouldn't need to dampen (stop from vibrating) the head with tape or an internal system in order to lessen the overtones because there won't be any.

If you use the techniques in this section to tune your drums and still can't get the sound you want, more than likely your heads are the problem (see "Choosing and Replacing Heads" later in this chapter). A few people do seem to have a drum-tuning deficiency. If you're one of the few who can't seem to tune your drum, don't hang your head in shame; just find someone who can do it for you and then ask that person to teach you.

Tuning a drum with lugs

Got a wrench and a few minutes? Well, that's all you need to tune up your lug-tuned drum. Lug-tuned drums are by far the most common style these days; drummers use lugs on all drumsets and many of the hand and stick drums in Chapters 15 and 16. For the most part, drums with this type of tuning system are pretty straightforward to tune.

Start by removing the drumhead and the rim from your drum, and putting the drum on the floor. Wipe the edge of the shell with a dry cloth to get off any dirt or dust. Next, put the head on the drum and then the rim over that. Then follow these steps:

1. **Tighten the lugs by hand until they're as tight as you can get them.**

   Work the lugs by going across the drum as you go around. Start with the lug at the top (12 o'clock position), go to the lug at the six o'clock position, back up to the one o'clock position, to the seven o'clock position, and so forth until you go all the way around. This method ensures that you get the head evenly set on all sides.

2. **Press down on the rim over each lug as you tighten it further by hand, following the same pattern around the drum.**

3. **After all the lugs are fully tightened by hand, gently press on the center of the head with your palm until you hear some cracking from glue on the head (be careful not to push too hard).**

   This pushing seats the head and forces it to make full contact with the shell.

4. **Using the drum key (tuning wrench), work around the drum in the same manner described in previous steps and tighten each lug one-quarter to one-half a turn until all the wrinkles are out of the head.**

   This process should take only one or two times around the drum.

5. **Check the drum's *pitch* (how high or low the sound is) by hitting the drum in the center of the head.**

6. **Continue going around the head using one-quarter turns until you get to a pitch that rings freely.**

   If you notice overtones or if the pitch isn't really clear, lightly tap the head with your stick about one inch in from each lug. The lugs should all be the same pitch. Adjust any that are out of pitch with the others until all are the same.

Repeat this procedure on the bottom head if you have double-headed drums. I usually like to get both heads tuned to the same pitch, but other people tune the bottom head slightly higher or lower than the top head. Experiment and see what you prefer.

Tuning a drum with a rope system

Rope-tuned drums look hard to tune but they're really not. In some ways, they're actually easier to tune than drums with lugs, because you don't have to worry about getting the drum in tune with itself.

The process for tuning a drum with a rope system is pretty simple. All you have to do is untie the loose end (usually the long section) from the rope so that it's free. You can find this section by noticing where the end of the rope is that's strung around the drum. To raise the pitch, feed the loose end of the rope under the next two vertical strands (keep the rope taut where it was initially tied off). Next, loop the rope back across the second strand to the first and go under that one again. Hold the drum securely (I usually rest my knee on it) and pull the rope tight until the first strand crosses the second and the rope is straightened out. Continue this procedure until you have the drum at the desired pitch. Tie off the loose end of the rope, and you're set to play!

Tuning the untunable

Many frame drums (see Chapters 15 and 16) are untunable — they don't have a hardware system that allows you to adjust the tension on the head. That doesn't necessarily mean that you can't adjust the pitch of the drum — you can as long as the drum has a natural skin head.

Because natural hide heads are affected by temperature and humidity, you can use these factors to adjust the tension on the head of your drum. Higher temperatures and lower humidity result in the head becoming more tense, thus producing a higher pitched sound. Likewise, lower temperatures and higher humidity result in a lower pitched sound. In most cases, you find that your drum drops in pitch, sometimes to the point where all you get is a "thud" when you hit it. This drop in pitch is especially evident in thinner-headed drums.

To raise the pitch of your untunable drum, place it in sunlight for a little while until the head warms up a bit. You can also hold it over a heat source for a couple of minutes (some people use a hair dryer). Be careful though: If you put the drum too close to extreme heat or leave it in the hot sun too long, the head will break. If you want to lower the pitch of an untunable drum, put it in the bathroom, close the door, and turn on the shower (don't put the drum in the shower though!). The humidity in the room will drop the pitch of the drum.

These are both temporary solutions to tuning an untunable drum. The drumhead will eventually readjust to its natural pitch, as determined by the humidity and temperature in your room.

Choosing and Replacing Heads

At some point you're not going to get the best (or any) sound out of your drum by tuning it, or you're going to want to change the type of heads you have on a drum to give you a different sound. This section offers some guidelines for when to replace the heads on your drums, how to choose the best heads for your purposes, and how to replace them.

Knowing when heads need replacing

I doubt you'll have any problems knowing that you need to replace a drum head when it breaks (pretty safe bet, eh?), but many drummers don't know what to look (or more accurately, listen) for when replacing a head that doesn't have a hole in it.

No cut and dried rules exist for replacing functional heads. Replacing your drumheads depends on your playing goals. Drumheads are expensive, especially if you have to replace all the heads on a massive rock kit at the same time. To keep you from pouring your money down the proverbial drain, here are some things to consider when thinking about replacing heads:

- ✔ **Can you tune the drumheads to sound good?** If you can get a good tone out of your drum, the heads are fine. If not, you need to replace them. This test is the only true measure of when you need to replace your drumheads.

- ✔ **Are there any dents or warps in the heads?** Dented or warped heads don't tune well, and they sound dead when you hit them. Some people say that you can get rid of small dents in plastic heads and extend their useful lives, but my experience is that the sound suffers and this fix doesn't last long enough to make the effort worthwhile. Get a new head if yours is dented, especially if you intend to record your drums.

✔ **Where are you playing?** If you only play in your garage or basement with your buddies, you can go longer before replacing your heads. In fact, you may choose to wait until they're broken before switching them out. On the other hand, if you want to record your drums, you need to change the heads at least every few days. I've even been in recording sessions where the drumheads were replaced a couple times a day. Granted, these frequent changes were likely because the drummer didn't really know how to hit the drums properly or the drums were set up in such a position that hitting them properly wasn't possible. (Check out Chapter 5 for some helpful guidelines on setting up your drums for ease of playing and optimal sound.)

Choosing replacement heads

If you play drums long enough, you'll have to replace your drumheads at least once, putting you in the position of having to make yet another decision to define and refine your sound.

Drumset and stick-played drums

The number and types of drumheads available are daunting, and choosing the right one for your needs can be difficult. I can't possibly cover all the types of heads that are available or all the types of sounds that drummers may want from their drums. Different types of drumshells affect which head sounds best — and the definition of *best* is totally up to the player. With all those disclaimers out of the way, I can offer some basic guidelines for choosing a replacement head for your drumset. Here's a short list broken down by drum:

✔ **Snare drums:** For snare drums I like basic coated heads like the Remo Ambassadors. This head gives a nice open sound. If I want to dampen the head, I throw a plastic ring on it (or, if I'm playing live, my wallet).

✔ **Kick drums:** For kick drums I like Remo Pinstripes or other oil-filled or "hydraulic" heads. These heads have a mellow tone and make tuning a large drum like the kick a little easier. Because most people tend to stuff a pillow or other dampening into the kick drum, the fact that the oil-filled heads have less resonance is fine. You can also find some bass drumheads that have varying degrees of dampening abilities, but I've found that a pillow is still more effective.

✔ **Tom-toms:** For tom-toms I go between basic clear heads like the Remo Ambassadors or the Pinstripes. The clear Ambassador heads offer more sustenance but they can get a bit *ringy* (the overtones can get to be too much on some drums).

✔ **Resonant heads:** For the resonant head (the bottom head on double-headed drums), I prefer clear Ambassadors for every drum I've tried because they resonate freely, which is what you want in a "resonant" head. I have known people who like the Pinstripes, though.

Hand drums

Hand drum drumheads last a lot longer than drumset or other stick-played drumheads because you're not whaling on them with a hard object (unless you have really hard hands). For some drums, you can get years, if not decades, out of the head that comes with the drum. I have a 40-year-old conga drum with its original head that sounds better than some of my newer congas. Of course, 40 years is nothing compared to the 300-year-old frame drum that's hanging on my studio wall. This one doesn't get played much, but its age and durability are good news if you have a drum with tacked-on heads, because replacing them really isn't a practical option.

A general rule for replacing hand drum heads is to stick with what came on the drum. If your drum came with a natural skin head, replace it with one. Likewise, if your drum came with a plastic head, go that route come replacement time.

The only exception to this rule is a thin-skinned drum that you're moving back and forth between a dry place and a wet place. If you fit this profile, be sure to put a plastic head on the drum. Most of you probably don't have to worry about this problem, but when I lived in the San Diego area and my studio was inland 30 miles and up 2,000 feet, I figured out that the plastic is best.

Replacing your heads

Replacing heads is basically the same process as tuning a head except you need to take the old one off first. To remove the head, simply loosen all the lugs, pegs, ropes, or other hardware holding the head on the drum's shell. Then proceed with the steps I outline in the "Checking Out Tuning Basics" earlier in this chapter to put the new head on and get it sounding good.

Caring for Your Drums

With all the pounding you do on your drum, you can easily forget that it's a somewhat fragile instrument that you need to treat with some care. This section explains how to take care of your new best friends.

In most cases, you can keep your drumshells and hardware clean with a little soap and water. Slightly dampen a cloth and wipe it gently over the shell to get dust and minor dirt off. Follow it up with a dry cloth and you're all set.

I don't recommend using any abrasive cleansers or scouring pads because they can scratch your drum. Also, avoid any cleaners with alcohol or petroleum based products in them because they can ruin the finish.

Handling hardware

For the most part, the hardware used on drums is pretty tough, and it's often coated with a chrome plating, which can handle a lot of wear. Keep the following three things in mind, however:

- **Keep it clean.** Dirt and grime may eventually ruin the chrome plating because it can hold moisture or contain chemicals that eat away at the chrome. You can keep your chrome clean with a damp cloth and a mild soap solution (dishwashing soap is fine). Just make sure that you wipe your hardware dry after you clean it.

- **Don't scratch it.** Make sure you don't scratch through the plating. After it's scratched, it will start peeling off the metal base.

- **Keep it dry.** If your hardware gets and stays wet or damp for a long period of time, it will rust. The rust will "grow" through the chrome plating, which will eventually start to flake off. If you start to see some rust, use steel wool. Start with the stuff labeled #0000 (this grade is the least abrasive; #0 is the most abrasive) and use a rougher grade if it doesn't get the rust off.

Also watch out for any hardware parts that come loose. The metal hardware on drums is generally attached using screws on the inside of the drum, so you have to get your screwdriver or wrench inside the drum to tighten it, and you often have to remove the head. I always tighten screws and bolts when I'm replacing a head because I have easy access at that time.

For hardware such as bass drum pedals, lugs, and cymbal and hi-hat stands that have moving parts, make sure that these parts function smoothly. I recommend lubing all moving parts with white lithium grease to keep everything moving freely. You can find white lithium grease at your local hardware store. Just apply it to the moving part, such as a hinge, and wipe off any extra that seeps out.

Cleaning cymbals

For basic cleaning, cymbals just need a wipe with a soft cloth. Because cymbals are made with a variety of metals often including copper, they tend to get tarnished. A lot of newer cymbals, however, have a special coating to make and keep them shiny.

Because every manufacturer has its own recommendations on cleaning your cymbals, I strongly suggest that you check with the company to find out how to care for its products. Every manufacturer has a cleaning product, and many of these products work for other brands of cymbals (some exceptions may exist). Personally, I haven't found one product at the local drum shop that works better than another.

I hate cleaning cymbals and like to do the absolute minimum to keep my cymbals looking good, so I follow these simple guidelines to keep them clean and reduce the amount of time I spend working on them:

- **Keep your fingers off the cymbals.** Treat your cymbals like really big CDs or DVDs, and hold them by their edges and handle them as seldom as possible (this rule is easy for me now that I no longer tour with them). The oils in your hand may react with the cymbals and discolor them. If you or someone else touches them, wipe them down with a clean, dry cloth right away. You may need to scrub a bit to get the fingerprints off.

- **Keep the cymbals dry.** Water can cause problems on cymbals, so if they get wet, dry them off right away. 'Nuff said.

- **Don't use any abrasive cleaners.** No steel wool, scouring pads, or polishes that use an abrasive. If your cymbals are discolored and you want to get the original color back, use a cleaner specifically for cymbals. You may need to apply the cleaner and wipe it off more than once.

- **Don't use solvent-based cleaners unless they're recommended by the manufacturer.** Solvent-based products can eat away at the finish, or worse yet, the cymbal's material.

If you have vintage cymbals like the Zildjian "K" series, especially the original Turkish ones, don't clean them with anything other than a damp cloth and a very mild detergent. And whatever you do, don't try to polish them up to a shine. They were made to have a dark patina on them.

Storing and transporting safely

When storing your drums, try to avoid extremes in temperature and humidity. Some people suggest a humidity-controlled room, but as long as your drums are in a reasonably consistent environment, they'll be fine. Try to avoid keeping your drum in direct sunlight because the finish will fade or the head may crack (natural skins only). If you have natural skin drums that you don't play very often, I recommend that you *detune* them by loosening up the heads so that they aren't under pressure. Of course, you'll have to tune them up every time you want to play them, but your heads will last much longer.

One of the great injustices of the musical instrument world is that drums don't come with cases. Most drummers would rather spend their hard-earned money on a new cymbal or drum rather than a case. I understand, but I strongly recommend that you get some cases if you intend to move your drums around much. While you're at it, get some cases for all your hardware. It makes moving it around a lot easier.

I can't tell you how many times I see a set of drums just thrown into the back of a car or pick-up truck without any kind of protection on them. Do yourself (and your drums!) a favor and get some cases for them. You don't have to buy the most expensive hardshell case — a soft, padded bag is fine. See Chapter 19 for some hints about the best drum cases.

Part VI
The Part of Tens

The 5th Wave   By Rich Tennant

@RICHTENNANT

COMEDY CAGE

"...and this time, just give me a rim shot after my jokes and save the paradiddle exercises for your own time."

In this part . . .

As a nod to the *For Dummies* family, I include a couple of lists of tens. In Chapter 21 you can discover ten great resources to help you continue your drumming journey, and Chapter 22 offers guidelines for finding the best teacher for you.

Chapter 21

Ten Ways to Expand Your Drumming Horizons

In This Chapter

▶ Attending classes and workshops

▶ Finding books, videos, and magazines

▶ Exploring Internet resources

As much as I tried to include everything about drumming in this book (as if that's possible, right?), I trust you want to know more than I can offer here. To help you along, this chapter presents ten avenues that you can explore to expand your drumming world. I introduce you to some classes and workshops, books, magazines, videos, and Internet resources, and give you some ideas to get you out in the world to connect with other musicians.

Checking out Classes

If your interest is in hand drums, especially African or Brazilian drumming, classes may be the ticket for you. Drumming classes are a great way to learn how to play well with others and to meet people who share your interests. Almost every city has an African drum or dance class, and Brazilian classes are becoming more common. The best way to find out about classes is to call your local music store or drum shop. You can also look on the bulletin boards of record shops, natural food stores, or colleges.

Visiting Clinics

More and more, top-name drummers are teaching clinics around the country. Clinics are a great opportunity for you to see drummers who you admire up close and to learn how they do some of the things that they do. These clinics are often sponsored by a manufacturer or a drum shop and are often free to attend. You can usually find out about drum clinics through your local music store, on major instrument manufacturer's Web sites, or in drum magazines.

Attending Workshops

Workshops are intensive classes that can last anywhere from a day to a week. They're often held in interesting places like retreat centers or resorts where you don't have the distractions of daily life to get in the way of learning. The advantage of a workshop is that you can intensively immerse yourself in a particular drum or style of drumming. You can find workshops for hand drums much more often than drumset workshops. Every year, for example, the Seattle area hosts a huge African drumming conference.

A great place to find out about workshops is the Internet, or you can check out the magazines that I list later in this chapter. Most decent-sized workshops are listed in at least one of these resources.

Exploring Drum Circles and Jams

If you just want to have some fun drumming with other people, a drum circle may be for you. A *drum circle* is simply a gathering of hand drummers (most often playing African-style or frame drums). They often meet once a month in a park or at someone's home. The meetings are rarely advertised. Nearly every city has some sort of drum circle that you can join. Some are very public where you can just show up with your drum and start playing, while others are private, requiring you to make arrangements ahead of time or to be invited to join. The best way to find out about drum circles is to ask around at your local drum shop or drum school.

Hand drums are often sold in a variety of stores, not just a regular drum shop. So check out "new age" stores or places that sell African or tribal art as well.

Perusing Books and Videos

Instructional books and videos can be invaluable to you, especially if you live in a small town or can't find a teacher to help you study a particular drum. With a book or video, you can study at your own pace and according to your own schedule. The good news is that you won't find a shortage of great drumming books and videos out there. Finding them is rarely a problem, but choosing a particular one can be daunting. A good place to start is . . . you guessed it . . . the drum shop. Another place is the Internet. Literally hundreds of resources can steer you in the right direction, even if you're interested in one of the more obscure drums (like the pandeiro or riq that I talk about in Chapter 15).

For starters, here are some places on the Internet that have large instructional video selections:

- **Drummer World:** www.drummerworld.com
- **Musicroom.com:** www.musicroom.com
- **Vintagedrum.com:** www.vintagedrum.com

Getting Online

No matter where you live, you can find other drummers to talk to and learn with as long as you have a computer with Internet access. A bunch of great online resources are dedicated to drummers and drumming. Here are a few of the more popular ones:

- **Drummer Cafe:** www.drummercafe.com
- **Drummer World:** www.drummerworld.com
- **Online Drummer:** www.onlinedrummer.com

Be sure to check out the forums on each of these sites. Being able to talk to other drummers is one of the best sources for tips, techniques, and tricks to help you along your way.

Reading Magazines

You can find several very good drumming magazines out there. These magazines can keep you up-to-date on new equipment, who's playing with whom, and what's happening in drumming. In fact, drumming magazines are probably the most useful resource for finding additional information on everything from books and videos to clinics and workshops. For easy reference, here's a list of the most popular drum magazines:

- ✔ **Modern Drummer.** *Modern Drummer* is published 12 times a year and focuses mainly on the drumset, but occasionally features a percussionist. You can check it out on the Internet at www.moderndrummer.com or call 973-239-4140.

- ✔ **Drum!** This magazine contains a lot of information on hand drums as well as drumsets. It comes out eight times each year. You can find out more about *Drum!* on the Internet at www.drummagazine.com or by telephone at 408-971-9794.

- ✔ **Percussive Notes.** *Percussive Notes* is a publication of the Percussive Arts Society (P.A.S.). P.A.S. is an organization that promotes education of the percussive arts (drumming). *Percussive Notes* contains more scholarly articles on drumming and drumming history than other magazines. It's published six times a year. P.A.S. also sponsors an international conference on drumming every year. Go to its Web site (www.pas.org) or call 580-353-1455 to find out more.

- ✔ **Not So Modern Drummer.** If you find yourself interested in vintage drums, *Not So Modern Drummer* is a great resource. This magazine offers information on old drums (mostly drumset components) and classified ads to help you buy and sell your drums. Go to www.notsomodern drummer.com on the Web. *Not So Modern Drummer* is published four times a year.

Joining a Band

Sooner or later you're probably going to want to join a band and play with some other people. You can usually find other musicians to play with by asking around at school or your local music store. You can also put up a flyer at local music stores or record shops. Be sure to include your name, phone number, and a description of the style(s) of music you want to play. One way to do this is to use familiar bands or musical genres to which you can compare your style (for example, "straight-ahead rock a la the Stones" or "electronica meets Metallica").

Forming Your Own Band

From big band great Chick Webb to jazz-fusion pioneer Billy Cobham, drummers have a long history of leading their own bands. You don't need to write all the music to be a bandleader; all you need are some basic organizational and leadership skills (you also need to have access to a deep well of patience).

Forming a band takes some time, but it can be well worth spending the time to be able to call the shots and play the exact music that you want. Of course, leading a band also means looking for the musicians, setting up gigs, arranging for the equipment (PA and lighting systems) your band needs, and lots of the other nonmusical aspects of the music business. If this is the route you want to take, the first thing you need to do is to find some other musicians who share your taste in music. (Hint: You find musicians the same way that you look for a band in which to play.)

Playing Open Stage

Depending on how old you are, you may be able to go to one of the many open stage nights available. *Open stage* essentially means that musicians are invited to just show up at a venue and play. These events are usually held at bars that feature bands the rest of the week. In most cases, a drumset is already there so you won't need to bring yours. However, if you intend to play a conga or another hand drum, you'll most likely need to bring one with you.

Most of the time, open stage means playing blues, jazz, or straight-ahead rock. Call the club to find out what type of music is generally played. If you're under the legal drinking age (21), you may not be able to participate in an open stage situation. Again, a quick call to the club can give you this important information.

Chapter 22

Ten Tips for Finding a Drum Instructor

In This Chapter

▶ Looking for and choosing a drum teacher

▶ Considering what you need from a teacher

▶ Examining cost, time, and expectations

---

*P*rivate lessons are without a doubt the best way to learn how to really play an instrument. You get instantaneous feedback and direction that can save you countless hours when learning new skills. Nothing can compare to the positive influence that a good private instructor can have on your playing. In this chapter, I provide some guidelines to make the search for just the right drum instructor easier. I present questions you can ask to see whether you and a teacher are compatible, and I help you understand when it may be time to move on to another teacher.

Test Driving a Teacher

Private instruction is a very personal thing. You should feel comfortable with your teacher. The greatest drummer or teacher in the world is worthless to you if you don't like or feel comfortable around him or her. Likewise, you'll probably find that quite a few qualified drum instructors in your area fit the criteria I list in this chapter. I recommend that you audition a few by taking one lesson from each of them to see which one you connect with.

A decent teacher won't a have a problem with you setting up an introductory lesson or two. After all, she doesn't want to teach someone she doesn't feel comfortable with or someone she doesn't think she can effectively teach. In fact, some teachers "audition" students and are very particular about who they'll teach. If you run into one of these teachers and he says that he won't teach you, don't take it personally or think that you're not talented enough to play well. This teacher may have a lot of reasons for not agreeing to teach you that have nothing to do with you or your abilities. Just move on and choose a teacher with whom you can study and be comfortable.

Knowing Where to Look

Unless you live in a small town in the middle of nowhere, you're likely to have a few qualified teachers in your area from which to choose. The first place to look is your local music store or drum shop. Most local stores offer music lessons. Those stores that don't will have a list of teachers in the area or at least a bulletin board where instructors can advertise.

If you don't have a local music store (or if one of those large music superstores took over your area, and the monster store doesn't have any decent referrals), you can ask people you know whether they have any suggestions for a teacher. Chances are you know someone who knows someone who knows a good drum teacher. You can also check the yellow pages of your phone book for music teachers. Look under "musical instruction" or "schools — music."

Understanding the Costs Involved

Some teachers charge a lot for lessons while others charge very little. If you go to a big-name teacher, you may pay upwards of $100 a lesson. Compare this price to the $20 to $30 you pay at your local music store. Keep in mind that the $100-per-lesson teacher may not be a better choice for you. Discovering what a teacher costs can be a good indicator of the level of student he teaches. Many times the more expensive teachers focus on advanced students and don't want to be bothered to teach beginners.

Another money consideration is the cost of books and other materials that a teacher expects you to buy. Some teachers write your lesson down while others work from a book (or two or more). A selection of books can cost you hundreds of dollars, and you may find that the money is better spent on more drums or the lessons themselves. At the very least, you have to take into account the cost of these materials when considering the cost of lessons.

Exploring a Teacher's Playing Style

Knowing what type of music a teacher plays regularly can give you some insight into her musical sensibilities. This knowledge can also tell you whether the teacher has a well-rounded background. Most teachers play many styles of music, but some teachers specialize in one area or another.

A drum instructor's experience and musical tastes will also color how she teaches all styles. A heavy metal drummer, for example, may have a hard time teaching the subtleties of jazz or Latin music. Likewise, a jazz drummer may not be well-versed in hip-hop. On the other hand, each of these drummers may offer a fresh perspective and open your eyes, err . . . ears, to music you wouldn't otherwise listen to, and that can help you broaden your musical horizons.

Don't use this question *alone* as the deciding factor about whether a teacher is right for you. Other things may be more important to you, such as what level of student she teaches or her expectations for her students.

Gauging a Teacher's Willingness to Teach to Your Interests

Most drum instructors teach all styles of music, but certain teachers lean more toward one style or another. A good teacher can show you how to play all styles of music. As a beginner, most of what you're focusing on is the foundation of playing with proper technique.

Being able to apply the drudgery of technique to a style of music that you actually like to play can be inspiring. One of my first teachers was a technique guy and believed in the importance of rudiments. He was also a very good jazz drummer and felt that all decent drummers should play jazz well.

The problem was I was ten years old and didn't like jazz. Like many kids, I wanted to rock. This guy was great because instead of forcing jazz down my throat, he showed me how to play the rudiments and how to use them in rock music. By making practice relevant to me and letting me see the practical implications of what could have been esoteric exercises, he inspired me to practice. If he had simply taught me the rudiments on the snare drum or forced jazz on me at this age, I probably wouldn't have been as inspired to practice every day.

I highly recommend that you start with a teacher who can relate to the styles of music that you regularly listen to and can create lessons that allow you to incorporate the skills he's teaching you into something that makes you want to practice. After all, the difference between a good drummer and a great drummer isn't usually talent — it's sweat and hours and hours behind the drums.

Starting Where You Are

So you find a world-class drummer in your area and, because you're just starting out, you think it's a good idea to study from the best. Well, this idea isn't necessarily a good one. Most of the time famous musicians are in high demand and have limited time to give lessons. As a result, most of them won't teach beginners. They prefer to work with players who have at least some rudimentary skills so that they can spend their limited time focusing on helping good drummers become great ones. This isn't to say that some famous or highly accomplished players don't teacher beginners. It all depends on what they like to do.

The key is to look for a teacher who teaches students within your skill level. As a beginner you want a teacher who understands the issues and challenges you deal with while developing a foundation for solid playing. Someone who primarily teaches intermediate or advanced students may not have the patience to deal with the relatively slow progress that building a foundation requires.

All that said, if you only know of a teacher who focuses on advanced players, give her a call because she more than likely knows a teacher who fits your needs. In many cases it's a past or present student of hers. This referral can be an advantage if you want to ultimately study with the guru herself — your beginning teacher knows which skills you need and when you're ready to move on up the ladder.

Another aspect of starting where you are is to honestly represent your skill level to a prospective teacher. Resist the temptation to say you're an intermediate player when you've never had a teacher. A prospective teacher will find out pretty quickly if you're over-representing yourself. It's better to go in saying you know less than more.

Getting a Sense of History

As far as I'm concerned, knowing where and with whom your teacher studied is important. Although a self-taught drummer may be a great player, he may not have a depth of understanding into some of the fundamentals that can save you time and frustration as you learn.

In Chapter 3 I relay a story of my experience when I first got to college and met my main mentor at school, Joe Porcaro. He had me relearn how to hold the sticks in order to move my playing up a notch. Had I previously had a teacher who had these skills himself, I wouldn't have lost months relearning something fundamental. And I had several very good drummers as teachers!

Knowing the history of a potential teacher can help you understand whether he has a solid technical foundation from which to build your skills. Here are some things to ask:

- ✔ **How long have you been playing drums?** If the instructor is teaching at a music store, she will have had to be playing a while and be fairly accomplished, but if the teacher offers lessons in her home (or yours), this question can help you uncover her level of experience.

- ✔ **With whom have you studied?** Again, you're trying to understand how qualified the teacher is, and knowing whom he has studied with can help you uncover this information. Someone who has studied with a world-class teacher or a teacher who plays the style that you want to play is more likely to provide you with information that will speed your learning.

- ✔ **With whom have you played?** This question can give you some insight into who this teacher is musically and provide more information about her musical tastes and abilities. If this teacher has a lot of experience playing with decent bands, she may be able to save you time by showing you shortcuts and giving you practical advice. Sometimes, a teacher who is out there playing will give you opportunities to play with others or sit in with her band. (In fact, years ago I recommended one of my students to a band that I was leaving, and he got the gig!)

Honoring Yourself

I can't put enough emphasis on finding a teacher you like, respect, and want to study from. I once had a teacher who was a great player. The problem was he wasn't very patient and I didn't feel that he was interested in what I wanted or what I thought. Going to a lesson with him was like boot camp, and he was the shouting drill instructor pushing my buttons.

My point is that even though he was a great player and I had a friend who liked studying with him, I didn't like his teaching style. I just never felt comfortable and I didn't enjoy sitting in a room with him for an hour a week.

This was a problem. Because I dreaded going to my lessons, I was resistant to practice the material he assigned for me, which resulted in me being unprepared for my lesson. And that furthered this destructive cycle.

I'm not saying that your teacher should be your best buddy, but you should at least like her and look forward to your lessons (most of the time anyway). If you don't, look for another teacher with whom you feel comfortable, even if he's not a better player than your first teacher. You learn the most when you want to go to your lessons and you like your teacher.

Trust your instincts when choosing a teacher. Go with the teacher you like and respect. He or she doesn't have to be the greatest player in the world in order to help you become one of the best.

Understanding Expectations

Some teachers expect a lot; others expect very little. What you're looking for here is a match for your level of commitment. Having too much or too little material to work on between lessons can be frustrating. A good teacher can gauge the amount of material to give you from week to week and focus on the areas that interest you at the time.

Another reason to look at expectations is to know what areas a particular teacher puts emphasis on. For instance, I had a teacher early on whose goal was to teach the drumming rudiments, and all the lessons I had with him focused on the rudiments, even when playing the drumset. This dedication to rudiments gave me a solid technical foundation that I can apply to any style of music. Later I studied with a teacher whose focus was on musicality. He didn't care how I held the sticks or what level of technical skill I had. What mattered to him was the sound I got from the drums and the way I interpreted the music (known as *feel*). So rather than correct me on my technique, he analyzed my feel.

Both these teachers were invaluable to me for different reasons, and I studied with each based upon what they had to offer and what they expected from me. Had I not known their approach and expectations and I wanted to learn musicality from the rudimental guy, we both would have been disappointed.

Knowing When to Move On

It's inevitable that you're going to outgrow your teacher at some point, and that's okay. I don't know any professional (or very accomplished amateur) musicians who only studied with one teacher while they learned their craft. The trick is to know when it's time to move on and to find a more appropriate teacher to continue with. You can use the tips I present in this chapter to determine whether your current teacher is no longer appropriate for you and to find a new teacher who can help you continue your progress.

Appendix

How to Use the CD

● ●

*I*f you pop the CD that accompanies this book into the nearest CD player, you can hear most of the rhythms contained in this book. Plus, as an added feature for the 2nd Edition, I've placed *every* music example on the CD in MP3 format. You can use the CD to help you figure out how to play a rhythm or to help you determine whether you like the sound of a particular type of drum (the traditional drums from Part IV, for example).

One very important part of playing drums is to develop an "ear" for how a particular drum or rhythm sounds. You do this by listening carefully to how the drum or rhythm sounds on the CD. Try to hear how the different tones of a drumset (Chapters 6 through 11) or drums (Chapters 15 through 18) relate to one another. Doing so eventually gives you the ability to pick out the drum part(s) among all the other instruments (guitars, bass, keyboards) in a song.

Several times in the book I tell you that you don't have to read music to learn to play the drums. This is where the CD comes in handy. All you have to do is listen to the rhythm as I perform it on the CD and play along with it or try to copy it. To help you with your reading, I recommend that you look at the rhythm in the figure as it plays on the CD.

Relating the Text to the CD

Throughout the book you see a black bar (the *track bar*) next to a rhythm in each of the figures telling you where that rhythm is located on the CD. Because a CD has only 99 tracks and because there are almost 400 rhythms performed on the CD, each track often contains more than one rhythm. The track bar tells you the CD track number for each rhythm as well as its time within that track (listed as minutes and seconds).

For Chapters 6 through 12 and 15 through 17, I play each rhythm on the CD two times through after a four-beat count-in. Chapter 13 has a count-in followed by one measure of a basic rhythm and then the rhythm that is written in the figure. I play all the solos in Chapter 14 once after a four beat count-in. Chapter 18 contains ensemble rhythms that play for 64 bars (that is, I play 64 times through the written rhythm in Figures 1 and 2 and 32 times through the written rhythms in Figures 3 through 6).

System Requirements

Audio CD players

The CD included with this book will work just fine in any standard CD player. Just put it into your home stereo system, and check out "CD audio tracks," later in the chapter, for the track descriptions.

Computer CD-ROM drives

If you have a computer, you can pop the accompanying CD into your CD-ROM drive to access the MP3 files that I included. Make sure that your computer meets the minimum system requirements shown here.

- A computer running Microsoft Windows or Mac OS
- Software capable of playing MP3s and CD Audio
- A CD-ROM drive
- A sound card for PCs (Mac OS computers have built-in sound support)

Using the CD with Microsoft Windows

To install the items from the CD to your hard drive, follow these steps:

1. **Insert the CD into your computer's CD-ROM drive.**

2. **The CD-ROM interface will appear.** The interface provides a simple point-and-click way to explore the contents of the CD.

If you don't have autorun enabled, or if the CD-ROM interface doesn't appear, follow these steps to access the CD:

1. **Click Start⇨Run.**

2. **In the dialog box that appears, type *d*:\setup.exe, where *d* is the letter of your CD-ROM drive.** This brings up the autorun window I describe in the preceding set of steps.

Using the CD with Mac OS

To install the items from the CD to your hard drive, follow these steps:

1. **Insert the CD into your computer's CD-ROM drive.**

   In a moment, two icons representing the CD you just inserted appear on your Mac desktop. Chances are good that both icons look like a CD-ROM. In addition, the Audio portion of the CD may automatically begin playing, depending on how you have your Mac set up.

2. **Double-click the CD icon labeled "Drums FD" to show the CD-ROM's extra content.**

   If you want to use your Mac's CD player to merely play the audio on the CD, you can either let it play automatically, or you can double-click on the icon labeled "Audio CD" to view the individual tracks. Double-click on a track to play it.

3. **Double-click the License Agreement icon, and then double-click the Read Me First icon.**

   This is the license that you're agreeing to by using the CD. You can close this window after you look over the agreement. The Read Me First text file contains information about the CD's programs and any last-minute instructions you may need in order to correctly install them.

4. **To install files from the CD onto your computer, just drag each file from the CD window and drop it on your hard drive icon.**

What You'll Find on the CD

You can access most of the rhythms contained in this book as CD audio tracks. But as a bonus, I've added all of the audio tracks in MP3 format for this edition.

CD audio tracks

Here is a list of the tracks on the CD along with the figure numbers that they correspond to in the book. Use this list as a quick cross-reference to finding more about interesting-sounding tracks on the CD.

Track	(Time)	Figure	Rhythm	Track	(Time)	Figure	Rhythm
1	(0:00)	6-1	1	5	(0:00)	6-13	1
	(0:09)	6-1	3		(0:08)	6-13	6
	(0:17)	6-1	5		(0:16)	6-13	8
	(0:25)	6-1	7		(0:29)	6-13	9
	(0:33)	6-1	9	6	(0:00)	6-14	1
	(0:41)	6-2	2		(0:08)	6-14	3
	(0:49)	6-2	3		(0:15)	6-14	5
2	(0:00)	6-3	2		(0:23)	6-14	7
	(0:13)	6-3	3		(0:31)	6-14	9
	(0:25)	6-3	5		(0:39)	6-14	11
	(0:37)	6-5	1	7	(0:00)	6-15	1
	(0:49)	6-5	2		(0:12)	6-15	2
	(1:01)	6-5	3		(0:25)	6-15	4
3	(0:00)	6-6	1		(0:38)	6-15	5
	(0:08)	6-6	3		(0:50)	6-16	
	(0:15)	6-6	5	8	(0:00)	6-17	2
	(0:23)	6-7	1		(0:08)	6-17	4
	(0:36)	6-7	2		(0:17)	6-17	6
	(0:49)	6-7	4		(0:25)	6-17	8
4	(0:00)	6-9	1		(0:34)	6-18	1
	(0:07)	6-9	3		(0:42)	6-18	3
	(0:14)	6-9	6		(0:50)	6-18	4
	(0:21)	6-11	1		(0:58)	6-18	5
	(0:30)	6-11	3	9	(0:00)	6-19	1
	(0:39)	6-11	5		(0:08)	6-19	6
	(0:47)	6-12	2		(0:16)	6-20	1
	(0:55)	6-12	3		(0:24)	6-20	4

Track	(Time)	Figure	Rhythm	Track	(Time)	Figure	Rhythm
	(0:31)	6-21			(0:14)	8-5	5
10	(0:00)	7-2		19	(0:00)	8-6	2
	(0:11)	7-3			(0:08)	8-6	5
	(0:23)	7-4	1	20	(0:00)	8-7	1
	(0:34)	7-4	2		(0:06)	8-7	2
	(0:46)	7-4	4		(0:13)	8-7	5
11	(0:00)	7-5			(0:22)	8-7	6
	(0:07)	7-6	1	21	(0:00)	8-8	1
	(0:14)	7-6	4		(0:08)	8-8	3
12	(0:00)	7-7	4		(0:16)	8-8	5
	(0:07)	7-7	5		(0:23)	8-8	6
13	(0:00)	7-9			(0:30)	8-9	1
	(0:05)	Sidebar 7-1			(0:39)	8-9	3
14	(0:00)	7-10	1		(0:48)	8-9	6
	(0:11)	7-10	2	22	(0:00)	8-10	1
	(0:23)	7-10	3		(0:08)	8-10	3
	(0:34)	7-11			(0:17)	8-11	3
15	(0:00)	7-12			(0:25)	8-11	4
16	(0:00)	8-1	1		(0:34)	8-12	2
	(0:07)	8-1	5		(0:42)	8-12	4
	(0:15)	8-1	6	23	(0:00)	9-1	
	(0:23)	8-2	1		(0:06)	9-3	
	(0:30)	8-2	3		(0:12)	9-4	
17	(0:00)	8-3	1		(0:22)	9-4	
	(0:11)	8-3	4		(0:27)	9-4	
18	(0:00)	8-5	2		(0:35)	9-5	
	(0:07)	8-5	3		(0:58)	9-6	

(continued)

Track	(Time)	Figure	Rhythm	Track	(Time)	Figure	Rhythm
24	(0:00)	9-7	1	30	(0:00)	9-21	1
	(0:06)	9-7	3		(0:07)	9-21	3
	(0:12)	9-7	4		(0:15)	9-22	1
	(0:19)	9-8	1		(0:24)	9-22	3
	(0:26)	9-8	2	31	(0:00)	9-23	1
	(0:32)	9-8	4		(0:08)	9-23	2
25	(0:00)	9-9	1		(0:17)	9-23	3
	(0:07)	9-9	2		(0:25)	9-23	4
	(0:14)	9-9	3		(0:36)	9-24	1
	(0:21)	9-9	4		(0:46)	9-24	2
	(0:28)	9-10		32	(0:00)	9-25	
26	(0:00)	9-11	1		(0:08)	9-26	1
	(0:06)	9-11	2		(0:16)	9-26	2
	(0:13)	9-12	1		(0:22)	9-27	1
	(0:20)	9-12	4		(0:30)	9-28	1
27	(0:00)	9-13	1		(0:35)	9-28	4
	(0:06)	9-13	4	33	(0:00)	10-1	1
	(0:13)	9-14	2		(0:12)	10-1	2
	(0:20)	9-15	1		(0:25)	10-2	1
	(0:27)	9-15	4		(0:37)	10-2	2
28	(0:00)	9-16	1	34	(0:00)	10-3	1
	(0:07)	9-16	4		(0:09)	10-3	2
	(0:14)	9-17	2		(0:19)	10-4	1
29	(0:00)	9-18	1		(0:27)	10-4	2
	(0:07)	9-18	4	35	(0:00)	10-5	1
	(0:14)	9-18	5		(0:07)	10-5	2
	(0:21)	9-19	1		(0:14)	10-6	
	(0:28)	9-19	3		(0:23)	10-7	

Track	(Time)	Figure	Rhythm	Track	(Time)	Figure	Rhythm
	(0:34)	10-8			(0:16)	11-6	
36	(0:00)	10-9	1	41	(0:00)	11-7	
	(0:12)	10-9	2		(0:07)	11-8	
	(0:24)	10-10	1		(0:15)	11-9	
	(0:33)	10-10	2	42	(0:00)	11-10	1
	(0:41)	10-11	1		(0:12)	11-10	2
	(0:51)	10-11	2		(0:24)	11-10	3
	(1:01)	10-12	1		(0:37)	11-11	
37	(0:00)	10-13	1		(0:45)	11-12	
	(0:08)	10-13	2	43	(0:00)	11-13	
	(0:17)	10-14	1		(0:11)	11-14	
	(0:29)	10-14	2		(0:19)	11-15	
	(0:40)	10-15	1	44	(0:00)	11-16	
	(0:49)	10-15	2		(0:09)	11-17	
38	(0:00)	10-16			(0:18)	11-18	1
	(0:08)	10-17	1		(0:28)	11-18	2
	(0:16)	10-17	2		(0:39)	11-19	
	(0:25)	10-18		45	(0:00)	11-20	1
	(0:34)	10-19	1		(0:08)	11-20	2
	(0:45)	10-19	2		(0:16)	11-21	
	(0:57)	10-19	3	46	(0:00)	12-1	
39	(0:00)	11-1	1		(0:07)	12-3	1
	(0:11)	11-1	2		(0:14)	12-3	2
	(0:20)	11-2	1		(0:22)	12-3	3
	(0:30)	11-2	2		(0:29)	12-3	4
	(0:41)	11-3		47	(0:00)	13-1	
40	(0:00)	11-4			(0:06)	13-2	1
	(0:08)	11-5			(0:15)	13-2	2

(continued)

Track	(Time)	Figure	Rhythm	Track	(Time)	Figure	Rhythm
	(0:24)	13-3	1		(0:23)	13-11	4
	(0:31)	13-3	2	55	(0:00)	13-12	1
	(0:39)	13-3	3		(0:08)	13-12	2
	(0:48)	13-3	4		(0:17)	13-12	3
	(0:56)	13-3	5		(0:25)	13-12	4
48	(0:00)	13-4		56	(0:00)	13-13	1
	(0:09)	13-5			(0:07)	13-13	2
49	(0:00)	13-6	1		(0:15)	13-13	3
	(0:09)	13-6	2		(0:23)	13-13	4
	(0:17)	13-6	3	57	(0:00)	13-14	R
	(0:26)	13-6	4		(0:08)	13-14	L
50	(0:00)	13-7	1		(0:16)	13-14	F
	(0:07)	13-7	2		(0:24)	13-14	F
	(0:14)	13-7	3	58	(0:00)	13-15	1
51	(0:00)	13-8	1		(0:08)	13-15	2
	(0:08)	13-8	2		(0:17)	13-15	3
	(0:17)	13-8	3		(0:25)	13-15	4
	(0:25)	13-8	4	59	(0:00)	13-16	
52	(0:00)	13-9	1		(0:12)	13-17	
	(0:07)	13-9	2	60	(0:00)	14-1	
	(0:14)	13-9	3	61	(0:00)	14-2	
	(0:22)	13-9	4	62	(0:00)	14-3	
53	(0:00)	13-10	1	63	(0:00)	14-4	
	(0:08)	13-10	2	64	(0:00)	14-5	
	(0:16)	13-10	3	65	(0:00)	14-6	
	(0:25)	13-10	4	66	(0:00)	14-7	
54	(0:00)	13-11	1	67	(0:00)	15-3	1
	(0:08)	13-11	2		(0:06)	15-3	2
	(0:16)	13-11	3	68	(0:00)	15-6	1

Track	(Time)	Figure	Rhythm	Track	(Time)	Figure	Rhythm
	(0:07)	15-6	3		(0:11)	16-20	2
69	(0:00)	15-9	1		(0:21)	16-21	1
	(0:09)	15-9	3		(0:31)	16-21	2
	(0:16)	15-10		82	(0:00)	17-3	1
70	(0:00)	15-13	1		(0:08)	17-3	2
	(0:09)	15-13	3	83	(0:00)	17-6	1
71	(0:00)	15-16	1		(0:06)	17-6	2
	(0:12)	15-16	3		(0:12)	17-6	4
72	(0:00)	15-19	1	84	(0:00)	17-9	1
	(0:06)	15-19	3		(0:10)	17-9	2
73	(0:00)	15-22	1		(0:20)	17-9	3
	(0:08)	15-22	2		(0:28)	17-9	4
	(0:15)	15-23		85	(0:00)	17-11	1
74	(0:00)	15-26	1		(0:08)	17-11	3
	(0:08)	15-26	2	86	(0:00)	17-13	1
75	(0:00)	16-3	1		(0:08)	17-13	2
	(0:07)	16-3	2	87	(0:00)	17-16	1
76	(0:00)	16-5	1		(0:07)	17-16	3
	(0:09)	16-5	2	88	(0:00)	17-19	1
77	(0:00)	16-8	1		(0:06)	17-19	3
	(0:08)	16-8	2	89	(0:00)	17-21	1
78	(0:00)	16-11	1		(0:06)	17-21	3
	(0:07)	16-11	3	90	(0:00)	18-1	
79	(0:00)	16-14	1	91	(0:00)	18-2	
	(0:06)	16-14	2	92	(0:00)	18-3	
80	(0:00)	16-17	1	93	(0:00)	18-4	
	(0:09)	16-17	2	94	(0:00)	18-5	
81	(0:00)	16-20	1	95	(0:00)	18-6	

Digital music

All the audio tracks contained in this book have been stored on the CD-ROM in MP3 format. To access these tracks, just fire up your favorite MP3-capable media player. You can even put them on a portable player! You'll find these bonus MP3s by browsing the CD-ROM on your computer.

Troubleshooting

If you have trouble with the CD-ROM, please call the Wiley Product Technical Support phone number: 800-762-2974. Outside the United States, call 1-317-572-3994. You can also contact Wiley Product Technical Support at www.wiley.com/techsupport. Wiley Publishing will provide technical support only for installation and other general quality control items.

Index

● *C* ●

BUSINESS, CAREERS & PERSONAL FINANCE

0-7645-5307-0   0-7645-5331-3 *†

Also available:

- Accounting For Dummies †
  0-7645-5314-3
- Business Plans Kit For Dummies †
  0-7645-5365-8
- Cover Letters For Dummies
  0-7645-5224-4
- Frugal Living For Dummies
  0-7645-5403-4
- Leadership For Dummies
  0-7645-5176-0
- Managing For Dummies
  0-7645-1771-6

- Marketing For Dummies
  0-7645-5600-2
- Personal Finance For Dummies *
  0-7645-2590-5
- Project Management For Dummies
  0-7645-5283-X
- Resumes For Dummies †
  0-7645-5471-9
- Selling For Dummies
  0-7645-5363-1
- Small Business Kit For Dummies *†
  0-7645-5093-4

HOME & BUSINESS COMPUTER BASICS

0-7645-4074-2   0-7645-3758-X

Also available:

- ACT! 6 For Dummies
  0-7645-2645-6
- iLife '04 All-in-One Desk Reference
  For Dummies
  0-7645-7347-0
- iPAQ For Dummies
  0-7645-6769-1
- Mac OS X Panther Timesaving
  Techniques For Dummies
  0-7645-5812-9
- Macs For Dummies
  0-7645-5656-8

- Microsoft Money 2004 For Dummies
  0-7645-4195-1
- Office 2003 All-in-One Desk Reference
  For Dummies
  0-7645-3883-7
- Outlook 2003 For Dummies
  0-7645-3759-8
- PCs For Dummies
  0-7645-4074-2
- TiVo For Dummies
  0-7645-6923-6
- Upgrading and Fixing PCs For Dummies
  0-7645-1665-5
- Windows XP Timesaving Techniques
  For Dummies
  0-7645-3748-2

FOOD, HOME, GARDEN, HOBBIES, MUSIC & PETS

0-7645-5295-3   0-7645-5232-5

Also available:

- Bass Guitar For Dummies
  0-7645-2487-9
- Diabetes Cookbook For Dummies
  0-7645-5230-9
- Gardening For Dummies *
  0-7645-5130-2
- Guitar For Dummies
  0-7645-5106-X
- Holiday Decorating For Dummies
  0-7645-2570-0
- Home Improvement All-in-One
  For Dummies
  0-7645-5680-0

- Knitting For Dummies
  0-7645-5395-X
- Piano For Dummies
  0-7645-5105-1
- Puppies For Dummies
  0-7645-5255-4
- Scrapbooking For Dummies
  0-7645-7208-3
- Senior Dogs For Dummies
  0-7645-5818-8
- Singing For Dummies
  0-7645-2475-5
- 30-Minute Meals For Dummies
  0-7645-2589-1

INTERNET & DIGITAL MEDIA

0-7645-1664-7   0-7645-6924-4

Also available:

- 2005 Online Shopping Directory
  For Dummies
  0-7645-7495-7
- CD & DVD Recording For Dummies
  0-7645-5956-7
- eBay For Dummies
  0-7645-5654-1
- Fighting Spam For Dummies
  0-7645-5965-6
- Genealogy Online For Dummies
  0-7645-5964-8
- Google For Dummies
  0-7645-4420-9

- Home Recording For Musicians
  For Dummies
  0-7645-1634-5
- The Internet For Dummies
  0-7645-4173-0
- iPod & iTunes For Dummies
  0-7645-7772-7
- Preventing Identity Theft For Dummies
  0-7645-7336-5
- Pro Tools All-in-One Desk Reference
  For Dummies
  0-7645-5714-9
- Roxio Easy Media Creator For Dummies
  0-7645-7131-1

* Separate Canadian edition also available

† Separate U.K. edition also available

Available wherever books are sold. For more information or to order direct: U.S. customers visit www.dummies.com or call 1-877-762-2974.
U.K. customers visit www.wileyeurope.com or call 0800 243407. Canadian customers visit www.wiley.ca or call 1-800-567-4797.

SPORTS, FITNESS, PARENTING, RELIGION & SPIRITUALITY

0-7645-5146-9

0-7645-5418-2

Also available:
- Adoption For Dummies
  0-7645-5488-3
- Basketball For Dummies
  0-7645-5248-1
- The Bible For Dummies
  0-7645-5296-1
- Buddhism For Dummies
  0-7645-5359-3
- Catholicism For Dummies
  0-7645-5391-7
- Hockey For Dummies
  0-7645-5228-7

- Judaism For Dummies
  0-7645-5299-6
- Martial Arts For Dummies
  0-7645-5358-5
- Pilates For Dummies
  0-7645-5397-6
- Religion For Dummies
  0-7645-5264-3
- Teaching Kids to Read For Dummies
  0-7645-4043-2
- Weight Training For Dummies
  0-7645-5168-X
- Yoga For Dummies
  0-7645-5117-5

TRAVEL

0-7645-5438-7

0-7645-5453-0

Also available:
- Alaska For Dummies
  0-7645-1761-9
- Arizona For Dummies
  0-7645-6938-4
- Cancún and the Yucatán For Dummies
  0-7645-2437-2
- Cruise Vacations For Dummies
  0-7645-6941-4
- Europe For Dummies
  0-7645-5456-5
- Ireland For Dummies
  0-7645-5455-7

- Las Vegas For Dummies
  0-7645-5448-4
- London For Dummies
  0-7645-4277-X
- New York City For Dummies
  0-7645-6945-7
- Paris For Dummies
  0-7645-5494-8
- RV Vacations For Dummies
  0-7645-5443-3
- Walt Disney World & Orlando For Dummies
  0-7645-6943-0

GRAPHICS, DESIGN & WEB DEVELOPMENT

0-7645-4345-8

0-7645-5589-8

Also available:
- Adobe Acrobat 6 PDF For Dummies
  0-7645-3760-1
- Building a Web Site For Dummies
  0-7645-7144-3
- Dreamweaver MX 2004 For Dummies
  0-7645-4342-3
- FrontPage 2003 For Dummies
  0-7645-3882-9
- HTML 4 For Dummies
  0-7645-1995-6
- Illustrator cs For Dummies
  0-7645-4084-X

- Macromedia Flash MX 2004 For Dummies
  0-7645-4358-X
- Photoshop 7 All-in-One Desk
  Reference For Dummies
  0-7645-1667-1
- Photoshop cs Timesaving Techniques
  For Dummies
  0-7645-6782-9
- PHP 5 For Dummies
  0-7645-4166-8
- PowerPoint 2003 For Dummies
  0-7645-3908-6
- QuarkXPress 6 For Dummies
  0-7645-2593-X

NETWORKING, SECURITY, PROGRAMMING & DATABASES

0-7645-6852-3

0-7645-5784-X

Also available:
- A+ Certification For Dummies
  0-7645-4187-0
- Access 2003 All-in-One Desk
  Reference For Dummies
  0-7645-3988-4
- Beginning Programming For Dummies
  0-7645-4997-9
- C For Dummies
  0-7645-7068-4
- Firewalls For Dummies
  0-7645-4048-3
- Home Networking For Dummies
  0-7645-42796

- Network Security For Dummies
  0-7645-1679-5
- Networking For Dummies
  0-7645-1677-9
- TCP/IP For Dummies
  0-7645-1760-0
- VBA For Dummies
  0-7645-3989-2
- Wireless All In-One Desk Reference
  For Dummies
  0-7645-7496-5
- Wireless Home Networking For Dummies
  0-7645-3910-8

HEALTH & SELF-HELP

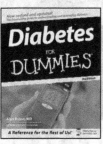

0-7645-6820-5 *†

0-7645-2566-2

Also available:

- Alzheimer's For Dummies
  0-7645-3899-3
- Asthma For Dummies
  0-7645-4233-8
- Controlling Cholesterol For Dummies
  0-7645-5440-9
- Depression For Dummies
  0-7645-3900-0
- Dieting For Dummies
  0-7645-4149-8
- Fertility For Dummies
  0-7645-2549-2

- Fibromyalgia For Dummies
  0-7645-5441-7
- Improving Your Memory For Dummies
  0-7645-5435-2
- Pregnancy For Dummies †
  0-7645-4483-7
- Quitting Smoking For Dummies
  0-7645-2629-4
- Relationships For Dummies
  0-7645-5384-4
- Thyroid For Dummies
  0-7645-5385-2

EDUCATION, HISTORY, REFERENCE & TEST PREPARATION

0-7645-5194-9

0-7645-4186-2

Also available:

- Algebra For Dummies
  0-7645-5325-9
- British History For Dummies
  0-7645-7021-8
- Calculus For Dummies
  0-7645-2498-4
- English Grammar For Dummies
  0-7645-5322-4
- Forensics For Dummies
  0-7645-5580-4
- The GMAT For Dummies
  0-7645-5251-1
- Inglés Para Dummies
  0-7645-5427-1

- Italian For Dummies
  0-7645-5196-5
- Latin For Dummies
  0-7645-5431-X
- Lewis & Clark For Dummies
  0-7645-2545-X
- Research Papers For Dummies
  0-7645-5426-3
- The SAT I For Dummies
  0-7645-7193-1
- Science Fair Projects For Dummies
  0-7645-5460-3
- U.S. History For Dummies
  0-7645-5249-X

Get smart @ dummies.com®

- **Find a full list of Dummies titles**
- **Look into loads of FREE on-site articles**
- **Sign up for FREE eTips e-mailed to you weekly**
- **See what other products carry the Dummies name**
- **Shop directly from the Dummies bookstore**
- **Enter to win new prizes every month!**

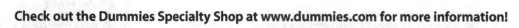